# The Class of '75

# Jack Batten

## The

# Class of '75

Macmillan Canada
Toronto

**Canadian Cataloguing in Publication Data**

Batten, Jack, date.
   The class of '75: life after law school
ISBN 0-7715-9178-0

1. Lawyers – Canada.   2. Women lawyers – Canada.
3. Practice of law – Canada.   4. University of Toronto.
Faculty of Law – Alumni.   I. Title.

KE330.B38 1992        349.71'092'2        C92–094313–6
KF297.B38 1992

1   2   3   4   5   JD   96   95   94   93   92

Cover design by Don Fernley
Cover photo by John de Visser

Macmillan Canada wishes to thank the Canada Council for supporting its publishing program.

Macmillan Canada
A Division of Canada Publishing Corporation
Toronto, Ontario, Canada

*This book is for Reg and Ruth Soward*

# CONTENTS

# ACKNOWLEDGEMENTS

Most of my thanks go to the members of the University of Toronto Law School class of 1975, who were so generous with their time and reminiscences, their patience and insights, and their hospitality. In the latter category, I was treated to wonderful food and wine in Sudbury, Ontario (by Bob Topp); in Paris, France (by Joel Saltsman); in the Victoria Hotel in downtown Toronto (by Leslie Yager); in the Parliamentary dining room in Ottawa (by Patrick Boyer, MP); in Puyloubier, Provence, France (by David Baker); and in many other spots, both domestic and exotic. Not only did I eat and drink superbly well, I had meals in places where small pieces of history were unfolding in front of me. One member of the class, the excellent law teacher Murray Rankin, took me to lunch in Victoria, British Columbia, on a day in November 1991 immediately before the day when the new NDP government of Mike Harcourt was to be sworn in. Rankin has worked closely with the New Democrats for years and was in an ebullient mood. We were eating in an elegant restaurant around the corner from the British Columbia legislative building. Across the room from us, there was a table of one older man and eight younger men and women. "That guy's saying goodbye to his staff," Rankin said of the older gent. "He's a Cabinet minister in the Social Credit government. Tomorrow he won't be."

Other thanks go to the Ontario Arts Council, whose grant helped pay for plane tickets and hotel rooms; to Marty

Friedland and Arnie Weinrib of the Faculty of Law at the University of Toronto, who consistently steered me in the right directions; to Garry Clarke and Julie Cruikshank for their kindness and generosity in Vancouver; to Sheree-Lee Olson for hustling the essential research; to Susan Girvan for her terrific editing and cheerleading; to Edna Barker for her enlightening (to me) copy editing; and to Marjorie Harris, without whose encouragement and love I'd never get a word written.

# INTRODUCTION

THE MEN AND WOMEN I write about in this book, with much admiration, entered the University of Toronto Law School in the autumn of 1972 and graduated in the spring of 1975. They're the class of '75, and they are, as you'll see, a remarkable bunch. But before I get to them, let me take you back to an earlier and possibly more humble time at the law school, back to the class of '57. I can speak with authority about that class. I was a member of it, not an entirely willing member.

I went into law school more by default than out of a driving ambition to emulate John Robinette. I didn't want to be a Robinette. I wanted to be a Norman Mailer. But I lacked the wit and courage to launch myself into literature or journalism. As an alternative, I settled on law. I joined the eighty-two other students who had presumably picked law, and the University of Toronto Law School, as a first choice in careers. Eighty-two students. That's how many started in first year at the school in September 1954. The number didn't remain that high for long. Four or five students were gone before the end of the first week of lectures, another twenty before the first month was over. The school's dean, Cecil Augustus Wright, weeded out the students. Throughout the autumn, he summoned people to his office and advised them they weren't up to scratch, didn't have the temperament, intellect, dedication suitable to the law school, that they should leave. They left. By the Christmas break, after we'd written a set of exams, after Dean Wright had made deeper cuts, we were down to fewer than forty students. By graduation day, Friday, June 14, 1957, thirty-one of us, the class of '57, survived. Only thirty-one, and I was one of them, me, the reluctant law student. It was amazing. How had I endured while others were axed in first year?

I developed a theory about my survival. The theory turned on Dean Wright's other job at the school. As well as running the place, he taught a first-year course in torts. A tort is a civil wrong, damage done by one party to another party's person or reputation. It's an intricate branch of the law, and Wright was the Canadian—maybe the world—authority on torts. He put together the case book on the subject. He influenced judges, lawyers, and academics. And he gave first-year students the benefit of his torts wisdom.

The man taught with style. He reminded me of William Powell in the Thin Man movies. Wright had a tidy moustache like Powell's, and he handled a cigarette with the same flair. He ran to weight around the middle, but he looked dapper in his dark three-piece suits. He exuded a tremendous aura of authority—it was not for nothing that his nickname was "Caesar"—and nowhere was the authority more on display than in torts class.

"We come in some fascination to the case of *Donoghue v Stevenson*," he said one autumn morning, speaking to the class from his seat behind a table at the front of the room. "A 1932 decision that gave voice to a central proposition in the area of negligence."

Dean Wright paused.

"Who would care to discuss *Donoghue v Stevenson*?" he asked, his voice deceptively benign.

His eyes dropped to the single sheet of paper that rested on the table beside his open case book. The paper listed the names of the students in the class. Dean Wright's finger moved over the list. In the class, we students tensed. One of us was about to be put on the griddle.

"Mr. Jones," Dean Wright said from the front of the room.

"Sir?" Jones said. (I use the name Jones here to protect the sensibilities of those students who got the heave from the class of '57 and haven't recovered.)

"The facts first, Mr. Jones," Dean Wright said.

Jones was off to a fast and sure start on the facts in *Donoghue v Stevenson*. Mrs. Donoghue was a shop assistant in Paisley, Scotland. She had gone with a woman friend to a local café for the Scottish equivalent of a ginger-beer float. They were served two dishes of ice cream and one dark opaque bottle of ginger beer. Each woman poured some ginger beer over her ice cream and ate the concoction. The friend tilted the ginger-beer bottle over the remains of Mrs. Donoghue's ice cream and emptied the rest of the bottle's contents into her dish. A decomposed snail plunked out of the bottle onto the ice cream. Mrs. Donoghue suffered an attack of gastroenteritis and emotional distress. She sued Stevenson, the unfortunate fellow who owned the aerated water company that made and sold the ginger beer with the snail in it. After a trial and appeals, the case reached the House of Lords.

"Lord, ah, Atkins's judgement," Jones said. He was out of the facts and into the law, and he was wavering. Two small pink circles bloomed in his cheeks.

"What does his lordship tell us, Mr. Jones?" Dean Wright prodded.

"A clear instance of omission here, sir," Jones said, trying to steady his voice. "That's, ah, at the root of the decision."

"Is that your view, Mr. Jones, or his lordship's?"

"Omission, sir, no doubt about it. Stevenson *omitted* to remove the snail from the ginger-beer bottle. That's it, where the defendant went wrong."

"Huggermugger."

"Sir?"

"*Huggermugger*, Mr. Jones."

Everyone in the class, including Jones, knew he was toast. Dead meat. Out of there. "Huggermugger" was the term Dean Wright invoked when he detected fuzzy thinking.

"One moment, sir," Jones said, talking quickly. "Responsibility. Now I've got it. Stevenson ought to have been *responsible* for not omitting the snail from the ginger-beer bottle."

Dean Wright's attention had returned to the class list, looking for another student to continue the discussion.

"*Sir!*" Jones refused to roll over. "Breach of an omission . . . no, it was a duty, that's right, a duty that Donoghue owed . . . no, wait, that *Stevenson* owed . . . so the snail in the bottle . . . Maybe it would have been a different result if the snail was whole, sir . . . I mean, *decomposed*, that's disgusting . . ."

What Lord Atkins said in *Donoghue v Stevenson* was that, in order for Mrs. Donoghue to succeed in her action against Stevenson, she had to show that Stevenson owed her some kind of duty and that he had breached the duty. There was no doubt that a breach occurred—Mrs. Donoghue did get sick from consuming the snail-infested ginger beer—but was there a duty? Here's how Lord Atkins answered the question in a few sentences:

"The rule that you are to love your neighbour becomes, in law, you must not injure your neighbour, and the lawyer's question, who is my neighbour?, receives in law a restricted reply. You must take reasonable care to avoid acts or omissions which you can reasonably foresee would be likely to injure your neighbour. Who, then, in law, is my neighbour? The answer seems to be persons who are so closely and directly affected by my act that I ought reasonably to have them in contemplation as being so affected when I am directing my mind to the acts or omissions which are called in question."

Three events followed Lord Atkins's pronouncement. The law received a workable definition of the biblical golden rule. Mrs. Donoghue collected three hundred pounds in damages from Stevenson, who should reasonably have foreseen he would injure someone in Mrs. Donoghue's position. And twenty-two years later, after failing to grasp the basis of Lord Atkins's decision, poor Jones got a summons to the dean's office, where he was invited to drop out of law school.

In Dean Wright's first-year torts class, he wasn't merely teaching torts. He was also sizing up the students, and discussions of such cases as *Donoghue v Stevenson*—the give and take, the grilling, the testing for huggermugger—probably made up the major part of Wright's assessment process. Reveal yourself to be a less than perceptive analyst of the decisions in the torts case book and, barring other weighty factors in your favour, you were on your way out of the class of '57.

What of me, then? What happened when Dean Wright called my name in class? Did I open my mouth and the wisdom of Chief Justice Sir Lyman Poore Duff popped out? Did I dazzle the class? Bowl over Dean Wright? Ensure my future in the school?

No.

Through the entire autumn of 1954, in fact through the winter and spring to the end of the school year, Dean Wright *never once* spoke my name in class.

Wright's eyes went to the class list, and day after day, they failed to settle on "Batten, J.H." How could it have happened? Was it because my name stood at the top of the list in alphabetical order and for some curious reason of habit or superstition, Wright skimmed over the first name? Or was it because Wright sensed I had the right stuff and he didn't need further reinforcement for his intuitive judgement in a classroom grilling?

I don't know. Well, actually, I realize the second explanation is wishful thinking. Whatever the reason, I passed invisible through Dean Wright's torts class. And if not invisible, then definitely low-profile, I proceeded through the three years of law school in the class of '57. I joined a study group of five classmates, and I wrote an article for the *Faculty of Law Review*, "Common Law: Its Elimination from the Criminal Code" (which I recently reread and concluded the author was either temporarily learned in one tiny corner of the law or bluffing). But I accomplished nothing that made me stand out from others in my year. *Stand out?* Are you kidding? My marks in third year included more Ds (three) than As (one), plus two Bs and two Cs. This sorry collection ranked me twenty-fourth at graduation, in the lower third of the class. Ahead of me, there were guys like Jack Ground, who became an Ontario Court of Justice judge; Calgary's Jack Major, the best litigation lawyer on the Prairies; and Ted Weatherill, who has gone on to become the chairman of the Canada Labour Relations Board. Below me was the guy who's our most famous class member, Alan Eagleson—the only one with a published autobiography and the man who used to run the hockey players' union and still runs international hockey. "How did they let you and me in that place?" Al says whenever he sees me.

I practised law for four years, then got out and became what I always had in mind for myself. A writer. But one thing stuck with me from my law school days, a realization that grew firmer with time. It was this: I had spent three years at a superior institution, at a school that is today the pre-eminent centre for teaching and research in law in Canada and, more, is one of the great schools in the common law world, right up there in the company of Harvard and Yale, Oxford and Cambridge.

It didn't rate in that category when I attended the school. Not quite. But it was on the way, and the man who propelled it was the dapper, demanding dean, Cecil A. Wright. Wright had been a brilliant student: gold medalist in history and political economy at the University of Western Ontario; gold medalist at Osgoode Hall Law School. He took a masters in law at Harvard and began a long career as the ace teacher at Osgoode. He was an industrious writer, Canada's leading legal scholar, celebrated inside the country and beyond. But he wasn't happy with Osgoode. It was a practitioners' school, controlled by the legal profession through the Law Society of Upper Canada. Students weren't to be burdened with legal theory or scholarship. Just nuts and bolts, the practical stuff. They spent only two full years at lectures, and the rest of the time was given over to apprenticing in a lawyer's office at twenty-five bucks a week. Wright argued for a three-year course of study toward a bachelor of laws degree, for a combination of the abstract and the practical. The law society turned him down, even after it named him dean of Osgoode Law School in 1948. Wright got fed up and took a walk in 1949— to the University of Toronto, where he established a three-year law school. He was starting from scratch, with the assistance of his colleague from Osgoode, Bora Laskin (later the Chief Justice of the Supreme Court of Canada), and he still had a fight with the law society on his hands. It refused to recognize the U of T Law School's graduates and forced us to submit to an extra year of studies at Osgoode, where we repeated courses we'd already taken at Wright's school. But by the end of the 1950s, Wright had won all the battles. The law society converted Osgoode into a three-year school, extended full recognition to the University of Toronto Law School, and opened the way for other universities to create their own law faculties. That was one legacy Wright left when he died in 1967—the spread of legal education. The other legacy, the one that affected me, was the establishment of a premier law school at the University of Toronto.

I wanted to write about the place. Al Eagleson and I probably wouldn't be allowed in the front door if we were students today. But I had gotten a whiff of the school's greatness, a feeling for what makes it a special place of learning.

But how to write about it? That was the question. And the answer was to write about it through the people, through the school's graduates. Heaven knows there's been a spectacular bunch of *them* in the school's less than forty years.

Two premiers of Ontario: David Peterson of the class of '67, and Bob Rae, class of '77.

An assortment of Members of Parliament: Ian Waddell, class of '67, and Paul Martin, Jr., class of '64.

Senators: Jerry Grafstein, '58, and Trevor Eyton, '60.

A mayor of Toronto: John Sewell, '64.

Tycoons: Trevor Eyton again, and Hal Jackman, '56, who also comes under the heading of Lieutenant-Governors of Ontario.

A black activist: Charles Roach, '61.

A feminist: Rosie Abella, '70, former head of the Commission on Equality in Employment and, as of 1992, member of the Ontario Court of Appeal.

A civil rights leader: Alan Borovoy, '56, general counsel of the Canadian Civil Liberties Association.

A newspaper editor: John Honderich, '71, editor of the *Toronto Star*.

A mandarin: Michael Shoemaker, '59, deputy commissioner of the RCMP.

A villain: Julius Melnitzer, '71. Just before Christmas 1991, in London, Ontario, where Melnitzer practised law and had one of his three homes (he also had a condo in Utah's ski country, not to mention a Jaguar XJS coupe, part ownership of a Stradivarius, et cetera, et cetera), he pleaded guilty to forty-three charges of forgery, fraud, and attempted fraud. The crimes turned mainly on a billion dollars' worth of phony stock certificates that Melnitzer used to con banks into lending him money and extending lines of credit. Bankrupt and leaving behind friends and law partners whom he'd chiselled, Melnitzer got nine years and was sent to one of the federal prisons in the Kingston area. At least three other graduates of the law school preceded him there, but Melnitzer's offences were the most flamboyant.

A priest: the Reverend Canon Donald Landon, '56, Anglican parish priest, the Diocese of Algoma in Ontario.

A philosopher: Jack Iwanicki, '55, professor of philosophy at the University of New Brunswick (and one of the best basketball players to come out of the school).

Enough of lists. You get the idea. The law school has produced, and is still producing, an accomplished, varied, influential, and colourful group of Canadians. In order to get a handle on this crowd, I decided to concentrate on one year, on one class. And for help in picking the class I would write about, I dropped around to the law school and chatted with a couple of professors who have been teaching at the place for some years.

The law school isn't where it was when I attended it. The university used to shuffle it into spare corners on and off the campus. In my first two years, the school occupied a cramped house, Baldwin House, in the shadows of the forestry and engineering buildings. For third year, we moved to Glendon Hall. It was spacious, almost opulent, surrounded by acres of rolling lawns, but its location made it a trial to reach, miles out in the sticks in a neighbourhood in northeast Toronto. In 1961,

Dean Wright installed the school in its permanent home, Flavelle House, a graceful building just south of the Royal Ontario Museum where Avenue Road blends into Queen's Park Crescent. Sir Joseph Flavelle built the house in the early years of the century. Sir Joseph came from humble circumstances in Peterborough, Ontario, where the name was pronounced Flavle, accent on the first syllable. Later, after Sir Joseph made his fortune in pork packing, he changed it to the classy French pronunciation, Flav-elle, accent on the second syllable. During World War One, Sir Joseph ran the Imperial Munitions Board, the organization that manufactured shells for our boys overseas. That made him a hero. He was also accused of using the war to earn unconscionable profits in bacon. That made him a villain. He weathered the good times and bad, and in 1939, on his death, he willed his house to the University of Toronto. The house had Corinthian columns in the front and back, an entrance hall with art nouveau scrollwork, a conservatory, drawing room, formal dining room, a billiards room in the basement, a servant wing, and rambling attics. When the law school got its hands on the house, everything was classrooms.

The two law professors I consulted were Marty Friedland and Arnie Weinrib. Both are graduates of the law school, Friedland in 1958, Weinrib in 1965. Friedland was the school's dean from 1972 to 1979; Weinrib has taught at it since the late 1960s. I told them I had three general criteria for the class I planned to write about. The class should include a significant number of women (enrollment is now fifty-fifty, men and women, but it wasn't anywhere close to that split as recently as twenty years ago). Its members should have been interesting as students from academic and personality points of view. And I'd prefer it if—no, I'd *demand* that—many of them are doing work today that's somehow intriguing.

Friedland and Weinrib agreed on the class, the one that stood out. It was the class of 1975, the class that entered the law school in September 1972 and graduated in the spring of 1975.

"It was a *very* bright class," Weinrib said.

"Yes," Friedland said, "and it had a lot of people I've kept track of over the years because their careers have been so fascinating."

I started writing letters and making phone calls and booking plane tickets. I didn't intend to visit all the members of the class. A representative number would do, somewhere between a quarter and a third of the members. There were 154 who joined the class at the beginning, and 164 who graduated at the end. It wasn't the same 154, plus a few, who proceeded together through the three years; some starters dropped out and some new people came in from other law schools in second and third years. But the turnover wasn't substantial, and there was no massive weeding out of first-year students in the Dean Cecil Wright manner. For the past quarter century, the screening process has taken place when students apply to get into the school. It's harder to win admission to the University of Toronto Law School than to any other law school in the country. These days, about 2,500 people apply for 170 spots; those accepted have to show at least an A-minus average in their pre-law courses. I was right when I wrote earlier that Al Eagleson and I wouldn't be allowed past the front door if we applied to the school today. Or if we'd applied in 1972 for the class of '75.

The people from that class, as I got on the job of interviewing and hanging out with them, turned out to be, as Marty Friedland had indicated, a diverse and brainy collection. There are lawyers who are making their marks in every branch of the law: in criminal law; in corporate-commercial; an impressively high number, in fact disproportionately high, in labour law on the union side. There are also more academics from the class of '75 than other classes have produced. The class includes three judges, a member of Parliament, and a university president. Who else? The scion of an important capitalist family. These are people in their early forties, men and women who are moving into positions of power in the country or, if not that, into places where they can change the ways Canadian life is led.

On the down side, one person from the class has been disbarred. But he doesn't really count, because he was admitted back to the profession a few years later. I'm told he welcomed the disbarment. He needed a break from the law.

A few others made odd fits at law school. Fred Gormley, for example. He was an older student, probably in his forties. He had a PhD in engineering, and in the years he was attending the law school, he held down a full-time job as vice president at Inco. He missed more classes than he made. But he managed to stick it out for three years and take his degree. He also left something of himself around the school. "Fred taught us a lot about living in the world," one of his classmates, Harriet Lewis, told me. I would have liked to interview Fred Gormley, but he died in the mid-1980s, running for a train in Union Station.

I didn't get to Fred Gormley or to the guy who was temporarily disbarred. But I got to the university president and the MP and the scion and to about forty other members of the class. From each of them, I was looking for anything they could tell or show me about what's going on in the country as they see it, what's happening in our institutions, in the profession of law, in their own lives. And I was seeking their views and experiences against the background of the one remarkable institution that's common to all of us, to them and to me—the University of Toronto Law School.

I think I found what I was looking for.

# CHAPTER ONE

## *The Bencher*

BOB TOPP, criminal lawyer and member of the class of '75, phones me from his office in Sudbury.

"I checked you out with Eddie Greenspan," he says.

"Really?"

"I got your letter asking to talk to me about this book of yours."

"And you called Eddie?"

"He's the best, correct? Nobody rates higher at the criminal bar, and he's a friend of mine."

I suck in my breath and run through my encounters over the years with Eddie Greenspan. I don't recall offending him.

"Eddie tells me you're okay," Bob Topp says.

"He does?"

"Says you're a man of integrity."

"Well, he went overboard there . . ."

"That's good enough for me," Topp rushes on. "Look, how'd you like to be my guest when the law society meets next month?"

"Whoo . . ."

"I'm a Bencher, you know."

"I didn't."

"At that meeting," Topp says, "I'm going to set off fireworks. Ex*plo*sive is what it'll be."

Since 1797, the Law Society of Upper Canada has kept a tight rein on the legal profession in Ontario. It sets standards for the province's 24,000 lawyers, administers the legal aid program, keeps an eye out for shady practices, and disbars lawyers who dip into their clients' funds or commit other transgressions. The society employs a staff of more than fifty lawyers (up from a mere five in 1980) to tend to its machinery. But the lawyers who run the show are those elected by their fellow members of the profession to sit on the law society. There are forty of them, they are called Benchers, and they serve a term of four years. Twenty of the elected Benchers must come from Metro Toronto, and twenty—a group that currently includes Bob Topp—from the rest of the province. In addition to the forty, in accordance with a piece of legislation passed by Bill Davis's Conservative government in 1973, the province appoints four non-lawyer lay Benchers. They enjoy the same powers as the elected Benchers and get better recompense; lay Benchers receive a per diem, while elected Benchers are in it strictly for the expenses and the prestige. All forty-four meet on the fourth Friday of each month to do society business—the meetings, in society parlance, are called convocations—and the members also serve on various of the society's twenty standing committees, which cover such areas as legal education, professional standards, and compensation. The latter is compensation to clients who have been bilked by dodgy lawyers.

Convocations are held in the Benchers' quarters in the east wing of Osgoode Hall, the building on Queen Street in Toronto that houses some courts and other legal offices, and on the appointed June Friday, I present myself outside the formidable wooden door marked "Benchers' Entrance." An escort is necessary to go farther, someone with a key to the formidable door. Getting into the Benchers' inner sanctum, a place seldom open to outsiders like me, is on a level with penetrating the Pentagon. On the other hand, there are far worse places in the city to stand

and wait. In Eric Arthur's splendid book on local architecture, *No Mean City*, he says Osgoode Hall "ranks highest among the historic buildings still left to us in Toronto," an edifice that "will never be dominated spiritually." The east wing is the oldest section of Osgoode, dating from 1829. Eric Arthur uses adjectives like "scholarly" and "classic" to describe it. They're good. So are "humane" and "approachable." The east wing seems a remarkably friendly piece of work. It's two and a half storeys high, has three arches through which you reach the main entrance, an Ionic portico above, and is constructed of brick that is weathered and reddish.

The formidable door opens, and a man bustles down the stone steps. He's wearing a dark summer-weight suit, white shirt, and figured tie. He's balancing a cup and saucer in one hand, trying hard not to spill the coffee in the cup. He has black hair going to grey, a pale, bespectacled face, and an ebullient air. His smile is of the ear-to-ear sort. Hello, Bob Topp.

"Isn't this a *won*derful building?" he says. "Come on in here. We're going to have some *fun* this morning."

Topp leads me through the door and into the Benchers' library, on the left side of the second floor. It has a high ceiling and large, beautifully crafted windows that let in plenty of summer sun. The room is set up for morning coffee. Men and women—the Benchers—are serving themselves and chatting in groups. Topp fetches me a cup, and in a voice that drops to the confidential level, he briefs me on the fun ahead.

"I'm going to let off fireworks," he says.

"You mentioned that on the phone."

"Here's the deal. When a lawyer is called up before the law society's discipline committee, and the committee recommends he should be disbarred or reprimanded, I think the lawyer should be able to appeal his conviction and punishment to the *whole* convocation. You follow me? Appeal his case to *all* the Benchers sitting together."

"Who *can* he appeal to?" I ask, hoping it's the right question.

"He *used* to be able to appeal to the entire convocation. Now he can't. We've just changed the procedure. Now the guy who's been disbarred or whatever can only appeal to *another* commit-tee of Benchers. I say that's wrong, and I'm going to drop a few depth charges in there this morning and see if I can't persuade my fellow Benchers to go back to the older, better, fairer way."

"I'm beginning to get it," I say. "You think the former method was more democratic."

"Absolutely."

Another man joins us, the only person in the room wearing a barrister's gown. His name is Jim Spence, and the gown signi-fies that he is the treasurer, or chief Bencher, of the law society. The Benchers choose the treasurer from among their own num-ber. He—or she, since there has been one female treasurer, Laura Legge in the mid-1980s—is elected for a term of one year, though it's the practice that, once elected and barring any outra-geous goofs, a treasurer will stay on for two terms. Jim Spence is at the beginning of his second term. He's a short, balding man and has a face that manages the feat of looking simultaneously intelligent and merry.

"At one time, probably for centuries in fact," Spence tells me, "the treasurer's duties were something that people could handle in their spare time. Not any more. As treasurer, I'm virtually on sabbatical from my own firm."

I ask how many hours he devotes to law society business.

"About seventy-five percent of my work week. When a group of Benchers asked me to stand for treasurer a year ago, I went to my firm to see what they thought. I'm with Tory, Tory, DesLauriers and Binnington. The firm's executive committee called a meeting to consider the situation. They decided it was my duty to stand. I couldn't have taken the job without their approval. It's become a problem for anyone who isn't in a large firm to serve as treasurer."

Spence gives one of his cheery smiles. "Incidentally, I'm the first treasurer in history to come out of Dean Wright's law school. Class of '66."

Chalk up another one for the old alma mater.

At nine-thirty, the Benchers move across the hall, under a

high glass dome, and into the meeting room on the east side of the second floor. The walls are hung with portraits of former treasurers. Cleeve Horne's angular paintings seem to be over-represented. A handsome formal table runs down the centre of the room. Jim Spence sits at the south end of the table, and about twenty Benchers range themselves along both sides. The rest find seats against the wall. It strikes me as rather a catch-as-catch-can arrangement for such a solemn body.

Things get even more random, in the most charming way, with the first order of business. Spence welcomes into the already crowded room seven people who are being called to the bar. These are new lawyers who, for one reason or another, were unable to be called at the annual spring convocation for all recent law school graduates. The seven are gowned. Five are women, two are men. One woman is black, another Oriental. All are accompanied by family members. The families have brought along one baby in arms and seven cameras. One picture taker steps on my foot.

"You have distinguished yourselves," Spence tells the new lawyers. "You honour us with your presence."

The baby cries, the new lawyers and families shuffle out of the room, and Bob Topp is asked to make his pitch. He stands at a small lectern set on the north end of the table and reads from a prepared text. His reading is passionate. Topp's eyes, slightly protuberant at rest, threaten to pop from their sockets when he grows enthusiastic. I'm beginning to think a high level of enthusiasm is his perpetual state.

"I rise today in some trepidation," he begins, "in an attempt to convince a majority of you that previously endorsed changes to the discipline procedure were a mistake and now ought to be reconsidered."

Topp tells his fellow Benchers that it won't look good to the public if the fate of a cheating lawyer is determined only by a couple of committees of the law society. There are three Ben-chers who sit on each discipline committee and seven on the appeal committee. That adds up to a tiny minority of Benchers who decide on an issue as crucial as whether or not to toss a lawyer out of the profession. Such a decision, Topp argues, needs the wisdom of everyone in the convocation.

"The public and the profession," he says, his voice rising, eyes leaping, "expect and have the right to receive the full consideration of *all* members, not"—Topp's voice drops dramatically—"some fraction thereof."

He peppers his argument with quotes from great men. G.K. Chesterton and Sir William Van Horne make their appearances in his text. So does Abraham Lincoln. "Government for the people, by the people, of the people." Topp sits down.

Colin McKinnon is first up to debate Topp. McKinnon is a slim, cool, hip-looking lawyer from Ottawa.

"In a court of law," he says, a note of exasperation in his voice, "we don't have *all* the judges in the province decide on a matter. We have one judge or a panel of judges. In an assault case, we don't have *all* the provincial court judges rule on guilt or innocence. We have one. It's the same principle here. We don't need *all* the Benchers to decide on a discipline matter. We have confidence that the Benchers who are assigned to hear the matter are capable of doing a proper job."

McKinnon takes his seat and almost immediately pops up again.

"By the way," he says, "as long as we're using quotes this morning, consider Winston Churchill when he said, 'We are resolved to be irresolute, decided to be undecided, adamant for drift.'"

Netty Graham, a lay Bencher from Petawawa, speaks. She has brown hair and stylish looks.

"For me, the most important function is discipline," she says, talking in a grave voice. "It's why I'm here, why the government appointed me, why I'm representing the public. So I support the motion. Discipline must be done by all the Benchers and be seen to be done by all of them."

The debate pitches back and forth for an hour. An equal number of Benchers speak on each side of Topp's motion. The rumpled man sitting against the wall beside me is growing restless. "This is ridiculous," he says. He shifts his weight for about the hundredth time.

Joan Lax steps to the lectern. She's an elected Bencher at her first convocation. She has small, attractive features and a spray of curled hair. She's an assistant dean at the University of Toronto Law School.

"I'm new here," she says, "but I didn't think *this* was what I was getting into. We've been debating for over an hour about something that seems relatively simple. Do we need to spend this much time on the motion? Can't we do something else? I don't know how this is accomplished, but can I move for a closure of the debate?"

"Put the question!" the rumpled man beside me calls out.

Joan Lax turns to him. "What?"

"Put the question!"

Joan Lax looks puzzled.

"Move that the question be put to the convocation," the rumpled man enunciates very clearly. The man is Lee Ferrier, a leading family law practitioner and a former treasurer. "Put the question, and that'll end the debate."

"All right," Joan Lax says. "I, uh, move that the question be put to the convocation."

Jim Spence calls for a vote on Joan Lax's motion. Hands are raised and counted. The motion carries by eight votes. The debate is ended.

Spence calls for a vote on Bob Topp's motion that the discipline procedure be changed to its previous form, which allowed the entire convocation to participate. Up go the hands. The count is taken. Bob Topp's motion fails by seven votes.

"Thank God for that," Lee Ferrier mutters.

"I thank everyone who took part in the debate," Jim Spence says from the head of the table. "It was of a very high quality. I particularly thank Messrs. Lincoln, Chesterton, and Churchill."

He prepares to move to the next order of business, a report from the chair of the Legal Education Committee. But Paul Lamek feels the need to comment on what has just taken place.

"This is a terrible precedent," he says. He is a portly lawyer with a cultivated rumble of a voice and the manner of Sydney Greenstreet. "There were still members here who wanted to be heard in debate when the motion to put the question was presented to the convocation. The idea of silencing Benchers"—I can almost hear the harrumph in Lamek's voice—"is most unwelcome."

At twelve-thirty, the Benchers adjourn for drinks and lunch. The drinks are served in the library. I get a vodka on the rocks and ask Colin McKinnon for the source of his Winston Churchill quote.

"A House of Commons debate," McKinnon answers. "He was criticizing Sir Stafford Cripps. Another time, he called Cripps the chinless wonder. This time, Churchill just said that as far as a matter before the House was concerned, the two parties, Conservative and Labour, were 'resolved to be irresolute, decided to be undecided, adamant for drift.'"

"I thought you might have made it up," I say.

"Got it from an excellent little paperback of Churchill quotes. I lent the book to a friend back in the 1970s, and he never returned it."

"Who was the friend?"

"A speech writer for Pierre Trudeau."

A petite woman with jet black hair and lovely skin introduces herself. She's Fatima Mohideen, a newly elected Bencher who practises in Brantford.

"I'm finding that law society business takes thirty-five percent of my time," she tells me. "There's so much to read if I'm going to be properly prepared for convocation. Also I have to come down to Toronto a few days each month for meetings of the committees I'm on. I work for a legal clinic in Brantford, and if it wasn't for their support, paying me while I'm doing law society business, I could never afford to be a Bencher."

We go downstairs to the society dining room, another gorgeous space. I'm seated to the right of Jim Spence. He's fretting over Paul Lamek's complaint.

"Paul's got a point," he says. "If I had to do this morning over again, I might not handle it the way I did. Joan Lax's motion caught me by surprise. It's something that has never come up before. Now I'm worried about my ruling."

Lunch is cucumber soup, poached salmon and asparagus, fresh fruit tart, and one glass of white wine.

Spence rises to propose a toast.

"The Queen," he says, lifting his wine glass.

A few clear voices repeat, "The Queen." The rest make a general mumble.

"That's always delicate," Spence says to me when he sits down. "Some of our people object to the toast. Some won't stand up. It seemed to go okay today."

I remark that the law society doesn't come across as the stuffy, conservative outfit that I had vaguely expected.

"That's an old perception," Spence says. "It used to be thought that the big powerful downtown Toronto firms controlled the law society. Whether that was true or not, it certainly doesn't apply today. The big firms couldn't control things even if they wanted to. Nor are they over-represented on the society. These days, we have a much more widespread representation among Benchers. Women, sole practitioners, people from small centres, minorities. We have one native Canadian Bencher, a Cree woman. With a group like that, I think we take a fairly adventurous approach to the job."

After coffee, before the Benchers return to convocation, Bob Topp laments the vote on his motion.

"They wiped me on the floor," he says to me.

"You lost only by a few votes."

"The motion crash-dived into the ground."

"*Bob!*"

"They blew me out of the water," Topp says. "But I'm not finished yet."

"How's that?"

"The change in discipline procedure has to be reviewed by the provincial government's Law and Justice Committee. When that happens, I'll be at the legislature making my representations."

Later, after the day's convocation is finished, I ask Topp about this passion of his over the discipline procedure. Why the determination to change it? Why the great concern about the law society's treatment of lawyers who've broken the society's rules?

It soon becomes clear that reaching out a hand to lawyers in trouble has been a kind of leitmotiv running through all of Topp's years in practice. The man really cares about his fellow practitioners who, one way or another, stumble into grief. And what is slightly odd about his compassion is that it originated, perversely enough, when, as an articling student to a Toronto criminal lawyer named Bob Crane, Topp helped to *nail* a lawyer who was up to his ears—or maybe his waist—in trouble.

The lawyer in question was an aging but obviously virile chap who was convicted in the United States under the Mann Act. It's a statute that punishes people who transport young girls across state lines for immoral purposes, and the lawyer, who practised in western Ontario and also maintained a string of show horses, ran afoul of it when he bedded the teenaged female grooms who accompanied him and his horses to shows in Pennsylvania and New York State. The law society's discipline committee summoned the lawyer to determine whether he should be disbarred in view of his Mann Act conviction. As is its custom, the committee named an outside counsel to conduct the prosecution. The counsel was Bob Crane, and Topp assisted in preparing the case. Convinced by the Crane case, the discipline committee kicked the lawyer out of the legal profession. The experience registered indelibly on Topp.

"Watching the discipline committee in action scared the hell out of me," he says. "These people had the power to take away your ticket, and in my business, that's the ultimate power. It may be the experience on that case that makes me take a careful approach to discipline all these years later."

Up in Sudbury where Topp practises, the bar, about 150

lawyers, is a particularly fraternal group. (One suspects Topp has much to do with this.) When the city's lawyers catch a whiff of panic emanating from one of their members, they take remedial action. It isn't hard to note a lawyer in trouble; a cheque submitted on the closing of a real estate deal that bounces will send up an all-stations alert. The instant that happens, or something equally grim, word circulates among other Sudbury lawyers that each is expected to chip in a pro rata share to fill in the defaulting lawyer's trust account. This accomplished, the lawyer's clients protected against possible loss of their money, the law society is notified, and justice takes its course.

Some northern Ontario lawyers, however, get in trouble and slip past the compassionate aid of their brethren. They're the ones who, in the years before Topp became a Bencher, arrived at his office in despair. Topp says he had no trouble recognizing them in his waiting room.

"They were the guys who showed up without an appointment very late in the day, five-thirty, six, something like that, and they always had a brown envelope in their hands. That, and a really forlorn expression on their faces."

The envelope contained a letter from the law society, or more frequently several letters, requesting their presence at an investigatory meeting.

"The guy'd usually had the notice for six months," Topp says. "He hadn't done anything about it, and the hearing was scheduled for the next day. It was a situation where the guy absolutely could not come to grips with the jam he was in."

Topp talks about one lawyer who got himself in just such a pickle. Topp went through the lawyer's desk and found a couple of dozen registered letters from the law society containing notification of proceedings against him.

"He was like a little kid," Topp says. "He thought the bad things would go away if he didn't open the letters."

Topp makes the point that not all lawyers, not all by any means, tumble into problems by fiddling with money in their clients' trust accounts. The grief is often more mundane. It's the result of a failure of nerve that leads to a kind of catatonia.

"The guy gets paralyzed," Topp explains, looking sad and amazed. "I don't really understand what happens. Maybe the guy can't handle booze or he's addicted to drugs or something. The upshot is that as a lawyer, he can *appear* to be practising, but not really practise. He can carry out a real estate deal, but he never registers the deed. He just reaches a point in the transaction where he freezes up."

This is precisely the horror that befell the lawyer who owned the desk where Topp discovered all the unopened letters. Topp negotiated his case before the law society and won his client the right to resign from the profession. It was a private humiliation, probably better than the public disgrace of disbarment.

Since Topp has risen to the rank of Bencher, indeed a member of the discipline committee, his duties have changed. Not his perspective, though. His experience acting as a hand holder to lawyers in dire straits gives him a sense of compassion when he's on the other end of the equation, on the end where he's the guy who helps to make the decision whether to take away someone's ticket. The right to confidentiality prevents him from discussing the disbarred lawyers whose cases he's sweated over as a discipline committee member, but he doesn't mind talking a little about an instance where he sat in judgement on a lawyer who had appealed his disbarment by a discipline committee to the whole convocation of the law society. Topp is out front on this case because it's already a matter of very public record and because he thinks the correct decision was arrived at.

It's the Harry Kopyto case.

Harry Kopyto (University of Toronto Law School, class of '70) may have been the noisiest counsel at the Toronto criminal bar. He had a shrill voice and persisted in crossing the line that divides dogged advocacy from possibly rotten courtroom manners. He drove Crown attorneys to distraction and caused judges to simmer and rage. Kopyto insisted his style was all in a good cause. His point was that he acted for clients whom other counsel scorned, the downtrodden, the afflicted, the dispossessed, and that in order to win these losers in life a fair hearing, he needed to bring *Sturm und Drang* to the courts. He knew he ticked off the legal establishment. He knew the Benchers weren't pleased with him. Heck, they'd been on his case since 1972, when a monitor on the bar exams caught him cheating. The law society made him rewrite the exam. And when big trouble came down on Kopyto's head in the spring of 1989, he expected it. "Those fuddy-duddies at the law society," he said in an interview, "have only one purpose in mind—to disbar Harry Kopyto."

Since Kopyto's practice consisted almost entirely of indigent clients, his main source of income was legal aid revenue. Someone at the legal aid offices noticed that three years of Kopyto's billings to the plan, billings that totalled $600,000 in cash payments, ran as follows: 1,894 hours in 1984; 3,596 hours in 1985; and 2,719 hours in 1986. The normal range of billable hours for a hard-working lawyer runs between 1,100 and 1,300. Ergo, either Kopyto was a spectacular example of burning the candle at both ends or he'd conned the legal aid plan by a few thousand hours. The law society assigned a three-man discipline committee (Bob Topp was not a member) to decide the case.

Kopyto came out firing in his own cause. He turned up in the law society's rooms on the first day of his disciplinary hearing in June 1989 with an entourage that included a blind woman in charge of recording the proceedings for him and a man carrying a sign with the plea, "Don't Harass Harry." Kopyto's defence — he acted as his own counsel—was an offence. Not only had he performed all the work shown in his legal aid billings, he told the discipline committee, he'd done *more*, hours of work that, magnanimously, he hadn't *bothered* to bill.

That contention failed badly when Frank Marrocco, the lawyer charged with presenting the case against Kopyto, observed that the 3,596 hours billed in 1985 meant that Kopyto would have laboured ten hours a day, seven days a week, fifty-two weeks a year. In addition, he would have had to shoehorn in time to handle the work he hadn't billed, time to eat, sleep, brush his teeth, and help his eleven-year-old daughter, Erica, with her homework.

Kopyto reversed field in a hurry and threw himself on the

committee's mercy, something a normal man might have intu-ited was in short supply. Okay, Kopyto admitted, he billed for twenty-four hours of work for one day in December 1986. He admitted that he billed seven hundred phone calls he didn't make and he billed for clients who had already paid him out of their own pockets. But, come on, he was *so* busy defending his unwashed clients he didn't have *time* to keep his records in apple-pie order.

The discipline committee found Kopyto guilty of profes-sional misconduct and recommended that he be disbarred.

Kopyto appealed to the entire convocation of Benchers.

"We gave him all the time he wanted in convocation," Bob Topp says. "Three days altogether, three days spread over a couple of months. We had other people up on disciplinary matters in the same period, but Kopyto was the guy we kept giving extra time. 'You need two more hours? Take three. Want to come back another day? No problem.' We leaned so far over backwards we almost fell on our heads."

Kopyto came to the convocation with a counsel this time, the black activist lawyer Charles Roach. Roach told the Benchers Kopyto's dilemma was a matter of "poor bookkeeping" and "sloppy habits." Kopyto testified on his own behalf. "I'm a workaholic," he said. "I would fall asleep at night with my dictation machine in my hands." Six character witnesses swore that Kopyto was a saint, and eleven-year-old Erica huddled at her dad's side, tears in her eyes.

Topp, remembering the convocation, looks about as stern as he gets, angry maybe.

"I didn't know the man before the hearing took place, Kopyto I'm talking about," he says. "I had no bias one way or the other, and at the hearing, I thought he and Charlie Roach gave a decent performance for their side. Another thing to keep in mind is that discipline cases are the toughest part of being a Bencher. I put myself in the shoes of the guy who's being disciplined and I think, there but for the grace of God . . ."

Topp takes a breath.

"That's one side of the picture," he says. And then his voice escalates. "The other side is that the legal aid fund is for people who don't have money to pay for their own legal problems. That's what really rankled with me about the Kopyto affair. The evidence satisfied me the man had taken money from the fund. *Taken* it. Taken it when other people needed it. That's a terrible, terrible thing."

On November 8, 1989, the law society disbarred Harry Kopyto.

"The law society," Kopyto said that day, "has just never run into a revolutionary socialist and Trotskyist who spends day and night fighting the system."

The cab driver who takes me from the Sudbury airport to Bob Topp's office is a dead ringer for Stompin' Tom Connors. It's rush hour on a humid August afternoon, and from the cab, the city looks flat and treeless. Mounds of smooth rock poke through the surface in the spaces between buildings. The skyline is dominated by a smokestack that might have come from the Land of the Brobdingnagians.

"Not a smokestack," the Stompin' Tom lookalike says. "A super stack. That's Inco's. It's built big and tall so's the smoke and shit won't land on the city any more. Now it blows where it oughta, all the way to Toronto."

Bob Topp's offices—a reception area, law library, space for three secretaries, Topp's working quarters—are on the second floor of a smart-looking five-storey building on one of the narrow downtown streets. He's recently moved in, and the smell of newness hangs in the air of his roomy corner office.

"This is a prosperous town, *very* prosperous," Topp says, on the boil as usual. "A miner who's been at Inco or Falconbridge for awhile, he makes seventy thousand a year. He'll have a house, a car, a cottage, a boat, a Skidoo. And you know what? All paid for. Lot of disposable income in town."

Topp has on one of his dark suits and a white shirt. He keeps a clean desk, and the office is furnished in solid no-nonsense taste, a desk of dark wood, sturdy armchairs, a sofa.

"They drink up here, *oh*, yes," he says. "In Sudbury, every activity is accompanied by a few drinks. Bowling, hunting, fishing, whatever, a drink goes with it. People finish work at five and they're talking about going home, they have three drinks while they discuss it. The down side is the police lay a whole lot of impaired driving charges. Helps keep a guy like me in business."

I smile at the small joke.

"Tonight," Topp says, "you'll have a chance to judge a little of that yourself."

"I will?"

"You'll love it," Topp says. "We're having a few people over to the house, about sixty, mostly lawyers and their wives. Some *beau*tiful Sudbury people."


Bob Topp, the party animal: fire-engine red Bermudas, white knee socks, white T-shirt featuring a parade of liquor bottles across the back, a rum and Coke in one hand, the other arm draped over a guest's shoulder while he tells a story about a Sudbury lawyer renowned for being intense but not acute.

"Everybody gets a kick out of this one," Topp says, leaning in, trying to keep from laughing all over his straight lines. "An Italian gentleman comes to the lawyer and says he's been charged with careless driving. 'Careless driving, no,' he says to the lawyer. 'Driving too close, yes.' So they go to court, and the lawyer's aggressive like always in his cross-examination. Finally he gets up to present his argument to the judge, and he uses his client's line. 'Careless driving, no, Your Honour,' he says. 'Driving too close, yes.' 'Thank you, counsel,' the judge says. 'The charge *is* driving too close. There'll be a conviction.' The lawyer hadn't *noticed* the charge. *Won*derful."

The Topp home, in a buttoned-down neighbourhood in the east end of the city called New Sudbury, has large, airy rooms, a swimming pool, and a view from the balcony that sweeps back to the lights of downtown. A bartender is manning a massive collection of wines and liquors in the kitchen. Out on the deck, the oldest of Topp's three kids, fourteen-year-old Daniel, flips hamburgers in the barbecue. And Topp's wife, Helen, a woman with a sunny, open face and all the time in the world to get social, works the room, an ingenuous smile and a piece of chatter for each guest.

"You probably heard about the moon walkers," a tall, grey-haired man says to me a trifle defensively. "Years ago when NASA was getting ready to send guys to the moon, they brought the astronauts to Sudbury for training. The kind of rock we got up here, it was the closest they could find to the surface of the goddamned moon."

"There're ten thousand Finns in Sudbury," a thirty-something lawyer says. His monotone and permanent frown identify him as one of them. "They came here in three waves: a century ago, then after World War One, and the last wave in the 1950s. My parents were in that last one. I practise real estate law. Most of the Finns in town come to me when they're buying or selling a house. Especially since last March, they come to me."

"What happened last March?" I ask.

"Teuvo Eloranta died," the Finnish lawyer says, no break in the monotone or the frown. "He used to be the other Finnish lawyer in town."

"Flea," I think the Crown attorney is saying. He is French-Canadian, muscular, feisty, a Jean-Paul Belmondo clone.

"Flea?"

"No, no, F. *Lee*," the Crown attorney repeats. "F. Lee Bailey, you know? That's what I call Bob. I phone up his office, I never say, 'Bob.' I say, 'Let me speak to F. Lee.' Bob is very good in court, you know. Just like F. Lee."

A beefy man with enormous hands introduces himself as a police officer and the former head of the Sudbury Police Association.

"Bob does all the work for the policemen in Sudbury," he says. "In fact, he acts for all the police associations across northern Ontario. A policeman gets in trouble, needs advice, Bob is the lawyer we call on. He gets in there and yells and argues and fights. That's because Bob understands the problems. He really knows what a policeman has to go through on the job."

"Why's that?" I ask. "Why does Bob have this special empathy?"

"Don't you know?" the beefy man says. "Bob used to be a policeman himself."


At ten o'clock next morning in his office, Topp talks about his years before the law.

"Born and raised in Regina," he says. "I got out of high school in 1965 and went straight to the Regina police force. Don't ask me why. I guess I was looking for a challenge, which is what I got. I started out on regular patrol work. Walking the beat. Midnight shift in the winter at thirty below, we used to wear a buffalo-skin hat and coat. With them on, you could fall asleep in a snowdrift and wake up in the morning perfectly warm. But *heavy*, oh, man, I was exhausted carrying that coat on my back for eight hours."

Topp asks his secretary to refill his coffee cup, black, no sugar. He got to bed at one after the party the night before and arrived at the office in time for a seven o'clock meeting. But, back in his uniform of dark blue suit and white shirt, he looks fresh and spruce.

"After two years on the Regina force," he continues, "I came east and joined the Ontario Provincial Police. It just seemed like a good idea. I was assigned to a town twenty-five miles west of here. Dowling. I got a taste of every kind of work. One homicide, a lot of multi-vehicular accidents on the highway, eight or nine traffic fatalities. There were times of great exhilaration, particularly when I investigated a major crime and made an arrest, and there were times of boredom beyond belief. I mean, you can only write so many traffic tickets without thinking you're having a very dull day. I got to testify in court a lot. It was my first taste of lawyers in action. The OPP didn't train us how to testify. But I realized the easy rule was just to tell the truth.

That turned out to be great preparation for practising criminal law."

Topp looks at his watch.

"Come on," he says. "We're going to court."

We walk a block and a half to Sudbury's low-slung, brick courthouse.

"A client of mine is coming up for sentencing," Topp says. "He was convicted in May and he's been out on bail. Today we argue about the sentence."

"What was he convicted of?"

"Aggravated assault and use of a firearm to commit the assault. Very serious matter we got here. Jail-time serious."

We enter Courtroom B. It's plain and functional and rather gloomy, without architectural flourishes but with lousy acoustics. Topp slides into a seat at the counsel's table. I sit halfway back in the public benches and try to figure out the judge's sex. The judge has elaborately styled grey hair, either long for a man or short for a woman, and a voice that's either soft for a man or deep for a woman. The clothes are no help; this judge wears a white shirt unbuttoned at the collar, no tie, under the traditional black gown. No earrings, but no moustache, either.

"Your Honour." Topp is on his feet. "I have a difficulty in speaking to the sentence this morning. I have no transcript of the proceedings before Your Honour in May when you registered a conviction against the accused. I submit, Your Honour, that I can't properly argue the matter of sentence without reference to that transcript."

"What's behind all this, Mr. Topp?" the judge asks.

"Perhaps Your Honour would allow me to call the court reporter who recorded the proceedings at trial?"

The judge nods, and Topp asks a man from the courtroom to step into the witness box. The man has mussed hair and a paunch.

"You are the court reporter who sat on this matter?" Topp asks him.

"Yes, I am."

"I understand you are unable to provide a transcript at this time."

"I won't have it ready for a year," the reporter snaps. "I'm far too busy."

"I've offered to have someone from my office help you. A secretary of mine could work on the transcribing."

"Oh, I couldn't allow that. It's impossible."

Topp shrugs at the judge, and he and the Crown attorney take turns offering alternatives—waiting a year until the transcript is ready, obtaining an order directing the court reporter to put the transcript at the top of his list—until the judge, announcing a fifteen-minute break to consider the next step, rises from the bench and leaves the courtroom. The judge is male.

"What I'm told is going on here," Topp says to me out in the hall, "is the court reporter has some beef against the province over a disability payment or something, money he's owed, and he's taking it out on the courts by going slow on the transcripts."

Topp shakes his head.

"Be right back," he says. "I got a couple guys in the jail next door who might be changing their minds about their pleas."

Topp leaves, and I talk to his client, the man who's sweating out the sentencing hearing. His name is Gerry Dubreuil. He's a short, heavy man in his early forties. He has black hair, dark eyes, and a round, worried face.

"I don't understand all this," he says. "I keep taking time off work to come to court and nothing happens. It's crazy I was convicted in the first place. It was all about my daughter and drugs. She was running with a bad bunch of guys who were into drugs, and I made her stay home. Some of these guys came to the house to liberate her. How do you like that? *Liberate* her, for Christ's sake, that's what they said. One guy was really violent. He broke the door. Put his fist through a wall. So I got my shotgun and drilled him in the leg. Then what happens? The person who gets convicted is *me*. The way I feel about it now, after everything I've had to go through, the only mistake I made was not aiming higher at that guy."

Dubreuil wanders into the courtroom. I wait in the hall, and a few minutes later, Topp hurries through the door from the jail.

"It never fails," he says. "Both guys in there told me they didn't do the crimes they're charged with. They wanted to plead not guilty. But neither guy can make bail. I told each of them, look, you're gonna spend three months in here before I can get you on for trial. All of a sudden, with both guys, it's, 'I wanta plead guilty.' I say, 'I thought you didn't do the crimes.' 'Never mind,' they say. 'Just plead me guilty.'"

I ask about Gerry Dubreuil.

"The judge on the case is real good," Topp says. "Experienced, smart, one of the best. But he blew this one. Gerry should never have been convicted."

The androgynous judge calls the court to order, and very quickly he, Topp, and the Crown attorney find a solution to the problem of the no-transcript sentencing hearing. The notes that the judge made for himself during the trial will be typed and made available to both counsel. In two weeks, when everyone has had a chance to digest the notes, the argument over Gerry Dubreuil's sentence will resume.

Out in the hall, Topp speaks to Dubreuil.

"Here's what you've got to focus on, Gerry," Topp says, his voice low, his head no more than six inches from Dubreuil's. "Think beyond the sentencing and focus on the appeal. We're taking this to the court of appeal, and I promise you they're gonna have one look at your conviction and toss it out. That's all they'll need, one quick look. You just focus on that, Gerry."

Topp pats Dubreuil on the shoulder and trots into Courtroom C to look after the interests of the two clients who've had second thoughts about their pleas. Courtroom C is a mate to Courtroom B except that it's on the side of the courthouse that catches the morning sun and is cheery with light. At the front of the room, crowded along both sides, a couple of dozen men lounge in chairs against the walls. They're the accused, who have been waiting in jail to have their cases heard. There are skinny men in dirty white singlets, fat guys with tattoos. Most are pale, most in their twenties. Their collective body odour leaves a rank cloud floating over the proceedings.

The court clerk calls the first of Topp's clients. He has a lanky build, Fu Manchu moustache, and a San Francisco 49ers sweater with Joe Montana's number on the back. The charge is read—driving a car with stolen licence plates and no insurance—and he pleads guilty. Topp points out to the judge that his client actually has a job and asks that the sentence be shaped around that fact. The judge is a man in his late thirties with a thick brown beard and a manner that is attentive, patient, and possibly a little bemused. He gives the lanky guy thirty days in jail to be served from eight o'clock Friday nights to six Monday mornings. Topp thanks the judge.

Topp's second client is called. The charge is breaking and entering, and the client is a teenager. He has pimples and fuzz on his face and a mouth that droops open. The Crown attorney recites the facts of the crime. The kid went to a stranger's house and said his father lived in the house across the street but was out and would the man help him get into his father's house. The man, divining correctly that the boy was lying, told him to beat it. The kid broke into the house across the street anyway and ran off with a VCR and a camera. The police nabbed him a few hours later.

"It wasn't a brilliant crime, Your Honour," Topp says to the judge. "You'll notice from this young man's record that he was in some trouble as a juvenile. But I point out, Your Honour, this is his first offence as an adult, and I ask you to keep that in mind in your sentencing."

The judge looks at the pimply kid as if he were gazing on a creature from another galaxy.

"You have plenty of time to change the path you're on," he says to the boy after a long pause. "I think you can. I hope you do. I, ah, wish you good luck."

He sentences the boy to sixty days in jail.

Topp and I leave the courthouse.

"That last judge, the guy with the beard," Topp says, "he's new on the job. He's probably catching on that most people who appear before him, the accused, they're not exactly from the segment of society that produces brain surgeons and rocket scientists."

In his office, Topp returns to his autobiography. In 1969, married a year, he left the Ontario Provincial Police and enrolled in Sudbury's Laurentian University as a full-time mature student. The desire for education doesn't appear to have sprung from any particular drive on Topp's part to better himself in a grand sense. It seems more intuitive, a step-by-step process as Topp felt his way towards a higher-paying, more absorbing job, maybe into a profession. Once on the path, though, he didn't fool around. At Laurentian, supported by his wife and by his own part-time process-serving agency, he rushed to a BA in a speedy twenty-four months. And a couple of weeks after graduation, he entered the University of Toronto Law School. That move apparently had its motivation in Topp's instincts, too, though some influence came from the example of a fellow OPP officer at the Dowling detachment, Brian Inglis, who left to take an undergraduate degree at McMaster University and a law degree at Toronto, class of '74. Topp followed in Inglis's footsteps and immediately found himself in a state of shock at law school.

"I was overwhelmed by the atmosphere," he says. "All these brilliant people, people with such wide education, MAs and PhDs, what was *I* doing with *them*? I was older than most of the others, too, and married. That made me even more different."

But if Topp was "terrified"—his adjective—he had at least sorted out from the beginning where he expected law school to lead him.

"Criminal law was in my mind all the way as what I'd practise. That was partly because I didn't see how a guy like me could get into the corporate law structure. But mostly it came from my police background. I was sort of taken with the idea that one day I'd go into court as a lawyer alongside the lawyers who'd cross-examined me when I was with the OPP."

One problem, though. Topp felt initially queasy making the switch from chasing criminals to learning how to defend them.

"I have to say I found the first-year criminal law course very difficult. I could grasp the principles, no trouble on that, but with my police training, I saw the fallacies in the principles, that the guilty could escape out the door. I had to push the old kind of thinking out of my mind, and I had to be careful sometimes what I said in class. I was a tad more shy about expressing myself than I usually am."

Topp didn't shake his apprehension over whether he could keep pace academically until the end of first year.

"The exam results came in the mail," he says. "My hands shook when I opened the envelope. But I looked at the marks and I'd done so well I surprised myself. After that, I thought, okay, I've managed to stay in the same pond with these people who have better educational credentials than me. Now, I told myself, *now* I've got the confidence to stick with them for two more years. And I did."

When I ask Topp for specifics about those years, he talks about concentrating on courses that would prep him for a career as a criminal lawyer, the advanced criminal law course, a seminar in advanced evidence, Eddie Greenspan's practitioner's course in criminal law, an extra constitutional law course. Then he slides into an anecdote that has nothing to do with academic life but plenty to do with the sort of guy Topp is.

"I came out of the law school's main door one day," Topp says. "And a teacher of ours, Ralph Scane, he was bending over someone who was lying flat out on the ground. At first, I thought, well, what's all this? Next thing, I realized the man on the ground had had a heart attack and Ralph was trying to do something about it, except he wasn't sure what or how. I'd had training in resuscitation stuff when I was with the OPP. It's actually very simple once somebody shows you. So I went to work on the man. His heart had stopped. Completely gone. No beat whatsoever. But I got him started again. The heart was beating, and just at that moment, an ambulance pulled up and whisked the guy away. Nobody knew who he was, and to this day, whenever I see Ralph Scane, we always say to one another, 'I wonder what happened to that man. I wonder if he lived.'"

During Topp's years at law school, Helen operated as chief breadwinner. She worked in the data base department at the *Toronto Star*. She also packed such delicious lunches for Topp that another student, Harriet Lewis, asked if his wife did take-out. In the summers, Topp picked up jobs that paid good money, one summer as the uniformed chauffeur for a corporate bigwig, another summer as a law clerk for the provincial government poring over a murky statute called the Land Speculation Tax Act.

When it came time for Topp to spend his year as an articling student with a law firm, he got lucky. Many students looking for experience in criminal law find themselves attached to broken-down barristers whose notion of training is to despatch their students on 10:00 a.m. runs to the liquor store. Topp articled with Bob Crane, a man who was not only sober but—reasonably rare among criminal lawyers—a stickler for detail.

"From Bob," Topp says, "I learned the value of keeping a written chronology of each case all the way through. It may sound simple-minded, but it's a way you win cases, just maintaining an up-to-date file that shows you what your client says, what the witnesses say, the physical evidence, the police's story, all the detailed stuff that paints the picture."

As soon as Topp was called to the bar, he and Helen caught the first train to Sudbury where Topp established himself as the hot new criminal lawyer in town. He turned no client from his door, a policy that has seen him represent police associations and accused murderers (twenty-six so far), businessmen in suits caught by the ubiquitous Sudbury impaired-driving patrols, and unemployed petty thieves on legal aid.

"Not high treason cases, I haven't done them, or insult to the Queen stuff, not it, either," Topp says in his office, smiling. Then, serious, "No hate literature cases. I'm not sure I could defend anyone who was charged with handing out hate literature."

"And you never had any doubts about acting for lawyers in trouble?" I ask.

Topp shakes his head solemnly. "None whatsoever."

Coming out of Topp's office on our way to lunch, we run into Helen. She works as Bob's office manager. She reviews a few routine business details with her husband. And one detail not so routine: a secretary has been blabbing secrets about clients to outsiders and has to be dealt with. Helen has also been waiting to say goodbye. She and the kids are off to spend a few days at her parents' cottage on an isolated lake north of Sudbury. Topp is staying home.

"No newspapers up there," Topp says to me out on the street. "I get frustrated in a place where I can't find three or four newspapers to read every day. We went on a trip to France one summer. Beautiful country, but, you know, it took me about fifteen minutes to get through the *International Herald Tribune*, and I had nothing else for the rest of the day."

We climb into Topp's big black Chevy van. Every July, he drives the family in it to Sarasota, Florida, for three weeks of sun, fish dinners, and newspapers.

"Hel*lo*, beautiful," Topp says to the hostess who shows us to a table at the restaurant he's taken me to, a gaudy spot called Marconi's.

"Hel*lo*, beautiful," he says to the waitress who brings the menus.

Topp orders a rum and Coke and talks about an inquest a few months earlier where he represented a twenty-five-year-old police officer.

"A guy dialed the Sudbury 911 number," Topp begins. "The guy had obviously been drinking. You can hear it in his voice. It's right there on the tape the police made of the whole call. The guy says, 'I have a rifle in my hands.' Then he says, 'I'm loading it.' You hear the sound of the working of the lever action on the rifle. The guy says, 'Well, I guess I got to go out and shoot one of them.' You hear him say that. You hear *every*thing."

Topp pauses. He takes a bit of rum and Coke and places his hands flat on the table, hunching forward.

"The guy puts the phone down. He doesn't hang it up. The receiver's still off the hook, and the tape on the other end of the 911 number's getting all of it, the sound of the guy's feet walking across the floor, the door opening. By this time, the cops are on the way. And on this tape, it's recorded, *all* of it."

Another pause, another sip of the drink.

"Here's what you hear. A policeman's voice, 'Police! Drop that gun!' Then another voice saying the same thing, another cop. 'Drop that gun!' Then quiet. Then a shot. Very sharp sound on the tape. Just one shot. That's all, and then a bunch of muffled voices and people running."

Topp straightens up, looks down at the table and back up to my face.

"The man with the rifle was dead. A young police officer had shot him through the head from forty feet away. That's a remarkable feat of marksmanship in itself when you think about it. One shot from forty feet, and he hit the target. But that was his job. His duty. He was faced by a guy holding a rifle who wouldn't put it down. The young officer had to shoot. But, hell, it was very emotional for him, *extremely* emotional. It was traumatic. And here's what compounded the young policeman's trouble—the rifle in the man's hands, the rifle he talked about on the phone, the rifle he was holding when he took the bullet in the head, it was . . . *empty*. Unloaded. Not a single bullet in the chamber. None."

Topp stares at me in silence for a moment.

"The young officer was put on administrative leave, and we went to the inquest. In the courtroom, the tape was played over and over again, all the voices and sounds from the time of the man's 911 call until he was shot dead. Then I got up in front of the inquest jury, and I said, 'Ladies and gentlemen, what you heard was the anatomy of a suicide. The poor man was trying to end his own life, and he arranged for a policeman to do the job.'"

"What happened?" I ask. "What did the jury find?"

"Exonerated everybody. They commended the police and the ambulance service, and we all went home."

Topp picks up the menu. "What do you feel like? The food here's *won*derful."

After lunch, Topp says, "Come on. I'll take you on the scenic tour of the city."

Sure, and second prize is two weeks in Beirut.

But Sudbury has surprises in store. The city, Topp tells me, is built around five lakes. He turns the Chevy van off a main thoroughfare onto an up-and-down two-lane road. A couple of minutes along it, and we're on a strip of land with big stretches of lake on either side. Houses that look as comfortable as old shoes sit by the water. On one dock, a woman in a bikini is sunning herself. Kids are splashing, fishermen are fishing, and farther out, where there's a brisk wind, sailboats spank across the water. Just beyond the horizon in all directions, I know there are office buildings and traffic jams and a giant smokestack. But here on the water, all is bliss. The woman in the bikini stands up, rises on her toes, and dives into the lake.

"*Beauti*ful," Bob Topp says.

# CHAPTER TWO

## *The Study Group*

HOWARD FELDMAN is fifteen minutes late for our appointment.

"What happened, I was way out in Mississauga discussing settlement with another lawyer," he says. "From the feel of the conversation, I thought it must be one of those meetings where you talk social until the last two minutes, then you go fast to the issues and wrap them up. But that wasn't it. It was more this lawyer way out in Mississauga was lonely. He wanted somebody to talk to. In circumstances like that, I couldn't tell the man I gotta leave."

Right away, I know I'm in the presence of a slightly offbeat sort of lawyer. Other things aside, Feldman is definitely a simpatico guy. It's in the eyes. They're dark and large, made larger by the thick lenses in the glasses he wears. The eyes invite confidences and return understanding. Feldman has dense brown hair and a brown beard flecked with grey. Both give him a faintly rakish air. In size, he's medium height and slim. He walks with a slight stoop at the shoulders, the way Walter Matthau walks in the movies. Feldman delivers lines with Matthau's timing, too.

"I got accepted in pre-meds when I came out of high school," he tells me. "But I made a terrible discovery. I can't stand the sight of blood. So I studied English literature. I thought I might write novels. But I made another discovery. I didn't have the talent to write novels. Or the discipline. I went into law."

Feldman practises family law. That figures. It's easy to picture him, the big dark eyes, all the patience in the world, sitting across the desk from a wounded husband or an outraged wife. He could handle the wounds and the outrage. But, as natural as the fit seems today, Feldman and family law, he arrived at it by a route that was circuitous and sometimes discouraging. Feldman had early doubts about where his career was headed.

"Sick, even," he says. "I felt sick."

We're taking a walk through the law school building. Feldman has asked to meet me here. He hasn't been back to the school in years, and he wants to check out what's new and what's intact from the old days.

"Whoa." Feldman stops in front of the framed picture of the 1975 graduating class, rows of small oval photographs, each student in coiffed hair, serious smile, the white fur of the Bachelor of Laws gown over the shoulders.

"In between Vickie Faulkner and Harvey Fine?" Feldman says, pointing. "Where I should be? Nobody, right? I didn't show on the day the photographs were taken. I was sick, and what was part of it, I was feeling alienated. For some reason, I had trouble getting an articling job. The interviews were going on around the same time as the picture taking, students getting interviewed by the big downtown law firms for articling positions. I don't know what it was, my looks, my style, whatever, all the firms turned me down. So I was thinking, the hell with it, why should I be part of a system, getting my photo taken and everything, that doesn't want to give me an articling job?"

Feldman talks about his family.

"My parents met in a displaced persons camp in Germany. Both came from small towns in Poland. At the start of the war, my dad was in the Polish army, 1939, and when the Germans invaded, they captured him. He escaped to the eastern part of Poland. The Germans hadn't got there yet. The Russians had. They took him into *their* army, and he fought the Germans again when they moved farther east in 1941. My dad spent the rest of the war working in a factory in Russia. By 1945, everybody in the family was dead except for an older brother and some cousins in Canada and Israel. My mother had a very bad time, too. She was in a concentration camp. She survived, but all she had left were a brother and a first cousin in Israel."

Feldman shrugs.

"Anybody whose parents went through a concentration camp," he says, "we have our own *meshuga*. Our own craziness."

In the larger picture, Feldman thinks he suffered from Jewish Prince Syndrome when he was growing up.

"This is typical in Eastern European families. Spoil the son. When my father had his hotel, what happened? My sisters washed the dishes, waited on tables. I played baseball and read books. My family treated me in special ways. But the catch was, later, by the time I got to university and began to think about things, I realized I had to do something in life to make up for the special treatment I got."

Feldman's father and mother arrived in Toronto in March 1950. Howard was born three months later, the second of three children, the first and only prince. His father got a job in a mattress factory. In 1956, Feldman senior and his older brother bought a variety store on Bathurst Street near St. Clair. Howard's father worked two jobs, in the mattress factory by day, in the variety store at night and on weekends. Everybody in both families, four adults and four children, lived in the rooms over the variety store. Howard remembers it as a happy time.

He was less thrilled a few years later when his father traded up from the variety store to a hotel in Hespeler. Hespeler is a town about sixty miles southwest of Toronto close to Mennonite country. The hotel had twenty-five rooms and a restaurant. Mrs. Feldman cooked nonkosher food in one pot for the customers, kosher food in another pot for the family. The Feldmans ate meals in a booth at the back of the restaurant, and teenaged

Howard longed for the cosmopolitan life at Bathurst and St. Clair.

"I moved back to the city when I took English at university," he says. "But one thing about the English course, I had too much time to think. Why did the war happen? Why did people like my parents have to endure what they did? What was my role in the world? Those kinds of issues I find very hot, very hard to handle. Maybe that's why I went into law. There's something concrete about law."

On an afternoon in early September 1972, before law classes began, Feldman went around to the school for a chat with Arnie Weinrib. Weinrib was talking to another student, and through the open door, Feldman could overhear the conversation.

"Well, my marks in my last year in arts," the student was saying, "they weren't, you know, that good."

"Sure, but we've accepted you," Weinrib said. He was the admissions officer, the man on the faculty who put together the package on each student, academic history, LSAT results, the application form with a personal statement from the student spelling out his or her feelings about law.

"But, ah, what I'm wondering," the student in Weinrib's office said, "with my background and everything, do you think I can hack law school?"

"Well, if you don't get an A in first year," Weinrib said, "I'll bounce you from here to Manitoba."

Feldman, out in the waiting room, clutched up.

"Arnie didn't say it in an aggressive way," Feldman remembers. "He isn't an aggressive person. He's a nice person. But the thing was, the reason I'd come to see him was that my *own* fourth-year marks in English weren't so great."

Classes began, and Feldman couldn't shake his uneasy feeling.

"There's a lot of pressure in first year, anyway," he says. "And I had the impression, the first couple of weeks, I was maybe in over my head."

Feldman leans forward a little, sharing something that's half secret.

"What saved my life was the study group."

Study groups are a tradition in law schools. Four, five, six students cloister themselves at regular intervals, perhaps once a week, more often as exams come closer, and analyze their courses. One session might focus on torts, the next time it's contracts, then it's criminal law. Everybody chips in ideas and interpretations, though sometimes, if the group hangs together for the whole school year—study groups can dissolve out of a lack of chemistry among the members or out of sheer ennui— one or two students might emerge as leaders. The leaders aren't necessarily the brightest, merely the most vocal. So, some dominate, some absorb. It doesn't matter. The strength is in the group, and all members come away with different levels of reassurance. A kind of academic and personal communing has taken place.

The study group that saved Howard Feldman's life numbered five guys. They came together almost immediately in first year, early in the fall of 1972, and they remained a group through the entire year. Even more amazing, their group was one of only two in the class that stayed together as a unit to the very end of third year.

The other four members of Feldman's group were Mike Mitchell, Joel Saltsman, Dave Baker, and Jim Blacklock. By any measuring stick, those four have had careers since law school that are long in accomplishment. Mitchell is a leading labour law practitioner. Baker is the founder and director of the Advocacy Resource Centre for the Handicapped, an organization that does just what the name says—it provides the legal power to handicapped people who are brave enough to fight for their rights. Blacklock is a senior counsel in the Ontario attorney general's office. Saltsman is a teacher and businessman in Paris, France. Solid men, all four, smart guys pursuing worthwhile careers.

Nobody from the group remembers which of the bunch first said, hey, guys, let's put on a study group. But everyone imagines Feldman must have been key to the organization. Mitchell, for one, is clear that, if not for Feldman, he would probably have wandered solo through law school.

"I wanted to be part of a study group," Mitchell says, "but I was a social klutz. Luckily I met Howard on the first day of law school in our property class. Howard is open to everybody, social klutzes included, and through his friendship, I ended up where I wanted to be—in a study group."

So Feldman was the group's point man, at least in the club-bable sense. He knew Saltsman slightly from the years when both attended the same synagogue in southwestern Ontario. He hit it off with both Mitchell and Baker in the very early days of law school. Mitchell had already struck up an acquaintanceship with Jim Blacklock. Somehow, *voilà*, a group.

"Our study group wasn't exactly like the way it is in *Paper Chase*," Feldman tells me. "You know that movie? The stereotype of 1970s law school. Very Harvard, very intense, very competitive. Ours wasn't exactly like that, but close enough. The group showed me what the other guys thought about cases, how much they were studying, where they put the emphasis. And there was a wide variety of approaches within the group. Dave Baker was less traditional and very creative. He'd look at cases from different angles than other people. Jim Blacklock was a straight, middle-of-the-road guy. He went at cases from a very logical perspective. I was the guy who benefited from all those approaches. These were bright, bright people I was in with. Take Joel and Mike, here were two guys out of the class of 150, they finished in the top five in the first-year exams."

But, for Feldman, the academic stuff, all the chatter about cases, didn't entirely define the group's final measure of significance. Maybe of more help to him was the psychological propping up the group gave its members, especially him.

"You start at law school, and it's an us–against–them situation," he explains. "Me against the system. I couldn't go it alone. I needed allies. And the study group is where I found them. I'm talking about more than just having people you can sit around with and bitch about your problems at the school. There's that, but there's more. There's the sense of collegiality you need as a student in a law school. You might eventually get that from the class as a whole, but you have to work up to that level, and what you start with is the study group. That's the first bonding."

When Feldman couldn't find an articling job after law school, he knocked around Europe for three months. Back in Toronto, he got taken on as an articling student at a big downtown Toronto firm, Thomson Rogers. He worked on the corporate-commercial side. It was an experience of mixed pleasures.

"I admire people of unique and powerful abilities, people like the lawyers at Thomson Rogers," Feldman says. "But I have trouble getting along with them. In some respects, I'm afraid of authority. I sympathize with the victims."

He left Thomson Rogers and spent his last two articling months in the company of the victims. They were his clients at the Parkdale Legal Clinic, clients with poor-people problems: landlords who gouged them, bureaucrats who baffled them, employers who stiffed them. Feldman worked for nothing and lived on his bar mitzvah bonds.

He was called to the bar and stood back for the job offers to roll in. None did.

"That confused me," he says. "I thought once you got through law school, it was, okay, where's the money, the big house, the Cadillac? I thought I'd made it. I'd graduated. So where were the rewards?"

An economic recession was on. It reached into the levels of the legal community where Feldman expected to operate, if he could just figure out which levels those were. He scrambled. A temporary job brought in a pay cheque for a few months. He moved forty miles east, to Oshawa, and practised a mix of law for two and a half years. At a depressing low, he collected unemployment insurance.

In the early 1980s, a friend of Feldman's in Toronto was

leaving his practice. Feldman took it over. It was a hodgepodge, a bunch of legal aid clients, different kinds of litigation, some clients who actually had money to pay their own bills.

"I did all kinds of stuff," Feldman says, "but what gave me the most rush were the family law files."

Maybe this was the answer to the big one, the question Feldman had been asking himself for years: "What's my role in the world?"

His role is to practise family law.


By way of definition, Feldman says, "Family law is essentially looking into people's bedrooms, their bank accounts, their closets, into their garages, their pension plans, into the lives and houses and assets of their girlfriends and boyfriends.

"Family law," he goes on, "is taking a hot situation and trying to make it cool.

"Family law," he says again, "is a combination of immediacy, hostility, empathy, aggression, destruction, comedy, suicide, urgency . . ."

"Hold it," I say. "*Suicide?*"

"Right near the beginning of my practice," Feldman says, "one of my earliest clients was a businessman who developed a drinking problem. He dropped all the way down the rungs, as far as skid row. His wife didn't want him to see the kids. We went to court, and the judge ordered that my client should have some access. He was supposed to see his children on a Sunday. Monday, the lawyer on the other side phoned me. He said my client hadn't showed up on the Sunday. The reason was he'd killed himself. It was—how else can I describe it?—very upsetting. It was devastating."


Feldman explains how a lawyer gets rich practising family law.

"By litigating everything. A lawyer who goes to court a lot, that's money in the bank, the lawyer's bank. If the lawyer has a client who comes in and says, argue every issue, go to court whenever you have to, destroy my spouse, then the lawyer's got it made. Even better, if this client has rich parents, and it's the parents who are paying the bills to destroy the spouse, the lawyer is really laughing."

Feldman has not gotten rich practising family law. He prefers to settle rather than to litigate. But this is a tricky area, litigation versus settlement, because, perhaps more than any other branch of the law, family law is charged with raw emotions.

"The clients come to your office," Feldman says, "and the thing always in the back of your mind is, this is a situation that is not starting off from a rational basis. The context is emotionally skewed. That's a given. Next thing, what you say to the clients will have an impact on how they're going to govern themselves throughout the whole of the case. You can rev their motors high and make them aggressive by the way you treat them. Or you can make them more reasonable. More reasonable is definitely better."

Feldman has a theory that in family law—probably in all areas of litigation—clients gravitate to the lawyers they were meant for, a match made in heaven or hell.

"Some lawyers have a mean, finicky, aggressive approach," he says, "and they tend to get the hostile clients who don't mind walking all over their spouses. What's behind this, the public wants to think there is a certain lawyer for them in their situation whatever their situation is. They want to think there are criminal lawyers who work miracles, who are champions of the innocent, who sometimes get guilty people off. In the family context, they want a lawyer who can crush their spouse. That's because *they* want to crush their spouse. Or perhaps they're afraid they'll be pushed around unless they hire a lawyer they perceive to be mean and finicky and aggressive."

I ask Feldman what category of clients he represents.

"Probably I get the more reasonable people," he answers. "The tendency is towards the less aggressive clients. I get more victims."

Victims, Feldman says, can be troublesome.

"The real problem comes when you get sucked in by the

victim clients. You end up doing extra work for them, sometimes very litigious work, without making a profit on it. Your
empathy for the client goes too far, and you lose money. The
only reward is you think you've done something right for a
person who's been victimized."

It gets worse. With victim clients, besides showing a financial
loss, Feldman finds himself under strains nobody mentioned in
law school.

"Clients on legal aid," he says, "they telephone, they write
letters. Repeatedly they do those things. There seems to be a
correlation between not being personally responsible for paying
the bills and inundating the lawyer with ideas and requests and
demands. Or clients who are retired or unemployed or disabled,
for them time takes on a different meaning. Where in a business
sense they could wait a month, in the situation of a family law
matter, a half hour is too long. They put stress on you."

Feldman thinks about what he's just said.

"Some family law practitioners, the smart ones," he goes on,
"they have social workers on staff in their offices."

I suggest that maybe, with the attitudes and style he has, he's
his own office social worker.

Feldman doesn't buy it.

Well, I say, he *sounds* like a social worker sometimes.

He isn't buying that, either.

$$\star \quad \star \quad \star$$

David Baker is brushing up on his French. He's come to the
right place, to Provence, the part of the south of France that has
many fine things going for it, sunshine, rosé, Cézanne, a landscape that rolls up from the Mediterranean in shallow valleys
and well-weathered mountains, a manageable landscape. Baker
is in the next to last month of a seven-month sabbatical-cum-
holiday from his job in Toronto as head of the Advocacy
Resource Centre for the Handicapped. ARCH, which Baker
founded in 1980, goes to bat for handicapped people in the
courts and wherever else lawyers can be effective. For his sab-

batical, he and his wife and two children are living in Puy-loubier, a village about a dozen kilometres due east of Aix-en-Provence, which is where I catch up with him.

Aix is small (population: 160,000), serene, and a university city. Naturally, the university has been around for a while, since 1413. The students, on the other hand, are young and gorgeous and incredibly chic, and make the streets practically sing with their *joie* and *esprit*. The city's main avenue, Cours Mirabeau, is short and ideal, about a kilometre long, lined on both sides by rows of plane trees that look as if they've been standing there since the Romans came through in the second century B.C. The avenue's houses are early eighteenth century, and its name is taken from Gabriel Riquetti, Comte de Mirabeau, an eloquent rogue who sweet-talked his way to the leadership of the National Assembly in 1790 and was only uncovered, after his death and after the naming of Cours Mirabeau, as being simul-taneously a secret agent for King Louis XVI.

Early on a warm winter afternoon, David Baker picks me up near the three-tiered fountain that defines the western end of Cours Mirabeau, and heads into the countryside. The car is a Renault station wagon. Baker says he's put plenty of miles on it, especially on a long family tour over Christmas and the New Year to Paris, London, Edinburgh, Holland, Denmark, Germany, and Austria. Aix falls behind, and the countryside begins to rise towards the mountain up ahead. It's Mont Sainte-Victoire. There are vineyards and a few trees, but green isn't the predominant colour of this landscape. Grey is, an elemental, ancient grey. The world out here seems stripped down to nature's essentials. It's as if we're driving straight into the movie version of one of Marcel Pagnol's turn-of-the-century novels, *Jean de Florette* or *Manon des Sources*. Baker reads my mind.

"We think we've figured it out," he says, gesturing towards a line of mountains to the southwest. "That's where they must have filmed the movies, where the books took place. Jean tried to start his farm up there."

Perfect.

Baker and I sit beside the desk in the room where he's established a writing space on the second floor of the small Puyloubier house. He has brought a computer from home to work on a few projects, mostly articles and reports, one called "Employment Systems for Disabled People," for the Ontario government, another called "Affirmative Action and the Charter of Rights." Baker is a big man. He wears glasses, and his dark blond hair is brushed back from his forehead in a long sweep. He gives off a palpable sense of calm. That goes well with his facial expression, which seems to say he's really interested in what other people are telling him, though in this case, I want him to tell things to me. He obliges.

"I remember Arnie Weinrib giving a talk when I was a U of T undergraduate about why a legal education was useful to have," Baker says. "I remember that talk very clearly. It was in the senior common room at Trinity College, the sun was coming in through the big windows, and Arnie was saying, 'All we care about at law school is quality.' He was very passionate about that, about quality and objectivity. I listened, and I wondered what Arnie would think of me. I thought, I'm tall and blond and a student at Trinity, which is WASPish and stuck-up and rich and useless, and he's this short, dark, intense Jewish guy. What's he think of me? After the speech, I went up and talked to him, I asked questions. What do we do about the disadvantaged? I was thinking of that even back then. Who has the power to accomplish things? I had the conversation with Arnie and I thought he was superb the way he talked to me. Toronto was the only law school I applied to."

The study group.
"We were like random atoms, the five of us," Baker says, "searching for a way to link up with something. We linked up with one another."

Baker went into first year not knowing anyone in the class. "I looked at people, just testing," he says. He was attracted to Howard Feldman because they shared a zeal for literature, to Mike Mitchell because they shared a zeal for NDP politics. The group evolved quickly—Baker, Feldman, Mitchell, Jim Blacklock, Joel Saltsman.

"It was a way of sharing the workload," Baker says. "But I don't think that was the main point about the group. The community aspect was more important to me. I looked at the group as like having someone to talk to about a novel I'd read."

Baker thinks he may have lacked something the others had for the law—intensity.

"I was always wandering off to political rallies and to extra English classes. I probably couldn't have articulated it at the time, but later on, I realized law school moves to a formula, and I'm only interested in change. A lecturer would say about his subject, 'This is how it is,' and I'd only think of how it could be something different."

In the civil procedure exam in first year, the students were asked to justify the hired-gun approach in legal representation, why it's proper for a counsel to go into court and act for whatever party has retained him.

"That doesn't cut it with me, the idea that it's okay to work for one side of an issue one day and for the opposite side the next day. It isn't right. I wrote an answer on the exam that argued against the hired gun. I got the lowest mark that I had the entire time I was at law school."

The person who taught the civil procedure course, a practitioner from downtown, was Ian Scott, perhaps the consummate counsel of his generation, strong on labour cases, and in the 1980s attorney general in David Peterson's Ontario Liberal government. Two years after the fateful exam, Baker articled with Scott and got a firm grounding in labour law. He admires Scott as a man and as a lawyer. But he hasn't changed his mind about hired guns. He's made a career out of acting only for people he thinks are on the side that is right.

Baker isn't a radical. That's not the word for him. Nor is revolutionary. He's a guy who figures out for himself what is just and then won't budge.

For high school, he attended the University of Toronto Schools, a small, private institution for smart kids, co-educational since the early 1970s but all male in Baker's day. He was the first boy at UTS to sport a Beatles haircut. The headmaster, a traditionalist in a three-piece blue suit named Brock Mac-Murray, told Baker his hair was setting a poor example around the school. Get it cut. Baker refused. There were discussions in MacMurray's office.

"We compromised," Baker says. "I agreed to flatten my hair with Brylcreem during the day. But I didn't cut it."

At law school, Baker was active in student legal aid, "active" being to understate his involvement by a few hundred degrees. In particular, in the summer after his first year, he brought legal aid to the Mental Health Centre on Queen Street West in Toronto. He went on the wards and talked to the patients. No legal person had ever before done that on a regular basis.

"It was a situation I perceived as basically one of domination of one group, the patients, by another group, the staff. That wasn't much good from a therapeutic point of view. The issue was that the patients had no rights. In the mental hospitals, the norm was mass-product health care, and no one, not the patients, had the power to protest. I was talking to people, including some psychiatrists who saw me as an instrument of change in the old methods, talking about people's problems and about finding a way to somehow help them by using the legal system."

Though he was busy over the next few years on other fronts, including work on a masters in labour law, which he didn't complete, Baker stuck at his idea to apply legal solutions to the problems of mental patients and of all the rest of society's handicapped. In 1978, he went to Washington and put in three months with Ralph Nader. His main assignment was to do research on the taxation of insurance companies (how do they avoid them, et cetera). He recalls the period as "a very happy time, working with highly motivated, very bright people who could earn fortunes in private practice but contributed to Nader for twelve thousand a year." What Baker was also up to in Washington was thinking through his scheme about linking law and the disadvantaged. When he returned to Toronto, he had developed the concept for the group that became the Advocacy Resource Centre for the Handicapped.

The basic premise was simple but, surprisingly, original: "I wanted an organization *of* disabled people, not *for* them."

In the United States, by contrast, Baker had seen lawyers and students active in public interest law, but, as he says, "They had no connection with the people they were acting for, no accountability to, for example, disabled people." Baker thought connection and accountability were central to long-term results. He invested a year and a half in networking and meetings to bring together representatives from the blind community, the mentally handicapped, from six or seven groups of people who were all in the same boat in a general sense but had never worked in concert. As a single unit, with Baker supplying the legal thrust, they could assert their rights. That was the idea.

It was in some ways a rough period for Baker. He earned some money doing jobs at the Association for the Mentally Retarded. But at the same time, he watched his law classmates beginning to shoot ahead in the big downtown firms.

"I have to admit," he says, "it sometimes got under my skin when guys from the big downtown firms would question what I was doing."

Baker persisted, and his concept fell into place. He got a board of directors with each disability group having one board representative. (The AIDS people would join a few years later.) On February 1, 1980, the Advocacy Resource Centre for the Handicapped opened offices over a public library in north Toronto. ARCH had three employees. One was blind. Baker was in business, ready to go to court and establish, under law, that disabled people have rights, too.

Action central in the Puyloubier house is the kitchen. The house is one of a row running up the hill of Avenue Pierre Jacquement, and it has the usual eccentric French layout. The main bedroom, architecturally, ought to belong to the house on the other side of the stone wall. The kitchen isn't big, but it's a friendly room, and the wooden table, good for six people, is a natural gathering place.

At the moment, the principal decor consists of birthday cards for Stoney Baker, just turned four. She has dazzling red hair and the loopy energy of the little kid in "Calvin and Hobbes." Her brother, Zeke, is nine, blond and formidably intelligent. He's responsible for one of the great one-liners. When his parents asked him if he wanted to go to the Nelson Mandela rally and speech in Toronto in 1991, he said, "What, *another* politician?!"

Birthe is the mother of these neat kids. She's tall and rangy and about the sexiest smoker since Simone Signoret in *Room at the Top*. The smoking's a problem. Birthe's husband and kids won't let her do it in a room or moving vehicle in which they are present. She's taken to leaning out of upstairs windows for a puff. She was born in Denmark, has a PhD in criminology from Cambridge, and when the NDP was in opposition in Ontario, she was a researcher and speech writer for the party. After Bob Rae was elected, she went to work in the whip's office. At the end of the Puyloubier sabbatical, there'll be an NDP job of some sort waiting at home.

Baker and I go for a walk through the village. It's all up and down on narrow streets that follow the rises and falls of Mont Sainte-Victoire's lowest levels. At the bottom of a hill, we're abruptly in the country. But first we pass expensive bungalows on large lots. These are the suburbs. Baker says he plays on the town team in regular basketball games on an outdoor court, town vs suburbs. There's a retirement home for members of the Foreign Legion at the edge of Puyloubier, and a legion cemetery. Baker has a neighbour who's an old Legionnaire, and he's picked up some legion lore. Members of the Foreign

Legion really were foreign—no French citizens allowed—and most had grim and secret pasts, a murder, perhaps, or a faithless wife or, most dramatic possibility of all, the murder of a faithless wife.

Baker and I keep walking, and he talks about the Dustin Clark case from 1983. It was the one that put ARCH on the map, or at any rate in the newspapers and on TV. Some people wanted to make a movie out of the case, but Dustin Clark told them to forget it. Not precisely *told* them, but then that's part of the story. Dustin Clark couldn't talk—and had difficulty doing some other tasks.

"Dustin was a young man who'd been institutionalized since he was a year and a half old," Baker begins. "His parents put him away. He had cerebral palsy. He couldn't talk, but he was a sharp guy. He wanted to move out of the institution and live a normal life on his own in Ottawa. Everybody was against it, his parents and the institutional system and the attorney general's office. Acting for Dustin, I knew I was in deep."

Baker was fighting the system big time on the Dustin Clark case. He brought the issue—should Clark be allowed to make his own choice for freedom?—before a county court judge in Perth, Ontario. It was Baker on one side and a line-up of heavy-duty counsel for the parents, the attorney general, and the various medical authorities on the other side.

"I felt as exhilarated as I've ever felt in litigation," Baker says. "The case stood for a whole group of people who had never been able to speak for themselves."

Most of the trial was a battle of experts, psychiatrists and psychologists for both sides, testifying, undergoing cross-examination. But the case, which lasted four weeks, came down to Dustin Clark in the witness box. He communicated by way of a Bliss board. It's a device invented by a certain Dr. Bliss that enables the communicator to get across his or her message by working a wide range of symbols on a board. Imagination is needed to manage the board. Imagination is necessary on all sides, in the questioning, in the answers, in the interpretation of the answers.

"Dustin testified for half a day," Baker says. "When he finished, he was dripping wet."

But his imagination on the Bliss board had meshed with the Perth judge's imagination. And when the judge handed down his ruling, he sprang Dustin Clark from his institutionalized life.

"The case," Baker says, "was about people who hadn't been taken seriously before. Now they were. Now they were getting listened to. They were getting the message across."

What of Dustin Clark?

He writes poetry, travels to countries he could only dream of in the institution, lives a life that he controls—and isn't doing a bad job of the controlling.


A decision by the Ontario Court of Appeal was delivered in another significant ARCH case in the summer of 1991. By this time, ARCH had grown to a staff of twenty-two. Each year, it was fielding twelve thousand inquiries from handicapped people who wanted to know their rights, turning away about twenty-five hundred cases that might have the potential to be litigated, and taking approximately one hundred cases to court. A matter involving two men named George Reid and Kenneth Gallagher was one of the cases that reached court and came to a far-reaching conclusion in the court of appeal.

Reid and Gallagher were confined to the Penetanguishene Mental Health Centre after they had been found not guilty of criminal offences by reason of insanity. At Penetang, doctors treated both men with anti-psychotic drugs, which were designed to suppress the worst symptoms of their illnesses—the delusions, hallucinations, the agitated behaviour. The drugs had nasty side effects—notably horrible facial tics—and when Reid and Gallagher regained their mental competence and were shown to be no longer a physical threat to themselves or others in the mental health centre, they asked to be taken off the anti-psychotic drugs. Penetang doctors refused. ARCH took the case of Reid and Gallagher to court.

David Baker didn't handle the courtroom work in the case. It's a measure of ARCH's present stature that the centre boasts counsel better than he is. Better than Baker, a guy who's argued five cases before the Supreme Court of Canada? The two lawyers on the Reid-Gallagher case were Anne Molloy and Carla McKague. "I'm especially not in Anne's league," Baker says. "She's a John Robinette of the future."

The case turned on the interpretation of the section in the Charter of Rights that guarantees life, liberty, and the freedom of the person. A provision in the Ontario Mental Health Act allowed for a review board to hear bids from attending physicians for orders authorizing them to give drugs to involuntary patients who were mentally competent and didn't want the drugs. That's what happened to Reid and Gallagher—the review board okayed the treatment against the two men's wishes—and Molloy and McKague argued that, wait, the Charter of Rights ought to override the review board provision in the Mental Health Act. The court of appeal agreed.

Mr. Justice Syd Robins wrote the court's thirty-eight-page ruling, and among many other opinions, he said: "To completely strip these patients of the freedom to determine for themselves what shall be done with their bodies cannot be considered a minimal impairment of their Charter right." Cautious phrasing, but the result was clear.

"What's important about the case," David Baker explains, "is that it swept away the last vestiges against the principle that even though you're in hospital against your will, if you're mentally competent, you can refuse treatment that doctors prescribe. That's the law in Ontario, a mentally competent patient has the right to choose how he or she is treated. That's the law, and one thing certain, it hasn't undercut the practice of psychiatry or anything else medical."

In this law, in Ontario's case law, and in its statute law, the province is in the lead in an enlightened approach to patients' rights issues. Not just in Canada—in the *world*. Germany has a developed program, Baker says, and Sweden's coming along. But Ontario's the best.

"I'm proud of what's happened in the province," Baker says. He lets a beat go by, and smiles. "The handicapped community is happy, too."

★    ★    ★

Jim Blacklock looks too gentle to be what he is. He's a senior counsel in the Ontario attorney general's office. Slim build, medium height, brown hair cut short on the sides, floppy on top, and a kindness in his face, a kindness in his voice. But then maybe I'm wrong. Maybe a Crown attorney doesn't have to look hard-edged and severe.

We talk in his house in north Toronto on a Thursday afternoon when he's taking a day off. He suggests we go down to the basement. He's established a mini office in one corner, a small desk, computer terminal to the side, a couple of mismatched chairs. He carries down two Budweisers and glasses.

"I've thought about changing careers many times," he says. "But I don't know what I'd do. Maybe teach high school."

Ah, there now, a schoolteacher. That's more what Jim Blacklock looks like, the teacher all the kids would remember, especially the shy ones.

Blacklock thinks one small impetus to form the study group came from what happened in class on the first day of Arnie Weinrib's property course.

"The first class was, what is property?" Blacklock says. "The vocal people tried to answer the question, and they got systematically destroyed. They'd come out with a notion, and Arnie would make it apparent that this was one of the silliest ideas of what property is he'd ever heard. That sprung us into togetherness and into a group."

Blacklock guesses he got in the group because he became friends with Mike Mitchell. "Over the years," he says, "I've felt close to Michael." He thinks Mitchell is brilliant.

"I'll tell you a story about Mike," he says. "This is the honest truth, this story. In first year, he never went to any of the civil procedure classes, ever. About two weeks before the final exams, he read the course materials and he asked me if he and I could sit down and talk about them for a couple of hours. I went over the stuff with him. We wrote the exam. Michael Mitchell stood first in the class in civil procedure."

What did each guy bring to the group?

"Mike was practical as well as smart. He'd been involved in politics, working in the Manitoba NDP government. He saw issues not just in an academic way, but he could bring them down to reality. That really impressed me. This person had actually been out in the political world getting things done.

"Joel Saltsman was just a very, very bright kid, and Howard Feldman had a tremendous sense of humour.

"Dave Baker was the wacko one in the sense that he would take an idea from a case and be very dogmatic and develop the idea through fourteen different principles that would lead him down the line to some absolutely startling conclusion."

What about himself? What about Jim Blacklock?

"I don't think I brought anything in particular to the group. The other people liked me and thought I was a decent person to be around. I wasn't a complete fool."

I forgot to say that, in addition to too gentle, Blacklock is too modest.


Jim Blacklock makes me feel secure. I'm a taxpayer, and he's the kind of civil servant I want on the job. He cares about his work, about the people of his province, about principles. He always has cared.

He says (and there isn't an ounce of sanctimony in this), "Part of me thought, even when I was a kid, that the public deserved good representation in court, and I was under the mistaken impression that lawyers in government were all hacks. So I wanted to go down there and really represent the public. Then I got to the attorney general's office and discovered they had a lot of very fine lawyers. I was glad to be in their company."

Blacklock grew up in Guelph, a small Ontario city. His father drove trucks for a living. His mother worked, too, but went to university when she was older and got an MA. Young Jim saved and went to the University of Western Ontario and studied history. He planned to teach high school. This is beginning to sound like a résumé politicians would give their right arms for. But Blacklock points out there's a dark side to his background. Well, darkish.

"I had a bit of a chip on my shoulder when I arrived at law school," he says. "I've always had this sort of small-town distrust of big-city intellectual types."

He entered law after only two undergrad years of history. Today, he thinks that was a mistake. "I'm not as well read as I should be," he says. The basement room he's talking in is lined with shelves of books. At the time, he had his reasons for leaving Western. Jobs teaching high school history were hard to come by in the early 1970s, and there was this girlfriend who lived in Toronto, and Blacklock's ambition to be a lawyer for the people hadn't gone away. He went to law school and had occasional but ongoing and fierce battles with disillusionment.

"I blew up one day in class in third year," he says. "I couldn't understand what the process was doing to us. I'd lost contact with a lot of my old friends. I found I had to work very hard and very long at law school, and I didn't think the school was well designed in terms of the human side. In class one day, I raised all of this. Maybe it's just me, I said, but I don't think the process of going through three years of law school is run with much thought to the students as people. It's just designed to produce young lawyers who have basic skills. It isn't a compassionate process. I said all of that, but I didn't get much reaction. I guess most people found law school a lot easier than I did."

Blacklock's wife comes down the basement stairs carrying an elegantly arranged plate of cheeses, crackers, and grapes.

"Something to help your conversation along," she says.

Her name is Claire. She is blond and sunny and beautiful. She's French-Canadian. Howard Feldman says, "With his

French-Canadian wife, Jim is the image of an integrated vision of the country." No exaggeration. The Blacklocks are the poster couple for national unity.

Blacklock articled at the Ontario attorney general's office, and after he was called to the bar, he was offered a job in the office on the criminal side (as opposed to the civil side). So were four other students. The AG was seriously short of bodies. The five new people were handed virtually all of the office's appeal work, arguing appeals by convicted criminals—appeals against their convictions, against the length of their sentences—or arguing appeals by the attorney general of acquittals or of sentences that seemed too lenient. Within six months, Blacklock appeared in the Supreme Court of Canada. He was twenty-five years old. He doesn't recall that first appearance, but he remembers his first time, earlier, before the Ontario Court of Appeal. It was a sentence appeal by a convict. The appellant wasn't present in court. He had filed his appeal, as he was entitled to, in writing and without benefit of counsel, asking that his sentence be reduced.

"Where is the appellant now?" one of the court of appeal judges, Mr. Justice Lloyd Houlden, asked Blacklock. "In an institution?"

"He's in Warkworth, My Lord."

"Of course, Mr. Blacklock, that's one of our best federal institutions."

Houlden was trying to be friendly and helpful, make the new kid feel at home. But Blacklock didn't get it.

"I don't know, My Lord," he said to Houlden. "Is it really? One of the best? Warkworth?"

"Well, you should. . ." Houlden started. He was going to say, "Well, you *should* know." But he stopped himself and modified it to, "Well, I'm sure you'll know next time."

"The court of appeal was very patient and generous with the five of us breaking in," Blacklock says. "But it was worthwhile for them to bear with us because we put a tremendous part of our lives into trying to do a good job for the court and for the province."

At first, Blacklock took a share of trials as well as appeals, but for the last seven years, he's done exclusively appeal work. There is no other lawyer in Ontario, apart perhaps from a gifted defence lawyer, an appeal specialist named Marc Rosenberg, who has had the same number and range of criminal appeals. Blacklock is the big hitter for the Crown, and he's gone up against the home-run people on the defence side, Rosenberg, Alan Gold, the Greenspan brothers, Eddie and Brian, Michael Moldaver before he was appointed to the bench.

"Is that what's made you step up a notch?" I ask confidently. "Arguing against quality guys like that?"

"No," Blacklock answers. Flat, categorical. "The thing that drove me was arguing before Arthur Martin."

In his day, which stretched very long, Arthur Martin was the greatest of all Canadian criminal lawyers. He defended accused murderers at a time when a jury's guilty verdict meant the noose. He defended bank robbers, escaped German POWs in World War Two, elderly Oriental gentlemen who supervised mah-jongg games. But you might not recognize Arthur Martin at work, not if your concept of a criminal lawyer is someone in a CNN trial from Florida, one of the guys on *LA Law*, a flashy mouthpiece. Martin's tools were scholarship, brevity, reserve, dignity. He's a bachelor, a race horse fancier, a quiet man. In the mid-1970s, he was named to the Ontario Court of Appeal, and given his background, he sat on many, many criminal appeals.

"Arthur Martin was my hero," Blacklock says. "He saw how important criminal law is to society. He had the human, caring, compassionate side along with the side that knew when to draw a line, knew when the law had to be a certain way and why it had to be that way. He listened to everybody in court, gave everybody a fair hearing, treated everybody with respect. And he was incredibly prepared on each case. He knew his law to an unbelievable degree. I appeared before him for nine or ten years, until he retired, and it was a constant seminar. The fact I'm still doing what I'm doing is the result of what I saw in Arthur Martin as a judge and as a man."


A week earlier, talking on the phone, Blacklock had told me he was on his way to Ottawa for argument before the Supreme Court in the Ernst Zundel appeal.

Zundel is a photo retoucher in Toronto, very deft at it, too. As an infamous sideline, he denies the Holocaust. That the Nazis murdered six million Jews, he keeps announcing, is definitely suspect. A hoax, in fact. In the early 1980s, Zundel published a thirty-two-page booklet to that effect. A woman named Sabrina Citron of the Canadian Holocaust Remembrance Association laid a charge against him under the false-news section of the Canadian Criminal Code. It's the section that prohibits anyone from publishing statements that are known to be false and that can cause injury or mischief to the public interest. A jury convicted Zundel in 1985. He appealed his conviction. The Ontario Court of Appeal overturned it and ordered a new trial. Another jury found Zundel guilty, and he got on the appeal merry-go-round again, first to the court of appeal, then to the Supreme Court of Canada.

"The only issue left is the constitutionality of the false-news section," Jim Blacklock said before he caught his plane to Ottawa. "Zundel's guilt is given, assuming the section is constitutional."

Zundel's counsel was Doug Christie of Victoria, British Columbia, a lawyer familiar to cases where holocausts are waved off and Zionist plots are conjured up. He acted for Jim Keegstra, the Alberta schoolteacher who peddles a line of goods similar to Zundel's.

"These laws," Christie told the Supreme Court, referring to the Criminal Code's false-news section, "are really instruments of thought control, which should be avoided in a free and democratic society. They violate the constitutional guarantee of freedom of expression."

Oh, no, Blacklock argued, it's not that complicated. "This

section of the Criminal Code can be used only against people who deliberately spread lies that harm the public."

Why, Christie said, under the section, "Galileo might have been convicted for spreading the news of his hypothesis that the earth revolves around the sun."

"In my opinion," Blacklock said, "Mr. Zundel is hardly in the position of Mr. Galileo."

The court reserved its decision.

"I'm glad it's over," Blacklock says back in Toronto, in his basement a week later. "It's cases like the Zundel appeal that're leading me to think seriously about getting out of the attorney general's office."

Blacklock makes me feel apprehensive when he talks about getting out. A good person like him, a good lawyer, leaving public service just when we can't spare good people and good lawyers? The reason behind his talk goes like this.

"I remember when I started out for the Crown, I'd go into court and talk about the merits of the case, about whether evidence was admissible to prove guilt, about whether the judge's charge to the jury was correct. Now I go into court, and it's, have the police screwed up in terms of observing constitutional rights? Has the Crown done something abusive so we're going to have to stop this case? Is there anything wrong with the legislation the case is founded on? I don't argue the merits of the case any more, and I find that much less personally fulfilling.

"It isn't especially satisfying to be put in a position where I have to justify the law. That isn't an easy process, justifying a law. Not because there's anything particularly wrong with the law, that isn't why I don't find it easy. It's more that we've never been in a mind set in this country to explain why we have this law or that law. We've never had to deal with such issues. Any law, you look at it and you think it's not done exactly correctly and if you were going to draft the law all over again, you might change a bit here, a bit there. On the other hand, if you have to sit down and draft the law from scratch and take everything into account, you probably wouldn't ever come up with the perfect solution.

"Anyway, since the courts have got into questions of the constitutionality of laws, into Charter of Rights arguments, I find my work not nearly as satisfying. I don't want to come off sounding like a redneck on this, but I've had bad experiences with the Charter. I have reservations about the Charter.

"I'm not having as much fun now, and it's making me think I might leave. Of course, I've thought that before, and I'm still here."

Blacklock and I go up the basement stairs. Claire is in the hall. She's holding a baby in her arms. Another child stands at her side, a pretty little girl in a pretty little dress. Blacklock tickles her and speaks in French. She giggles and answers in French. Claire asks me, in English, if I've had a good talk with her husband.

"Terrific," I say. I'm at the door ready to leave.

"*Au 'voir*," the pretty little girl in the pretty little dress says to me.

This family isn't a poster for national unity. It's the video.

$$\star \quad \star \quad \star$$

David Baker describes Mike Mitchell as the father figure of the study group. Mitchell looks like a father figure. Judging from the old class photos, he looked like one when he was in his early twenties. He's a hefty man, packing a few pounds around the middle, but he carries the weight with a kind of magisterial grace. He speaks in a low voice, sometimes causing the listener to lean forward to catch what he's saying. It's worth the leaning; Mitchell, as Jim Blacklock says, has a very quick mind. His smile is warm and agreeable, and seems to come, at the end of statements, as a reward for listening.

There are other reasons for identifying Michell as the study group's father figure. He was the only married member. Many of the meetings took place in the living room of the apartment he and his wife were renting. And Mitchell, of the five, had a past of intriguing work. For a year, after he took an arts degree at the University of Toronto in 1970, he served as executive assistant to Sid Green, a Cabinet minister in Ed Schreyer's NDP government in Mitchell's home province of Manitoba.

Mitchell, being Mitchell—principled and unyielding on his principles—drew a moral from his experience on the political inside that shaped his later career.

"I learned that it is terribly important if you're in government to have something to go back to," he says. "You can't be dependent on your position in government if you want the freedom to tell people on policy matters they can say what they want and you'll say what you want. You can't do that unless you have some other job or career to fall back on. In the Manitoba government, I saw former schoolteachers who had no desire to return to teaching, reporters who didn't ever want to work on newspapers again. They became political junkies, and they compromised themselves all over the place. They said things they didn't really mean or believe. They did it because they had no more life outside politics and government."

This lamentable state of affairs, in Mitchell's view, got underlined, printed in block letters, punctuated with exclamation points when Pierre Trudeau invoked the War Measures Act in 1970.

"In Ottawa, Tommy Douglas and David Lewis for the NDP were fighting tooth and nail against the Act," Mitchell says. "But in Manitoba, Schreyer pretty well supported it. An executive assistant of his said that every day the NDP opposed the War Measures Act, the party dropped a point in popularity. One of the Cabinet ministers said as soon as the FLQ kidnappers were caught, they should be put against a wall and shot summarily. That was the atmosphere. On the left wing of the party, a man named Cy Gonick got up at a public meeting and articulated the reasons it didn't seem necessary to take away Canadians' civil liberties. The Manitoba government hung Gonick out to dry. They allowed him to be shouted down. That was a big lesson to me. People in government, NDPers, avoided saying what they really thought, that they, too, might have doubts about the War Measures Act, because they were afraid they'd lose their positions, that their chances of promotion up the government ranks might vanish, and they had nothing else they wanted to return to."

Mitchell made his own decision.

"What happened over the War Measures Act was a formative influence in my deciding to go to law school. I think now I left government too early because I was enjoying the actual work so damned much. But I went voluntarily. I thought I'd see if I could stomach the idea of becoming a lawyer in order to practise labour law."

At law school, Mitchell stood fifth in the class in first year and hovered just below that neighbourhood in second and third. He articled with Jeffrey Sack, a leading labour practitioner on the union side in Toronto, and after his call to the bar, he stayed with Sack's firm. He acted for steelworkers, machinists, construction workers, Metro Toronto's cops, the University of Toronto's faculty association, and all of Ontario's doctors. The firm, now called Sack Goldblatt Mitchell, grew from four lawyers in 1977 to seventeen in 1992. If it isn't first among Toronto's labour law firms in brains, effectiveness, and negotiating skills, then it's second in all those qualities. Not bad for a guy who was wondering about law and his stomach.

Mitchell has a particularly Mitchellian analysis of the study group's value.

"It provided the focus for debate, for arguing about what some things in law meant, why other things were stupid. The group wasn't a way to learn the material. Nobody went to the meetings to find out what the stuff was all about. Most of us knew that from studying on our own. What the group was about was thinking."

Mitchell shifts in his chair. We're talking in Sack Goldblatt Mitchell's offices in the Atrium complex in downtown Toronto.

Mitchell has a William Buckley way of sliding sideways in the chair as he talks.

"Thinking is hard work," he says. "The group made it easier to think. It forced us to think. Talking in a group like that, other people came up with ideas, and that meant I had to do my share. I didn't *have* to, but I was stimulated to. That carries over to what we do in this office today. A bunch of us sit around and talk through problems and issues and approaches. We're thinking. It's out loud, but it's still thinking. For me, it all started in the study group."

Mitchell makes the point that, among the members of the class of '75, he isn't the only one who's gone after a career in labour law, not by a long shot. There are about a dozen who've taken a similar route. Mitchell gets even more specific when he mentions that the dozen labour law people came not merely from the one class but from a particular third-year seminar. It was a seminar in labour arbitration, and it was conducted by a teacher named Stan Schiff. Schiff is himself a graduate of the law school, class of '56, who was hired by Dean Cecil Wright in the late 1950s. He is a short, erect, precise man, and he is a teacher with exacting standards.

"It wasn't like most seminar courses where a couple of people dominate and the rest float," says Jim Hayes, who was one of the dozen. "In the arbitration course, *every* person was equally thoughtful about the subject, equally enthusiastic, equally full of ideas."

Hayes gives a giant share of credit to Schiff.

"He was like a circus ringmaster," Hayes says. "I don't mean that pejoratively. I mean he controlled the stream of conversation masterfully. The discussion never stopped moving."

Well, *occasionally* it stalled.

"Stan expected you to be super prepared and sometimes I wasn't," says another of the dozen, Rob Prichard. "Stan would slam his book down and say, 'This person is not prepared,' usually meaning me. 'I'm not going to teach.' He'd be ready to walk out. But everybody was so caught up in the material that someone like Mitchell or Hayes would say, 'I'm prepared. Maybe I could address the point.' That'd take me off the hook, and the discussion would race ahead."

Prichard adds one more line about the seminar. "I got a B-plus in the course, which, from Stan, was a hell of a grade."

One of the keys to the seminar's success was that, in addition to analyses of arbitration topics, Schiff arranged mock arbitrations. The students took turns arguing arbitrations against each other, one student as the lawyer for the union and one as the lawyer for the employer, with Schiff playing the arbitrator. (Mitchell recalls that a mock arbitration was how he first got to know Prichard, by arguing against him.) Each student also got a crack at sitting as the arbitrator and deciding the case before him.

"It was an excellently structured course," Jim Hayes says. "That's natural—Stan is a very structured person."

And so an extraordinary number of Schiff's students, a majority, wound up after graduation doing labour law, on one side or the other, union or management, full-time or part-time.

"What made that surprising," Mitchell says, "is that when we graduated, labour law was a relatively small and difficult field. You had to be very determined to get into it, determined, and lucky or good, or both."

The names from the Schiff arbitration seminar read like a list of candidates for the Labour Law Hall of Fame:

Mike Mitchell.

Jim Hayes, whose firm, Cavalluzzo, Hayes and Lennon, is either first among Toronto labour firms in brains, effectiveness, and negotiating skills or second to Sack Goldblatt Mitchell.

Rob Prichard, who, among his other careers, sat for many years on arbitration panels, the third member, the neutral arbitrator agreed to by the union and management representatives. (He sat, for example, on the critical arbitration between the *Toronto Star* and the newspaper guild.)

Bernie Fishbein, in the top ten or better in the class through all three years and now a leading labour practitioner at the firm of Koskie and Minsky.

Tom Kuttner, who teaches labour law at the University of New Brunswick.

George Grossman, who practised labour law on the management side for several years before leaving to run his family's large contracting firm, Belmont Construction.

And others.

Were there any exceptions? David Baker. He was one of the people in the seminar, but, as we've seen, he had other dreams, other purposes.

There's a kicker to the story of the Stan Schiff seminar and the class of '75. Mike Mitchell explains it:

"All the time we were in law school, for many years before and after, Schiff took jobs outside the school sitting on arbitration panels. He was an arbitrator, and when I was a young lawyer starting out and arguing arbitrations for employees, I would appear before a board and who would be sitting there? My old teacher, Stan Schiff. All of us in the class ended up arguing before him. He was as he'd be in the seminar—he had very high expectations."

Mitchell remembers that, in the second-year labour law course taught by David Beatty, one of the questions on the final exam centred on a bargaining unit of academics. What kind of problems would confront such a unit? It seemed a slightly far-out concept in 1974, a bunch of university teachers organizing themselves into a union. But eight years later, in real life, Mitchell found himself in exactly the situation posed in David Beatty's exam question. He and his firm were retained by the University of Toronto faculty association, which was going to the mat with the university administration principally over the issue of binding arbitration.

It's fascinating to take note of some wheels within wheels. Rob Prichard, with whom Mitchell had first formed a friendship when they argued the arbitration case in Stan Schiff's seminar, had in the intervening years joined the U of T Law School staff and became a member of the faculty association's bargaining committee. In the fall of 1983, the law school appointed Prichard to be its new dean. His predecessor, Frank Iacobucci, was elevated to the position of university provost. Iacobucci had been dean from 1979 to 1983, and before that, he taught at the law school, one of the best liked professors on the staff, friendly, gregarious. Mitchell had been a student of his. Now, as provost, Iacobucci was one of the key university officials with whom Mitchell had to negotiate. To Mitchell, Iacobucci still seemed friendly, gregarious—but a hard-nosed negotiator.

"The difficult question before us," Mitchell says, "was whether there was going to be binding arbitration to settle disputes between the faculty and the university over salaries. The university resisted binding arbitration because they saw it as giving away all their power. Something else the university desperately didn't want was for the faculty to be unionized. The faculty didn't really care about becoming unionized anyway, and they were not unionized in the end, but the faculty people were adamant about binding arbitration. They didn't want the university deciding on its own what the salaries would be without the faculty having any further recourse. That was the dynamic we had to deal with."

The compromise that Sack, Mitchell, Iacobucci, and others struck was creative. That's Mitchell's adjective. He has another adjective to describe the compromise. Crazy.

"Here's what we agreed to," Mitchell says. "There would be arbitrations over salaries, but they would be binding one year out of two. Binding one year, not binding the second. As a compromise, that's unique and a little odd. *Quite* odd. But it's still in effect today and it seems to be more or less working."

Two large points of more than passing interest emerge from Mitchell's experience in negotiating the settlement of the university–faculty dispute.

One, what Mitchell was doing—negotiating—isn't what labour lawyers usually do. Their work falls generally and tidily into three areas. They help unions get organized and proceed through the certification process. They argue on behalf of unions and individual workers before arbitration boards over such matters as the hiring, firing, promoting, and paying of employees. And when disputes get really serious, when, for example, issues arise that lend themselves to arguments under the Charter of Rights, then labour lawyers go to court on behalf of the union clients.

But negotiating for a union? Not usually.

"Lawyers for the management side have historically done a lot of negotiating," Mitchell says. "But union-side labour lawyers do very little. That's because the unions regard negotiating as *their* business. If unions don't know how to negotiate, what do they exist for? Management, from the 1930s and earlier, always walked into negotiations flanked by their teams of lawyers. They still do. Old-time union leaders hated lawyers. The only ones they could tolerate were people who identified with the union cause and happened to be lawyers. The leading labour law firm going back to the 1950s in Toronto was Joliffe, Lewis and Osler. Ted Joliffe had been the Ontario CCF leader, and David Lewis was headed for the national leadership of the NDP. They were the lawyers who the union people trusted to negotiate. But beyond that, there wasn't much scope for negotiating by labour lawyers."

Until the 1980s, when the scope broadened.

And this dovetails with the second large point emerging from Mitchell's negotiating experience on behalf of the University of Toronto faculty association. The group for whom Sack Goldblatt Mitchell was doing the negotiating wasn't a traditional blue-collar union. It was a group new to such concepts as labour relations and arbitration and unions. These people— university academics—were professionals, white-collar workers who, in earlier times, probably saw themselves more in step with management above than serfs below.

The faculty association wasn't the first white-collar organization that Mitchell found himself representing, and they're doubtless far from the last. In the late 1970s, the residents and interns in Ontario's hospitals—twenty-five hundred medical people—retained the Sack firm to represent them in prying better working conditions and pay out of the hospitals. The negotiating proved to be complex, just a trifle ugly, and decidedly protracted, lasting almost five years. But Sack, Mitchell, and company succeeded in winning for the residents and interns the rights they wanted, the power to bargain and arbitrate. Almost a decade later, in January 1990, Ontario's entire medical profession hired the Sack firm to go head to head with the government over extra billing and related issues.

Doctors? Interns? University professors? What's going on here?

"It's true we seem to be acting for more white-collar groups in the last few years," Mitchell says. "It's curious in a way. White-collar people, professionals, find it difficult making the decision to organize and arbitrate and retain labour lawyers like us. Thinking of themselves as trade unions is a tremendous leap."

Mitchell does another sideways shift in his chair and smiles benignly.

"It's a big change in labour law," he says, "the middle class discovering the benefits of collective bargaining."

Mitchell *does* look like a father figure.

★　　★　　★

Joel Saltsman lives in the eighteenth arrondissement in Paris. It's to the northwest, in a quarter of the city called Clignancourt, sloping down the hills beyond Montmartre. I'm staying at l'hôtel Olympiades on a secluded Clignancourt square. For 230 francs, I get a room that's clean, fairly quiet, and not big enough to swing a cat in.

On the Sunday I'm to meet Saltsman, I set out at noon for an advance tour of his neighbourhood. The February sun filters weakly out of a cloud-bright sky, and all I notice at first are the bare trees, the glistening cobblestones, and the passers-by with their upturned coat collars. It might be a better day for nursing an armagnac at a café's zinc counter than strolling the streets.

But there's something enchanting about the quarter. Seedy in places, but enchanting.

I get myself lost on streets that twist around pretty little squares. There seem to be three or four cafés at every corner. Most of them, I begin to notice, specialize in North African dishes. The skin shades of the people on the streets run from ebony to *café au lait*.

I go into a noisy bistro looking for couscous. My mistake, I've hit on a place that serves Italian. The waiter is short and speedy, a face like Charles Aznavour's. He wears a tuxedo spotted in red sauce. He brings me spaghetti Bolognese and red wine in a handsome jug. I feel wonderfully Parisian.

"American?" the Charles Aznavour waiter asks me.

"Canadian."

I feel much less Parisian.

I walk some more, back towards Montmartre, and try to see the streets as Toulouse-Lautrec and Maurice Utrillo painted them a century earlier. It's a stretch—there's definitely no Moulin Rouge in sight—but the hilly streets and the old buildings, which somehow manage a balance between the elegant and the tawdry, seem like the real article.

Joel Saltsman arrives on schedule at the Olympiades. He has black curly hair and a slight build. There's a reserve about him, a reticence. He wears glasses and looks youthful. He's one of those men whose face will always carry a reminder of its adolescence.

I ask about Clignancourt.

"This used to be a Jewish district," Saltsman says. "But not all that long ago, the Arabs displaced the Jews. The quarter's more like Algiers than Jerusalem now."

"Explains all the guys in burnooses."

"It's a really appealing neighbourhood to live in," Saltsman says. He sounds like a Canadian who's made himself right at home in this especially exotic corner of an exotic city.

We walk a few blocks to Saltsman's place. It's an apartment on the ninth floor of a building that's not particularly old, not particularly grand. The view out the living room window looks

south and up to Sacré Coeur, the massive Romanesque–
Byzantine church that sits at the top of Montmartre. Sacré
Coeur seems to be floating out there on the skyline above the
narrow chimneys and steep tile roofs. It's like having your very
own living Utrillo on permanent display.

Saltsman introduces his wife. She's Lydie, dark and *gentille*
and very pretty. It's Lydie who drew Saltsman to Paris. He tells
the story. It's a love story.

"I was over here on a holiday from Canada in the spring of
1989, here in Paris," Saltsman says. "But the weather turned
terrible, wet and cold. I wanted to go someplace warm for a few
days. A travel agent got me a reservation in Sicily. One afternoon there, I took an excursion to a site called Agrigento. It was
very interesting, this ancient Corinthian colony. But what was
more interesting, I met a young woman who was on holiday
from Paris with her parents. She was Lydie, and before I went
back to Canada, I knew I'd marry her. Which I did. But Lydie's
an only child, and her parents didn't really want her to be as far
away as Canada. So I moved to Paris."

Saltsman smiles. "All the rest, the other details of our meeting, I'm saving for the Harlequin novel I'll write in another
lifetime."

Saltsman's father was semi–famous, as famous as an NDP politician can be without getting elected premier of a province. His
name was Max Saltsman, and he owned a thriving dry–cleaning
chain in Galt, a large town southwest of Toronto. A businessman and a New Democrat? It gets better. Max Saltsman had
flamboyance, he had all the colours except grey, he laughed on
public platforms, a joke teller, a concocter of half nutty schemes.
(You've heard the one about annexing the Turks and Caicos
Islands in order to keep Canadian winter tourist dollars in
Canada?) He was not remotely like the average doctrinaire,
professionally solemn NDP parliamentarian.

Max made it all click. His business success defused voters'
suspicions he might be a radical terror (in fact, on social issues,

he leaned to the conservative side, though on economic issues, he stayed in harmony with his party). His bonhomie showed he was a regular guy. And besides, he came up the honest way, politically speaking, the earned way: Galt school trustee, Galt alderman, narrowly defeated candidate in the 1963 provincial election.

A federal by-election was called in 1964, the riding of Waterloo South, in Max's back yard. Despite all of the above, nobody gave Max a prayer. Waterloo South had been Tory since Confederation except for a brief Liberal interruption in the 1950s. Max won the by-election. This wasn't a mild upset. This was Cassius Clay knocking out Sonny Liston for the title in the first round. This was colossal, and Max made it stick. He kept on winning elections—relying largely on his own reach-out-and-touch-the-people brand of direct democracy—until he had held a seat in Parliament for fifteen years.

As an MP, Max got respect and laughs. He was NDP financial critic for twelve years, clever and prickly at the job, and when David Lewis resigned as party leader in 1975, Max shaped up as the front runner, before Ed Broadbent made his plans known. The laughs—well, there was the Turks and Caicos private member's bill (it didn't get to the floor of the House, though it accounted for many, many columns of newsprint) and another private member's bill that would send to jail, on charges of destroying food, farmers who registered their discontent by dumping crops on Parliament Hill (same fate). Max suggested that doctors who left Canada to practise in the United States should repay the $100,000 that Canadian taxpayers had invested in their education; that housewives should receive pensions; that citizens should get a $50,000 government credit as an alternative to subsidized education and housing. Max's fellow NDPers didn't chuckle when he supported the War Measures Act in 1970 and wage and price controls in 1975. He followed his conscience and was as effective as an opposition MP could be. He made his own choice to step out of federal politics in 1979. He died of cancer in 1985.

One might speculate, if one were psychoanalytically inclined (or a nosy parker), that growing up with an original like Max Saltsman for a father, a gregarious public force, could be a burden on a young man, could dampen some parts of life. For Joel Saltsman, that doesn't seem to be the case—except in one rather crucial area.

"I was never enthusiastic about politics," he says. "I didn't have any desire to get involved myself, and something as important as managing one of my father's campaigns, on that level, no, that wasn't me."

Which isn't to say that Joel checked out of his father's political life.

"I used to organize the Young Democrats in the riding. 'Young Democats,' my father called them. We'd decorate an old pick-up truck with flowers at campaign time and drive around putting up signs. But I was never what you'd call an activist. On the left, of course, and I organized debates at school on subjects like Canada's involvement in Vietnam. But I wasn't comfortable with public protest."

Which isn't to say, either, that Saltsman had a difficult relationship with his father.

"Especially when I was going through university, we were very close. We talked on the phone for hours. He used to call me late at night and tell me what was going on in his life. I learned a lot about politics that way, about politics from the opposition point of view, about him . . . ."

Saltsman's voice, soft at the normal level, fades off. But there's no missing the sound in his voice. A sound of great affection.

"In my father's life, my role was very much on the private side."

Like Jim Blacklock, Saltsman entered law school, barely out of his teens, after only two undergraduate years. Unlike Blacklock, he blossomed in the atmosphere and subjects of first-year law. It was a dream year, and not just because, at the end of it, he finished fourth in the class.

"I must have worked hard, but I have no memory of slogging

it out," he says. "It was such sheer pleasure. The work was highly intellectual without being theoretical. Which suited me perfectly because I enjoy studying, learning new ideas and concepts, but I don't have a good mind for theory. I'm more at home at the tree-top level."

And there was this: "It was a delight to develop and express ideas of my own in an environment where my ideas were treated with as much respect as those of the teachers, the judges, and the textbook writers."

Intellectual nirvana. And where did the study group fit in? It provided the warmth. Saltsman loosens up when he talks about the group. His best smile comes out. The talk isn't enlighteningly specific. Oh, the time he went snowshoeing with David Baker and Baker's fiancée, Birthe. Baker's wedding. Marvelling at Jim Blacklock's early resolve to go into prosecution work, so young and so definite. Sitting around Mike Mitchell's living room puzzling over property, "the one subject of all subjects that defied common sense." Nice snapshots from the past. A group of five such disparate guys: Howard Feldman, the son of an innkeeper, and Baker, a product of a private school but an idealist. Different backgrounds, but emotionally it worked. Saltsman, speaking of the group, is a man not so much remembering a part of his past as coddling it, feeling the warmth again.

The trouble with first-year law, though not with the study group, was that it ended, and for Saltsman, the rest was anticlimax.

"To me," he says, "the second and third years were largely echoes of the first in terms of method and concepts. The point is, at law school, you acquire tools of analysis, organizing, applying solutions. You learn them and you apply them to different areas. So I learned all of that in first year, and the rest, in the next two years, was repetition, to me, anyway."

This slant on things—a quick grasp, satisfaction, followed by a flagging interest—is a pattern repeated in Saltsman's later career. Pardon, *careers*. Looking back on law school, he wishes it could have gone another route. "I've often regretted there wasn't a convenient way of doing just one year of law and then proceeding on to something else without the stigma of being a law school dropout."

Still, smart cookie that he is, resourceful, Saltsman found ways at school of keeping himself involved. In second year, constitutional law was the subject that interested him most, so he concentrated on it and got the class's highest mark in the exam. In third year, taking up administrative law as a specialty (it still is), he wrote an article in the field, specifically on a new appeal procedure that had been introduced for disputes over doctor–staff privileges in hospitals. It was published in the *Ottawa Law Review*. Saltsman's overall standing in the class slipped off, though not much. He'd been one of the six A students in first year. In second and third year, he got Bs—but good Bs.

"Many of the other people saw their studies as a means to an end, practising law," Saltsman says. "For me, the studies were pretty much an end in themselves."


Saltsman tells an anecdote from his articling year. He articled at Weir and Foulds, an established Toronto firm, strong in litigation.

"I went to court with Jack Weir once. He was a senior partner, a litigator of the old school, very oratorical, you know, almost florid. He seemed to have a way with judges in the court of appeal, and that's where this case was that I was the student on. It was an action to complete a real estate deal that had gone sour, and I thought our side was hopeless. I couldn't understand how it'd got to the court of appeal. I asked Weir about this. He said, well, the client wants to appeal and I'll do my best. I wondered, how on earth can he say anything? He has no law in his favour.

"Weir stood up in court and he didn't talk about the law at all. He told the story of his client from the client's point of view. He said, well, we recognize our errors and sins, but let's put them aside and consider all the possibilities. Weir lost the appeal in the end, but what a story he told. I wanted to say, yes, yes, I believe you.

"It was a great lesson in advocacy, but not something I could do. For that matter, I didn't enjoy articling. I didn't feel at ease in the role I was asked to play, didn't feel I could be myself, whatever that was. It was partly my fault. I was very young and shy. I did a reasonably good job, but I was relieved when I could leave and go back to school."


Saltsman's life after law school has been like no one else's in the class. Peripatetic, exploratory, not blown by the four winds but driven by intellectual and personal curiosity. Many jobs. Many places. Teacher, salesman, lawyer, editor, consultant. England, Vancouver, Calgary, Ottawa. It's no puzzle that he makes his home today in an Arab quarter of Paris. It might be a mild surprise—or perhaps not—if his address was somewhere in Patagonia.

For one year, 1977–1978, Saltsman went to the London School of Economics, studied more administrative law, took a Master of Laws degree.

For two years, he taught at Osgoode Hall Law School. This was a revelation.

"For one thing, I felt like an impostor. The conventional line about a teacher like me is that he should get across the impression to his students he isn't telling them everything he knows, that he's holding something back and has this great wealth to draw on. Well, I didn't have a fund of experience or anything else to draw on. I was teaching people more or less my own age, and some of them had better educations than I did. I was going in front of these students and telling them everything I knew and hoping the hour would end before I ran out."

Next choice: more study.

"Whenever I feel at a dead end," Saltsman says, "I go back to school. And I've never regretted it."

But what he returned to study, at the University of Toronto, wasn't law. It was English literature.

"I didn't want to go through life without reading Shakespeare. I didn't want to miss the chance of sitting in a class with Northrop Frye."

The summer before he took the English courses, Saltsman read all the books on the curriculum.

"I was following Virginia Woolf's advice. Read a novel the first time for the story, the second time for the nuances."

And what were the benefits of his year among the great works?

"I didn't stay long enough to get a BA, but I read *Middlemarch* twice."

Time to find a real job.

"I didn't want to practise law, and if I hung around Toronto, I'd feel self-conscious about not being a lawyer like everybody else in my class. It was better to go far away and not have people looking over my shoulder."

He moved to Vancouver and was the BC sales rep for Richard DeBoo, a publisher of legal textbooks.

"I was good at it, but it became boring."

Then he tried lawyering.

"I was twenty-nine. That seemed old enough to give people advice about buying a house and getting a divorce. I did it for two years, and I'm glad I tried, but I found law didn't allow for much self-expression. What I was doing, thousands of others could do as well. I felt like a generic lawyer."

Next career: editing.

Next stop: Calgary.

Saltsman worked for Carswell, the major legal publisher in Canada, editing textbooks.

"It was as literary as you can get and still be in law. And I discovered I had a flair for editing. I could put some of myself into the work. I admire lawyers who practise and write books at the same time. That seems ideal."

Saltsman was gifted enough as an editor and administrator

that Carswell assigned him to open an editorial office in Ottawa. Two years later, still in Ottawa, he went out on his own as a consultant, mostly in the administrative law area, mostly with federal government offices. Then came Lydie and Paris.

His new career?

Saltsman smiles. "Back at school. I'm taking a one-year French MBA course."


Lydie takes a break from looking after four-month-old son Daniel and serves a meal. Just what happened to be in the refrigerator, she says. Small pizzas, avocado salad, scrambled eggs, cheese, dates, white wine, coffee. Wonder what she puts together when she's really trying.

Saltsman remembers something that amuses and baffles him.

"I kept diaries," he tells me. "After I got your letter about coming to see me, I went back to the diary during my law school period. At the beginning, it's a very introverted, private series of writings. Then it records the ordinary comings and goings of my life, successes or failures with women, a young person's stuff. But—this is the part that astonished me—there is virtually nothing about law school. Success or failure there? In class work? Almost a blank."

He tries to account for the curious omission.

"I plunged into law when I wasn't sure of myself. There might be some explanation in that. I've always regretted that I went to law school after only two years of undergraduate school. There were things I wanted to study at university that maybe I didn't get around to because I was young and insecure."

As he talks, Saltsman is getting away from the point about the diaries, but he seems to be leading someplace.

"Each time I've started something new in school, a different course, law school, each time I would think to myself, I'll do something purposeful. The exception was the year I took English literature. That was because I decided to learn something I was interested in. The other times, it was to do something more purposeful than what I'd done before."

It's easy, reciting Saltsman's job and study history, to pin a label on him: dilettante. This is the guy who took tenor saxophone lessons in his mid-twenties. He heard jazz in his head. He thought about making jazz. "I learned enough from the lessons to understand the complexities of jazz," he says, "but not enough to play them myself." Still, dilettante is all wrong to describe Saltsman. At worst—which isn't bad—he's entered a long process of sorting through temporarily absorbing careers until he hits on one with an appeal that's closer to permanent. Paris, marriage, fatherhood, and an MBA seem a good bet as a beginning to an ending.

# CHAPTER THREE

## *The Member*

PATRICK BOYER is telling me he isn't in good odour with his boss at the moment. His boss is Brian Mulroney.

"Well, let the chips fall where they may," Boyer says.

It's a Tuesday morning, nine-forty, in late November. I'm in Boyer's office, Room 238 in the West Block on Parliament Hill in Ottawa. Boyer is the MP, Progressive Conservative, for the riding of Etobicoke-Lakeshore in the west end of Toronto.

"I voted against a government bill the other day," Boyer says. "It imposes a very unfair tax, that's what the bill does. This is basically a piece of bankruptcy legislation, and it says, among other things, when a company goes bust, the employees are entitled to get paid their back wages and benefits. That's very worthy, no question, but to raise the money for the fund to pay the employees, the government wants to impose a new payroll tax on businesses, school boards, local government, right across the spectrum. Which is what I object to and why I voted against the bill. The whole thing should be handled within the unemployment insurance system, and let the employees get paid through it. Not *another* tax, my gosh."

Boyer is sitting behind his desk, very erect, suit jacket on, tie knotted just so. He has statesmanlike hair, adventurous hair, long, with dramatic swirls on the sides and back. A proper guy, but his face gives away something else, a boyish face, remarkably smooth and free of lines for a forty-five-year-old, earnest, keen. On the wall to his right, there's a photograph of Boyer and his dad taken on the night of Boyer's first election to the Commons in 1984. Beside it hangs a framed piece of scrollwork that begins, "Nothing in the world can take the place of persistence. . . ."

"Whenever a question comes up about conflict of interest, especially if it's a Cabinet minister involved, the media like to interview me," Boyer says. "That's because I wrote most of the report for the 1983 Task Force on Conflict of Interest. One night, this was a few years ago, I was lined up to go on the *Journal* and talk about the Sinc Stevens thing, when he was in trouble over conflict. I was getting ready to drive over to the CBC studios. A call came through from Erik Nielsen's office. The PM was out of the country, and Nielsen was acting prime minister. Don't go on the *Journal*, they said on the phone, you can't do it, we forbid you. So I deferred. I didn't appear on TV. But today, if they perform the thumbscrew act on me, I go ahead and do what I think's right. The PM doesn't like it? That's his problem."


Going in, some homework done on Boyer, I think I'm clear on three aspects of the political man, that (a) he's inordinately literate as MPs go, literary even, politically philosophical; that (b) he tends to viewpoints that come out maverick; and that (c), because of either (a) or (b), the big shooters in his party might be keeping him from rising as high in responsibility and decision-making as he merits.

Not that Boyer has been entirely shut out. He's chaired two Parliamentary committees, on equality rights and on the disabled and handicapped. True, any old hack backbencher can do a chairing job, but Boyer propelled his committees to take stands and do things. Further up the power scale, he was Joe Clark's Parliamentary secretary at External Affairs for two years and is now PS to Marcel Masse at Defence. True again, maverick MPs are often made Parliamentary secretaries to keep them quiet, but shutting his mouth isn't Boyer's style.

Boyer also writes, and we're not talking pamphlets here, or cheery letters to bedridden constituents. We're talking books, three published in the 1980s, *Political Rights: The Legal Framework of Elections in Canada, Lawmaking by the People: Referendums and Plebiscites in Canada*, and *Money and Message: The Law Governing Election Financing, Broadcasting and Campaigning in Canada*. Forget the top-heavy titles, the books are looked on as the current last word on Canadian election law. In a more accessible vein, Boyer is closing in on the final chapters, after twelve years of research, interviewing, and writing, of his James McRuer biography; McRuer, "Hanging Jim" to some, a civil libertarian to others, was Ontario's chief justice from the 1940s to the 1960s, and after that the chairman of a provincial commission on civil rights, and through it all, until he died at ninety-four, a man who generated legends it would take twelve years to track.

Journalists love Boyer. Small wonder. He returns their calls, and the words "no comment" do not cross his lips. On the very November day of my visit to Ottawa, Boyer's name turns up twice in the *Globe and Mail*. Jeffrey Simpson's column calls him, in more than passing, "the excellent Tory MP," and Graham Fraser, in a piece about the 1942 referendum on conscription, quotes Boyer for two key paragraphs and acknowledges him as "one of the few experts on referendums and plebiscites in Parliament." Simpson's column is about referendums, too, coming out in favour of one on the constitution and leaning on Boyer for support. The *Globe* should put Boyer on retainer as its referendum resource.

Going further back in the clippings I've rounded up, an item in the December 9, 1990, "Heard On The Hill Column by John A." from Parliament's own tabloid, the *Hill Times*, says this: "Patrick Boyer is being totally wasted by a government and by a prime minister who need talent rather than some of the dead weight they have in the Cabinet." A mere Cabinet minister? A year earlier, Doug Fisher's *Sun* column had a more lofty projection for Boyer: "Possibly the party leader in a few years."

Allison Stodin is sitting across the desk from Boyer. A huge, unsteady stack of documents, letters, memos, paper miscellany, occupies much of the desk territory between them. Stodin has a notebook in her lap.

"External say they don't know when your plane leaves yet," she says to Boyer, consulting the notebook. "Thursday, yes, the day after tomorrow, but not the exact time."

"What route do I take?" Boyer asks.

"Toronto to Zurich and nonstop from there to Kiev."

"Not bad."

Stodin's head is in the notebook. "No, wait, my mistake, one stop between Zurich and Kiev."

"How about coming back?"

"Return the following Thursday through Vienna and Paris."

"Somebody from External going to brief me before I go? I mean, I don't want to go over and stand around gawking like a tourist."

"Not External, somebody from Elections Canada. That's arranged for tomorrow. They'll tell you what to look for on voting day in Kiev, the logistics and so forth."

"Fantastic, Allison. Next?"

Allison Stodin is, by title, Boyer's executive assistant. By task, she does the typing, telephone answering, copying, scheduling, idea bouncing. She's Boyer's sole Parliamentary employee, a well-groomed woman in her early thirties, history graduate from Carleton, seven years on the Hill, three with Boyer, knows the ropes but isn't pushy with her expertise.

"Kiev?" I ask.

Boyer explains about Kiev. On the Sunday coming up, Ukraine votes in a referendum to confirm or overturn its Parliament's declaration three months earlier of independence from the Soviet Union. The vote is expected to favour overwhelmingly the creation of a Ukrainian republic, but to make sure everything is on the up and up, Ukraine's government has invited Canada to dispatch three impartial observers who will, somehow or other, monitor the voting. Boyer is one of the three designated to look over the voters' shoulders in and around Kiev.

"If Canadians go in and say, okay, no corruption in the voting process," Boyer says, "it's like the Good Housekeeping Seal of Approval. We have that reputation in the world. Did the same monitoring thing in Nicaragua, some African countries, Haiti. Well, yeah, Haiti, the election was well run. It was just too bad the army tossed out the people who got elected."

Allison Stodin carefully lifts a thick bundle of papers wrapped in elastic bands from the trembling pile on the desk.

"Defence issues package," she says to Boyer. "It arrived an hour ago."

"Part of the job, Parliamentary secretary to the Defence minister," Boyer tells me. "Keep up to speed on our role in Yugoslavia, that kind of thing, sexual orientation in the armed forces. In case *Canada AM* asks me to go on live tomorrow or whoever."

He hands me the bundle of papers. Nothing stamped "Classified" in red ink, nothing M would slip to 007 for his eyes only. Most of the stuff is photocopies of CP stories and *Globe* editorials.

"That reminds me," Boyer says to Stodin, "get this framed, okay?"

He has in his hand a photograph of a navy ship rolling in the ocean. The ship is the *Protecteur*, a supply carrier that was one of three Canadian vessels to get in on the Gulf War, and Boyer, in his Defence PS capacity, rolled in the *Protecteur* over the previous weekend during a naval exercise in the Atlantic.

"See the gun midship here," Boyer says, holding the photograph at eye level. "That's a fifty calibre. I fired it. Gets rid of a hundred rounds in a real big hurry."

He looks a little longer at the photo.

"Went up in a Sikorsky helicopter, too."

"What about *People's Mandate*?" Stodin asks. "We should talk about it."

"This is a big disappointment." Boyer levers a fat manuscript out of its support position at the base of the paper mountain. "But not terminal."

*The People's Mandate* is a book, as yet unpublished, in which Boyer offers what may be his final, ultimate, definitive, conclusive case for a national referendum on the constitution. The book analyzes the nature of democracy from every angle, lobbying, opinion polls, special interest groups, party discipline, and the place in this churn of pressures for referendums and plebiscites. A small publisher, Dundurn Press, planned to bring out the book in the spring, but backed away on the grounds that it lacked the resources to handle such a mighty undertaking.

"My idea," Boyer says to Stodin, "is we make copies of the first chapter and send them to four or five of the top publishers. Allison?"

"With a personal letter from you."

"To whoever's the president, editor, whatever the head person's called at each publisher."

"Um, McClelland and Stewart?"

"This book says things nobody else is telling the country."

"Penguin, ah, Key Porter. . ."

Boyer gets some personal rocks off in *The People's Mandate*. Towards the end of chapter fifteen of the manuscript, I read, "Although I never intended it when I began this book, I realized when reading the analysis I have made that the role of being a member of the Parliament of Canada is like being a Canadian soldier in the 1942 Dieppe raid—fodder in an intended ambush to satisfy the larger workings of the system's grand design."

"Macmillan. . ."

The phone rings.

"Jean's due to call about now," Stodin says.

Jean Webster is the woman who runs Boyer's riding office, and she's checking in from Etobicoke-Lakeshore. Boyer puts her on the speaker phone to free up his hands for note-taking and date-confirming.

"The Canadian Ukrainian Congress, Patrick," Webster says, her voice bouncing tinnily in the room, "they're throwing a freedom rally in front of Toronto City Hall next Wednesday and they want you to address them."

"Wednesday? Next Wednesday? I'll be *in* Ukraine next Wednesday."

"Send them a message, then? Something to be read at the rally?"

"Okay. . . . No, here's what we do. Corinne can deliver the speech for me."

"Pardon?"

"Corinne Boyer, the wife of the member, you remember her?"

A laugh comes down the line. "Oh, *that* Corinne. I didn't quite hear you."

"What else?"

"For the riding Christmas parade, which is coming up in, ah, four weeks, do you want a car, something open maybe you can ride in?"

"No car, definitely not. I'll walk and hand out pins and something else for the kids. I'd look ridiculous in a limo. Plutocratic."

"Candy canes?"

"Huh?"

"To hand out for the kids?"

"Great, and round up some Young PCs to walk alongside me."

"Ah, let's see, an invitation to Knowlton Nash's Christmas brunch. Sunday, December 8."

"I've got in my book that's the Sunday for our own riding Christmas party at the Mimico Cruising Club."

"Right."

"Regrets to Knowlton Nash," Boyer says. "How's the Christmas party coming?"

"Hot cider, cookies, carols. The invitations are out."

"That Monday night, I've got to be in the House for a vote, and then, yeah, Tuesday and Wednesday the conference on Canadian foreign policy in Toronto?"

"Is there a problem?"

"The PM's Christmas party is Wednesday night. I ought to show my face."

"Oh, well, the conference schedule has the round table discussion at three on the Wednesday afternoon followed by concluding remarks."

"I'll play it by ear which plane to catch back to Ottawa."

"This is looking further ahead," Jean Webster says, "but Royal Canadian Legion Branch 217 is celebrating a fiftieth anniversary on January 12 and would appreciate your attendance."

"What day of the week's that?"

"Sunday."

"Supposed to be a day of rest, Sunday."

"So they say. Eleven o'clock service at St. Elizabeth's Church and then to the Legion Hall."

"Oh, church, too. Okay, roll it in and I'll go to both."

"Corinne, too?"

"Absolutely."

"Well, that's it for this morning, Patrick."

"Thanks, Jean. . . . Oh, hey."

"Yes?"

"January 12, remind me to wear my legion pin."

Boyer clicks off the speaker phone and calls to Allison Stodin in the next room.

"Allison, not just one chapter of *The People's Mandate* to those publishers. Send the first three. I want them to understand where I'm coming from."


Patrick Boyer, with his boyish looks, candour, and keenness, could only have grown up in rural Ontario. And he did, in the town of Bracebridge, about two hours north of Toronto. He's the fourth in a line of Bracebridge male Boyers. The first Boyer, James, made his way from Stratford-upon-Avon to New York City around 1860. He and his wife left the United States during the Civil War and settled in Bracebridge. James did some law clerking around Bracebridge, but mostly he got into the newspaper business, the *Muskoka Herald*, and that—publishing, editing, writing, typesetting, ad selling—set the course for male Boyers over the next century. James's son took his turn running the *Herald*, and so did his grandson. The latter's name is Bill, and he is Patrick Boyer's father.

Patrick Boyer grew up in an apartment over the *Herald*.

"Pine wood floors, the smell of newsprint, I loved it," he says. "I learned to set type pretty young."

He played hockey in the winters and led canoe trips in the summers, down the Moon River, down the Mattawa. He got great marks in history and English, and came close to flunking maths. He was a Queen's Scout. He hung out with the gang at the Thomas Company Café, drinking coffee and gasping on cigarettes. One week, a bunch from his high school class put out an issue of the *Herald* all by themselves, wrote the stories, rounded up the photographs, sold the ads. Boyer's boyhood reads like *Tom Sawyer* without the fence-painting scam.

In 1955, Bill Boyer was elected to the Ontario legislature as a member of the governing Tory party. Patrick was ten at the time. When he was twelve, after two years of watching his dad hand-holding constituents, parcelling out aid, mainstreeting in Muskoka, he decided what his future must hold: he would edit and publish the *Herald* and he would be an MP in Ottawa. That was the master plan.

Both Boyer and his father managed to square the two juxtaposed professions, politics and journalism, the one that runs things and the one that picks holes in the way things are run. Boyer summed it up in a passage from the manuscript version of *The People's Mandate*: "The fact that my father was both the newspaper editor and the district's elected representative, who could thus write his editorials to interpret what was taking place because he understood from direct participation what was intended, set for me an implicit model of the participant observer. I was sensitive enough, too, to the obvious conflict—or was it confluence?—of interest. As an answer to it, I often repeated what others said—that they found our family's newspaper to be fair and balanced in its coverage. These comments came from supporters of rival political parties in response to election-time coverage."

On his feelings about journalism, Boyer told me, "As a kid I got the idea that until something had been written about, it hadn't happened. If the Bracebridge boat works was on fire, it wouldn't be real until the story was written. That was my instinct. It still is."

In step with the master plan, Boyer headed for Carleton University's journalism course. On enrolment day, he stood in line to sign up. A boy in a parallel line, Larry Pratt, struck up a conversation.

"What're you registering for?" he asked.

"Journalism," Boyer answered, and outlined the master plan.

Pratt was baffled. "Why would you spend three years learning how to write stories when you could use the years to study economics, philosophy, politics, all the subjects that are going to tell you what you're talking about when you finally get to write your stories?"

"Good point," Boyer said.

Though he'd been a star debater at Bracebridge High, he couldn't muster a convincing rebuttal to Pratt. He stepped out of the journalism line and into the arts line. At Carleton, he took honours in political science and economics.


Boyer says, "I've always overextended myself."

On the scale of understatement, that belongs alongside, "Michael Jordan plays a little basketball." From childhood, Boyer has been a compulsive doer, fixer, organizer, writer, speechifier. But never a dabbler. He attacks full bore. In the years after Carleton, he: worked as the expert on housing and urban affairs in the office of the federal leader of the opposition, Bob Stanfield; was Montreal stringer for CBC radio's *As It Happens*; reported for the North Battleford, Saskatchewan, *News-Optimist*; toured South America; delivered speeches, in the role of the party's young conscience, at Progressive Conservative policy conferences; served as executive assistant to Arthur Wishart, attorney general in the Ontario Tory government.

He also got married, on August 15, 1970.

Corinne Boyer is no slouch when it comes to credentials. Born in Delft, the Netherlands town where they make faïence pottery, she got a degree in fine arts at the Royal Academy of Art in The Hague and another in modern languages at the University of Madrid. She worked for Spain's government in the Netherlands, promoting Spanish tourism, and for Holland's government in New York City, promoting Dutch culture. She speaks English, French, Dutch, German, and Spanish, and in a pinch can deliver in Portuguese and Italian.

One winter evening a few years after they were married, Patrick and Corinne were driving north of Toronto on Highway 11, no cares on their minds, a free night, dinner ahead with friends in Newmarket. A car speeding south spun out of its lane in a crazy wavering arc and smacked front end to front end into the Boyer car. Patrick's head whiplashed, back, forward, and crashed against the steering wheel. The car careened off the highway. When it stopped, it was on the edge of a cemetery. "Except for the seat belts we'd buckled up," Boyer says, "we would have been dead." Patrick needed two operations to fix his mashed nose. Corinne's injuries were internal and they meant the Boyers would never have children.

At the office of Arthur Wishart, the Ontario attorney general, where Boyer was executive assistant, something dawned on him. An anomaly? A curiosity? A joke? Only two people on the large staff weren't lawyers, the chauffeur and Boyer.

"My thinking on lawyers," he says, "was that they probably played an important role in society, but it was specific and boring. Drawing wills, doing real estate deals, writing contracts. But I went to a federal-provincial meeting of attorneys general in Halifax. The agenda was divorce legislation, crime, civil rights, gun control. These were lawyers talking about issues that were at the heart of how modern society was working. I thought, well, if I'm intending to become a Member of Parliament some day where laws are debated and interpreted, the laws that regulated all the things the attorneys general were discussing, it made sense for me to go to law school and become a lawyer."

In Boyer fashion, he didn't confine his law school years to law. He ghost-wrote magazine articles for an MP. He conducted interviews in the Ontario Historical Studies series, interviews with aging Ontarians who had brushed against the province's history. He took classes towards a master's degree in history, and wrote his thesis, titled, *George Drew and the Revival of the Conservative Party in Ontario*. He received the MA in December 1975. It would have come earlier if the traffic accident hadn't slowed his pace by a step.

At law school, Boyer founded the University of Toronto International Law Society, wrote two articles for the *Faculty of Law Review*, and oh, yes, took classes. Not always with élan. "A lot of what we studied, I found inconsequential," he says. "I persevered because I knew where I wanted to end up. I saw the law as training for later public life."

Probably Boyer's biggest kick in law school came from associations with people whose minds he admired. Everybody in the class, Boyer says, was "intellectually superior." He liked that, at least partly because, intellectually superiorwise, he had no trouble staying the route, even when he was also occupied elsewhere.

After he graduated, he joined Fraser and Beatty, a large, venerable, correct, practise-law-in-the-classic-sense downtown Toronto firm. Boyer, however, managed to slide sideways in the firm, away from the correct and classic to the bold and newfangled. His public service interests led him to act for settlements and hamlets in the Western Arctic during the structuring of Inuit land claims. His journalism background helped him practise communications law, representing the Global TV network, *Esquire Magazine*, *Newsweek*, various book publishers, some authors. It must be an indicator of Boyer's political (if not diplomatic) skills that he did these sorts of law in a firm where performing an apple-pie-orderly job of drafting supplemental trust indentures was considered the measure of a real lawyer. Furthermore, he made the new stuff seem . . . *significant*.

Not all went swimmingly, though. Boyer handled the paperwork for dentists' wives and others who took advantage of the lavish tax write-offs in financing Canadian films in the early 1980s.

"I went to a screening of one of those movies," he says. "I knew the effort that'd gone into it, well, my effort, anyway, doing the legal end and having in mind thoughts of the powerful movies coming out of Australia at the time. I left the screening and walked up Yonge Street, it was raining, and I had to clap a hand over my mouth to keep from throwing up. Less than garbage. A total waste. Never again, I told myself, no more of this movie work."

September 4, 1984. A federal election was scheduled for this date. Time, at thirty-nine years of age, for Boyer to toss his hat in the ring. But the exact ring? A veteran Tory named Stan Darling had a lock on the riding up home, Parry Sound-Muskoka. St. Paul's was a consideration, the riding a couple of blocks from the apartment building where the Boyers were living. But Barbara McDougall was making noises about running there.

Boyer chose Etobicoke-Lakeshore. A tough call by all objective criteria. As long as anyone political could remember, the riding had been Liberal except for a blip in the early 1970s when it went NDP. It was working-class and ethnic, nine thousand Ukrainian-Canadians, thousands of Italian background, a sizable Polish community. Boyer licked his lips and rubbed his hands.

"Really, it was the kind of riding I wanted all along," Boyer tells me. "You take St. Paul's. Most people who live there are well-to-do, well educated, they have connections. If something goes wrong for them, something needs fixing, they don't call their MP. They're plugged into more direct levels. But in Etobicoke-Lakeshore, the constituents are on the underside of the system. If something bad happens for them, a plant closing, they're intimidated, they roll over. All they've got between them and defeat is the MP. And that's what I've always wanted, a chance to be of use."

Boyer knew how to mobilize a campaign. Hadn't he, ten years old, learned at Bill Boyer's side? "My dad was never a parent who pushed me in any direction," Boyer says. "All he'd tell me is, be sure you don't let good opportunities go by." Photo ops, for instance. At the time of the election, a handful of passionate Polish-Canadians, supporting their Solidarity brothers back home, went on a hunger strike outside the Polish Consulate on Lakeshore Boulevard in the heart of the riding. Each day and night, the gaunt, defiant men, on the pavement, in sleeping bags, Solidarity signs, flashing their fingers in Vs. Boyer was almost as constant as the hunger strikers, standing on the roof of a car outside the consulate, loud-hailer in hand, cheering on the strikers' cause. Click, click, went the newspaper cameras. People in the riding, Polish, Ukrainian, Middle European, fiercely anti-communist, got to know Patrick Boyer.

After each Boyer appearance on Lakeshore Boulevard, an underling from the consulate phoned his campaign office. Please, a transcript of Mr. Boyer's speech last night? For our records?

The answer was always the same.

"There is no transcript. Mr. Boyer speaks from the heart."

How could he lose?

On election night, Etobicoke-Lakeshore cast 44,856 votes. Boyer got 19,902. He won with a plurality of 44.78 percent.

Re-election in 1988, Etobicoke-Lakeshore was the only riding in the country without a Liberal on the ballot. This was not a strategy, this was a mystery. The putative Liberal candidate, parachuted in from Montreal, seldom appeared in the riding, and at the eleventh hour, in the quick blink of a period between the times when the deadline for nominations closed and when the ballots were printed, the elusive Liberal sent word from Montreal of, perhaps, a heart attack and of, definitely, his withdrawal. The NDP wheeled in its big guns. Without a Liberal to split the vote, Boyer looked vulnerable. Ed Broadbent toured the riding twice. But Boyer won with figures almost a duplicate of 1984's—45,529 votes cast, 20,405 for Boyer, a 44.81 percent plurality.

The house where Patrick and Corinne live, purchased after the 1984 election, is in a neighbourhood that's a delicious geographical secret from Torontonians like me who get disoriented and snotty when we're pried out of the centre of the city. The house is on Lakeshore Boulevard, a real boulevard, too, broad and gently curving, wide enough for streetcar tracks going both ways and four lanes of cars, and lined with thick, leafy trees that muffle the traffic sounds. The house is behind a waist-high stone wall. It has the look on the outside of a large English cottage. A one-hundred-year-old maple stands on the front lawn, and behind, two blocks south, is Lake Ontario with a long view looking downtown to the east. It feels very European out here. Geneva, maybe. But it's the part of Toronto that used to be called Mimico (and still is by the older merchants) and is now the posh part of the riding of Etobicoke-Lakeshore.

Inside, Corinne has done the rooms in bright colours and flowery patterns. The paintings on the walls are optimistic. Two rooms are for Patrick's business. One is a small and formal office on the first floor where he receives delegations and political friends. The other, on the second floor, is his writing room. Writers accustomed to garrets, or even to ordinary-sized offices, would weep at such a room. It's enormous, windows letting in southern light, many tables and desks, filing cabinets, space for research, for manuscripts, for . . . stuff. "Along here, this is everything on the McRuer biography," Boyer says, conducting a tour. "And those papers, the piles along the far wall, they're *People's Mandate*." For just one moment, I am seized in a spasm of jealousy.

A block to the west of the Boyer house is the Polish Consulate, still open but in friendly hands now. The Boyers are invited to receptions. On the consulate walls, among the photographs, some are of Boyer. They show him out front, loud-hailer in hand, proclaiming his union with the hunger strikers.

When Boyer went to Ottawa in 1984—this isn't Frank Capra, but close—he spoke his mind. Goodyear in the United States closed down a plant in his riding, fifteen hundred people out of jobs, and at the same time, the Tory government was paying Goodyear $30 million in duty remission assistance for a new plant in Napanee, Ontario. That made Boyer mad. He stood up in the House of Commons and said so. "An absolute farce" is what he called his own government's decision over the closing and the $30 million. The Conservatives knew they had some sort of oddball in their midst. What other MP woke each morning at five o'clock to write books for two and a half hours?

The jobs Boyer was assigned in the Commons had the look of window dressing and the sound of ceremony. Chairman of a 1985 Parliamentary committee to have a gander at all federal institutions and programs in light of the section in the Charter of Rights that guarantees equal rights to all Canadians? Oh, sure, make a report and watch it turn yellow. Collect dust alongside ninety-nine percent of committee reports. But Boyer knows his Parliamentary rules. Standing order 60, to be specific, very seldom used, almost a secret. Table your report, invoke standing order 60, and the government is obliged to respond to the report within 120 days. Here was a shock. The Boyer equality report wanted the government to allow women soldiers into combat; to treat gay people like regular people; to cut out mandatory retirement in federal departments and agencies; to deliver the goods on equal pay for work of equal value in areas where the feds have jurisdiction; and to follow through on eighty-one other proposals. Boyer hardly expected the proposals to progress immediately to legislation—gay rights in 1985?—but he forced his own government to face the future of laws in areas that are out front and touchy.

Chairman of the Parliamentary Committee on the Disabled and Handicapped. Something personal kept Boyer's focus on this one. A horse in Colorado kicked him in the leg. Boyer had to get around in a wheelchair. Or not get around. "What I learned," he says, "is that, to go from point A to point B, people with disabilities have to go through the whole alphabet." Right off the bat, before the committee was a year old, in December 1985, Boyer wangled $16 million out of the Secretary of State to launch a program for improved services to the handicapped. Not a whole lot, but a start where there had been nothing.

On a spring Sunday in 1989, Boyer was pouring cement for a new room in the basement of the house on Lakeshore Boulevard.

"Patrick!" Corinne called down the stairs. "The prime minister is on the phone for you!"

"You think I'm falling for that one, Corinne? Forget it."

"Patrick! It *is* the prime minister!"

"Okay, you've had your joke. Now let me do my cement work down here."

"Patrick, *honestly!*"

Boyer went up to the telephone.

"Patrick," said the voice on the line, as deep as the echo at the bottom of a canyon, "I'd like you to give Joe Clark a hand at External Affairs. Parliamentary secretary."

It was April Fools' Day, but it was also Brian Mulroney on the phone.

The new job got Boyer out of the country. He arranged contacts, understood alliances, met people of authority, mouthed policy (but made none). When Mulroney invented the Constitutional Affairs Ministry in the spring of 1991, put Joe Clark in charge of it, and installed Barbara McDougall at External, Boyer and his Parliamentary secretaryship moved over to Marcel Masse at Defence. Same learning role, same middling responsibility, spokesperson when the minister isn't in reach of the cameras and microphones.

"Do you know what I call Parliamentary secretary, the initials PS?" Boyer says. "Push and shove. That's what you have to do if you want to accomplish anything. Actually, now that I think about it, that's also what people do to you in the job. Push and shove."

Corinne Boyer joins her husband and me for lunch in the Parliamentary dining room. She is slender, a modish dresser, and wears her blond hair cut short like a medieval pageboy's. Her face is long and narrow, and has pink blooms as if she's just come in from a skate with Hans Brinker. The Parliamentary dining room, on the sixth floor of the Centre Block, is a surprisingly cheerful place, an underlay of formality in the heavy furnishings and thick carpets, but, on top, noisy and bustling and heartening. The buffet looks spectacular. Corinne, after she married Boyer, worked in the Ontario attorney general's office and for the province's ombudsman. Since 1984, she's devoted herself to Boyer's Parliamentary career, addressing envelopes, delivering speeches, nothing too humble for her or too daunting. At lunch, she talks of Patrick's courtship.

"We met on a blind date," she begins.

"In New York City," Patrick puts in. "I was down from Montreal for a weekend, and mutual friends introduced us."

"I was working for the Dutch Foreign Affairs ministry. And it was so funny, you know. I was invited to go away for the weekend with some friends out on Long Island. I said to them, 'But I have just met this nice Canadian.' 'Okay,' my friends said, 'bring him along.' Well, Patrick and I had the whole weekend to walk on the beach, just walking and talking, and that can make or break a relationship."

"We found we were on the same wavelength," Boyer says. "I came back six weeks later and asked Corinne to marry me."

"Yes, you know, but Patrick had another question. He asked, 'What do you think of being a politician's wife?'"

"How did you answer that one?" I ask.

Corinne lifts an eyebrow. "What did I know of politics? Listen, what did I know of Canada? I had never been there."

A woman stops by the table. She is small, intense, about sixty years old. She's carrying a plate of salads from the buffet table.

She executes a careful kiss on Corinne's cheek. Boyer introduces her to me. The woman is Sheila Finestone, the Liberal MP for Mount-Royal, Pierre Trudeau's old riding. She gives Boyer an especially warm smile, chats for a few minutes, and moves away to join a group of a dozen people at a large table in an alcove.

"All of them are Liberals," Corinne says, nodding in the direction of the alcove.

"A year ago," Boyer says, "some of them spoke to me privately. This was when I was upset with my own party. They asked me if I'd cross the floor and join the Liberals."

"Did you consider it?" I ask.

Boyer smiles, but before he can answer, Corinne speaks.

"The one thing that makes me so mad," she says, "is when people say, oh, these MPs, they get such money. They are lucky, so much money just for being an MP. That is so *wrong*. Patrick could make four times as much if he were still a lawyer at Fraser and Beatty. Plus he would have much more free time."

"Corinne's the one in the family who keeps track of finances," Boyer says to me.

"Patrick never thinks about money," Corinne says. "When he became the Parliamentary secretary to Joe Clark, it meant he had to give up the small connection he still had to Fraser and Beatty."

"The conflict of interest rules apply to PSs exactly the same as to Cabinet ministers."

"Except PSs don't have big staffs like Cabinet ministers. You have to do all the work and study and reading and everything yourself."

"It's fascinating work, most of it."

"Of course it's fascinating, but you should have some help."

"I have you," Boyer says to Corinne. They smile, and their smiles have the effect for the moment of excluding me and everyone else in the Parliamentary dining room.

Question Period in the House.

Boyer takes his Commons seat. Corinne and I sit in the

Members' Gallery. Down below, Jean Chrétien is haranguing Brian Mulroney about something. Boyer's seat is three over and two up from Mulroney's. The subject of Chrétien's harangue is the government's cavalier treatment of Prairie farmers. Mulroney stands up to answer. He seems shorter than on television, and freakishly wide across the shoulders. He looks like he left the hanger in his suit jacket.

Corinne says to me sotto voce, "Do you know a little trick Patrick and I have?"

"What?"

"When I'm in Toronto, Patrick will move around the floor during Question Period until the television cameras are on him and I can see his face. Then I phone him and say, you look tired, you need more sleep, or have you been eating good meals?"

"That's nice."

"It's how we communicate."

The argument on the floor over whether the government is or isn't lending a hand to Prairie farmers doesn't seem to be going anywhere. Corinne and I leave. So, down below, does Boyer.


We're in the lounge off the government side of the House. Tory MPs are murmuring into one another's ears, selecting drinks from a choice of coffee and tomato juice, shouting into telephones. A man hurries up to Boyer.

"This is first class, Patrick," he says, excited, shaking a Xerox of a newspaper column in one hand. "First class, I assure you of that."

The man stands very close to Boyer as he speaks. He has rough good looks and a forceful manner. The column he's holding is from the previous Saturday's *Toronto Star*, and it calls for a national referendum on constitutional reform. Boyer—who else?—wrote the column.

"I tell you what you do, Patrick," the man says. "Print more copies of this, one for each guy in the Quebec caucus."

Boyer introduces the man.

"Meet Jean-Pierre Hogue, the member for Outremont."

Hogue leans close to me.

"The situation between Canada and Quebec," he says, talking quickly, "it is top dog and underdog, and it is the underdog who must make the change. That's where change always comes from. In a divorce, who makes the divorce? The wife. Same thing here. The dog on top gives it to the dog on the bottom. Therefore, if the situation is to be changed, it must come from the underneath, the bottom dog. You understand?"

I try not to look baffled.

"It is very simple," Hogue says, and abruptly is on his way.

Boyer shrugs. "Jean-Pierre is a practising psychologist in Montreal."

Back in his office, Boyer asks Allison Stodin to print up enough copies of the *Star* column to cover the Quebec caucus.

The phone rings. It's Susan Riley of the *Ottawa Citizen*. She wants to talk referendum.

"Don't forget the committee meeting," Stodin whispers at Boyer, tapping a finger on her wristwatch. "In fifteen minutes."

"Susan," Boyer says into the phone, "I'm tired of living in a country that calls itself a democracy where the leaders are afraid to trust the people with something as important as the constitution."

On the end table beside the sofa where I'm sitting with Corinne, there's a handsome, luxurious book of photographs, *Elephants: The Deciding Decade*. I turn the heavy pages. Elephants in the wilderness, families of elephants, elephants that look as old as the world, young elephants as cute as Babar. At the front, the book's editor, Ronald Orenstein, has signed it with a fulsome and personal greeting to Boyer. I ask Corinne about the salutation.

"Oh, yes," she says in a low voice, "Patrick is very concerned with saving the elephants."

*Elephants*, too?

"My argument, Susan," Boyer is saying on the telephone,

"is, with so many provinces, Quebec, British Columbia, probably Saskatchewan, and who can tell how many others, all of them holding referendums anyway or talking about it, why not hold a national referendum rather than a number of disjointed, differently worded referendums across the country?"

Corinne, voice still low, explains more about elephants, about the International Green Corps. The latter is an idea Boyer has been pushing, an environmental equivalent of the International Red Cross, an outfit that would mobilize the response to ecological disasters, the *Exxon Valdez* crackup, the oil blowouts during the Gulf War. Elephants fit in here somewhere. Boyer travelled to a meeting of a working group on elephants in Lausanne a year earlier.

"Did you know," Corinne asks me, "poachers in Africa kill two hundred elephants every day? Or is it three hundred?"

"A piece of history, Susan," Boyer says into the phone. "Australia. In 1900, they put it in their constitution, article 498, check it out for yourself, any amendment to the constitution had to be ratified in a direct vote by the people. Since 1900, Australia's tried thirty-two times to amend the constitution, and only eight times the people voted in favour. So you see, the whole thing about a referendum isn't an alien concept in a parliamentary democracy."

Allison Stodin is in the doorway, holding up her wrist with the watch on it.

"Ten minutes," she says in a stage whisper. "You're already ten minutes late for the committee meeting."

"Susan, it's an abdication of national leadership not to bring a referendum forward in a positive fashion," Boyer says on the phone. "Gotta run, Susan."

He hangs up.

"Patrick," Corinne says, "is it two hundred elephants that African poachers kill every day or three hundred?"

"Three hundred." Boyer turns to me. "You know the treatment of elephants is criminal. . . ."

"Patrick!" Stodin breaks in. "The *meeting!*"

The meeting is of the Standing Committee on Human Rights and the Status of Disabled Persons. (These Parliamentary committees change names about as often as the Belgian Congo.) Boyer, long gone from the committee's chair, is present to nudge along a pet project. It came to him one day, years earlier, when he noticed groundskeepers scooping coins out of the fountain that surrounds the Centennial Flame on Parliament Hill. Boyer asked about the destination of the coins. General revenues. How much? A thousand dollars a year, more, possibly two thousand, three. Tourists tossed them in, you know, like *Three Coins in the Fountain.* Boyer introduced a private member's bill directing that the money from the fountain finance a program of grants to disabled people to study ways in which they can get in on activities in Parliament. The bill bounced back and forth for years—the Senate returned it to the Commons for retinkering—but finally it became law. Today's committee meeting is to discuss implementation, details, public relations aspects.

"It's very, very hard to get a private member's bill passed," Corinne says to me as we rush to the meeting.

"Really?"

"Jean Chrétien had one that changed the name of the airline to Air Canada. And, let's see, Lynn McDonald, she got one passed, an anti-smoking bill. And the other was Sean O'Sullivan's."

"Yes?"

"To make the beaver our national symbol."

The meeting is in a room as big as a hockey rink. It used to be the Reading Room, where MPs could browse over books and magazines in immense silence. Now it's an awkward chamber for conferences. The words of people at one end of the long table reach listeners at the other end seconds after the speakers' lips stop moving. Six committee members are present, huddled together, and at a remove, six bureaucrats. The two blank-faced men with beards are from the Department of Public Works.

"Those guys'd slow down anything," Boyer says from behind one hand.

The meeting proceeds in lurches. But gradually, with Boyer providing more than his share of prods, matters shake down. A plaque to be placed on the fountain explaining the use of the coins, at first estimated by Public Works to cost eleven thousand dollars, is scaled back to one thousand. A time and place is arrived at for a public announcement inviting disabled people to apply for grants. Photographs are arranged, advertisements, other bits and pieces. The meeting adjourns.

"Thanks for coming," one of the civil servants says to Boyer, a man named Bill Young from the Political and Social Affairs Division of the Parliamentary Library. "It wouldn't have got off the ground without you."

Boyer looks pleased.


In Boyer's office, I ask him what sort of Progressive Conservative he is. How does he label himself? As he answers and answers . . . and answers, I begin to rethink the wisdom of asking the question. I have a plane to catch in two hours. Boyer is giving me a lecture on the history of the Conservative Party in Canada, verbal footnotes included, references to learned authorities, a selection of quotes, all of it filtered through his own relentless analysis machine.

Mentions of Sir John A. Macdonald and Confederation Conservatism go by, Robert Borden and Public Interest Conservatism, R.B. Bennett and Social Conservatism, Diefenbaker and his inclusionary approach. We're closing in on contemporary conservatism. "Mulroney is cut from the same cloth as Sir John A.," Boyer says. "The patronage system is fine by him, and he favours the broad approach to bringing everyone together."

Now, at last, for the future. "The next phase will be Democratic Conservatism," Boyer goes on. "That's how I see myself, a Democratic Conservative. I favour a non-elitist, populist approach to conservative values. Let's emphasize community, family, self-reliance. Not individualism, no, no, that's Reagan and Thatcher. It doesn't equate with my kind of radical Toryism based in a strong sense of community."

"Patrick," Allison Stodin interrupts from the doorway, "you've got Roy Romanow's reception over in the Wellington Building."

Saskatchewan's premier is in Ottawa with 130 farmers to promote federal aid to agriculture. After the reception, Boyer must be in the House for a six o'clock vote and afterwards, a long dinner meeting of the PC Ontario caucus.

"Allison," Boyer says, "would you let Corinne know it'll probably be eleven anyway before I'm back at the apartment."

Boyer gets a thoughtful look.

"What I've been telling you about the evolution of conservatism, Macdonald to the present," he says to me, "I have plenty of material on that in my writing room at home, research, my own ideas, and it is definitely a book. My next book, a historical study of how the party's changed and evolved and where it's headed. The trouble with too many people around here, around Parliament, they think history is what happened two weeks ago."


The following Sunday, in Ukraine, with Boyer invigilating, eighty-four percent of the country's registered voters—the population is fifty-two million—go to the polls. Ninety percent of the eighty-four percent favour their country's independence. Ukraine is now a separate republic. Next day, Monday, Brian Mulroney announces from Ottawa that Canada extends diplomatic recognition to the new government of the new country. Canada is the first Western nation to make this large gesture.

A week later, Boyer phones me. He is in Toronto, and he sounds even more upbeat than usual.

"A thrilling series of events over there," he says. "As soon as the vote was certain, I got on the line to Barbara McDougall in Ottawa. I urged her we should go first in recognizing Kravchuk's government. He's the president, Leonid Kravchuk. I was quite forceful with Barbara. People who were with me at my

end of the call agreed I was forceful. Later, very late at night
Ukraine time, we got word at the Canadian Consulate in Kiev
about Mulroney's statement on recognition. We decided—we,
that is, me and the Canadian Consul General and a person from
External—we decided we would take the news to President
Kravchuk personally. Well, first there was the long drive out to
his villa in a forest, then I thought the guard dogs might eat us
alive. But we got in, well into the early hours of the morning by
this time, and Kravchuk was very pleased and very gracious.
Cognac, caviar, toasts, a good conversation. This had tremendous meaning for him, that a Western country had opened
diplomatic relations with the new Ukraine."

"And you were there."

"Just like the old Walter Cronkite TV shows I watched when I
was a kid, *The Twentieth Century*. 'It was a day like any other day,
only you were there.'"

"A moment of history."

"Well, I'm privileged in my job," Boyer says. "Listen, tomorrow I'm going to be seeing people in my riding office most of
the day. Why don't you come down and sit in? Constituents
with the most unbelievable problems, it's fascinating."

I say I'll take a pass.

# CHAPTER FOUR

## The Downtown Lawyers

ACCORDING TO DAVE MURPHY, and to John Whyte, too, here is how events unfolded.

Murphy ordered the king-sized Manhattan on the rocks. So did Whyte. Murphy began to talk about his doubts and dreams. This was over lunch in the winter of 1987 at Ed's Warehouse, a restaurant on King Street West in downtown Toronto (perpetual *plat du jour*: roast beef by the slab). It wasn't the first lunch in the restaurant where Murphy had aired his feelings to Whyte. The pair had met two decades earlier in residence at the University of Toronto's Trinity College and formed a friendship that persisted through the years together in law school and into practice in downtown firms. By anybody's standards, Murphy had it made. He was a partner at Blake, Cassels and Graydon, rising in commercial litigation, pulling down a hefty income, a bachelor with a condo looking over Lake Ontario and a place on a lake in the cottage country north of the city. For that matter, Whyte had a swell career of his own as a partner specializing in insolvency law at the firm of Strathy, Archibald.

"People think I'm doing so fantastically well in law," Murphy said to Whyte. "Got a great career, great firm, great future. But the thing I keep thinking, is that all there is?"

"Peggy Lee recorded the song."

"I'm serious."

"Dave, I *know* you are."

"Living the kind of life I am, all the hours I put in at the office and in court," Murphy said, "I really have only half a life. I'm getting stultified, you know, one-dimensional. Guys who work on Bay Street, guys like us, it's a really narrow existence we have outside the law."

"Listen, I sympathize with what you're saying to me," Whyte said. "But what *do* you want out of life? As if I haven't heard this before."

Murphy leaned back a little, the Manhattan in his hand, expansive, letting his thoughts float. "If I could find a job that would let me live as well as I do now in the material sense, but on the other side of the world where there's no winter, some exotic place but with Western influences, some place where there's a slower pace, time for reflection, time to do something besides law . . . a place like that, I'd be gone. I'd be out of here."

"Sounds like a movie."

"Sure, and here's more scenes for the movie. Somewhere that has a cultural scene, I'd want that. But physical attractions, too. Mountains. Water would be good, a location close to the sea. And . . ."

"All right, all right." Whyte held up his hand. "This is all terrific for you to fantasize about. You're a bachelor, no ties, nothing to hold you back."

"That helps."

"More than just *helps*."

"Okay, it helps a lot."

"I don't like Toronto winters, either," Whyte said. "If there was a warm climate where I could go and practise law and be compensated like I am now, hell, I'd find that pretty tempting."

"That's what I'm talking about."

"But, Dave . . . you *know* this is the difference in our situations . . . I'm *married*. A wife, two little daughters, you think that doesn't change the picture?"

"Makes it tougher, all right."

"Makes it impossible, is more like it."

"Well," Murphy said, "all I know is I've got to have a life, and it isn't in a big downtown Toronto law firm."

As it developed, Dave Murphy got out, *way* out, all the way to Hong Kong. The switch to Bay Street dropout came about through a series of seemingly unconnected events.

Murphy had a court date in Vancouver in the spring of 1988. He flew to the coast for a trial that was projected to last a few weeks. But the case was settled suddenly and unexpectedly. On the spur of the moment, Murphy decided to take the first long holiday since he joined Blake, Cassels in 1978. He headed for a part of the world that had always appealed to him, the Far East. For four weeks, he poked around Japan, Malaysia, Hong Kong, and eight or nine other places in the Asia–Pacific region. When he returned to Toronto, he brought back a sense of enchantment with what he'd seen and sensed.

In the summer of '88, Murphy had conversations with Professor Michael Trebilcock of the U of T Law School. Murphy had taken classes from Trebilcock years earlier, but the two didn't get acquainted until they discovered they had summer cottages in the same area. And in talks between the two, Trebilcock, who is arguably Canada's finest legal scholar, encouraged Murphy in musings he was having that he might prefer to teach law rather than practise it.

In December of the same year the pieces fell into place: an advertisement turned up in the *Globe and Mail* requesting applicants for a lecturing job on the law faculty of the University of Hong Kong.

Murphy answered the ad. A few months went by without acknowledgement from Hong Kong, enough time to make Murphy think maybe he'd hallucinated the whole thing, the ad and his response. But in April 1989, he took a long-distance call at Blake, Cassels. The man on the other end was in charge of recruiting the new lecturer in Hong Kong.

"We were rather surprised you wrote to us, Mr. Murphy," the man said.

"Surprised? Why?"

"You are very well established in a large firm in Canada," the man answered. "It would not seem likely you would want to come to us."

"It may not seem that way, but I'm absolutely sincere."

"Perhaps you are experiencing a midlife crisis."

"It isn't a crisis," Murphy answered. "It's a natural progression."

The man from Hong Kong said he'd get back to Murphy. He did, and after several more phone calls, he offered Murphy the job.

"I accept," Murphy said. "But I'll need a piece of paper from you. Before I resign here, burn all my bridges, I need to have a contract in my hands."

"It will be in the mail."

Alas for Murphy, the contract took several weeks to reach Toronto. Murphy agonized. He was walking around the office keeping a secret he shared with only one of his partners, turning down cases without being able to explain that he didn't expect to be around long enough to take them to trial or settlement.

At last, the contract arrived, and Murphy, the monkey off his back, went to the managing partner at Blake, Cassels to hand in his resignation.

"You're *what*?" the managing partner said.

"Going to teach in Hong Kong."

"Yes, yes, I heard that. But *why*?"

Murphy didn't bother to go into detail about his doubts over the law and his place in it. Instead he spoke to the managing partner in language any downtown lawyer would understand.

"The tax advantages of the move are tremendous," Murphy said. "And nobody can beat the benefits package the law faculty's offering me."

"Well, why didn't you say so?" the managing partner said.

By the following September—1989—Murphy was in Hong Kong, gone from Toronto winters, gone from a life style he had found oppressive, gone from a job in the law—a partner in a major, maybe *the* major, downtown Toronto law firm—that most lawyers would kill for.

Dave Murphy doesn't *look* like a flaming rebel.

I meet him on a summer morning when he's back in Canada for two purposes, to ride horseback through the Rocky Mountains and to open his cottage. He's a tall, fit, athletic man. He has thick hair and a resemblance to Christopher Reeve, Superman in the movies. If anything gives away the revolutionary lurking in Murphy, it might be his voice; it turns burrowing and intense when he gets on the subject of his radical change of job, home, and way of life.

But before he talks about how he got out of the practice of law, he tells me how he got into it. He decided on law, he says, when he was a kid growing up in Barrie, Ontario. The persuader was the summer jobs he had with a local lawyer, first as the little guy who swept the floors for ten dollars a week, then as the eighteen-year-old who wore a tie and closed real estate deals and appeared in small claims court. This, Murphy thought, was the life. He studied political science at the University of Toronto, took a master's degree at the London School of Economics, and at last enrolled in law school, which, maybe to his surprise, he found kind of dull.

"I'd just come from LSE, one of the most exciting years of my life," he says. "By the time I got to law school, I just wanted to get it done and go to work."

Murphy must have shown some smarts, though, because after the Bar Admission course, he was picked, along with a U of T law classmate named Bob Rueter, to clerk for a year with the Ontario Court of Appeal. Slow learners don't get that job. From the court, he proceeded to a plum position on the commercial litigation side of Blake, Cassels. The litigation people at the firm are one of the best kept secrets in Canadian law, held in something like awe by other litigators, but practically invisible as far as the media, the public, and probably the rest of the profession are concerned. The litigation leaders at Blake, Cassels are men named Jake Howard, John Brown, Jim Garrow, Burt Kellock, high in talent, low in profile, which is the way their clients like it. Dave Murphy joined these august ranks, and fairly quickly found himself taking a hand in some of the key cases affecting the Canadian financial community in the 1970s and 1980s. He was on *Wotherspoon v Canadian Pacific Limited*, a courtroom drama in which the title to chunks of land in the very hearts of downtown Toronto and Montreal were up for grabs. He was in cases that involved stock frauds, takeovers, professional negligence, high-level banking, and a scandal in tuna fish.

"It wasn't really the work that eventually got to me," Murphy says. "The work was great, often very exciting, and I'd never say a bad word about Blake, Cassels as a firm. My problem was with the rest of my life. *It* was practically nonexistent."

The natural question, leaping ahead in the story, is, by contrast with Murphy's past existence, how goes life for him in Hong Kong?

I ask the question, and Murphy grows positively elegaic describing his large apartment that overlooks the South China Sea, his neighbourhood on a rocky coastline ("kind of Mediterranean in its atmosphere"), his range of activities from golf to Chinese brush painting to classes in Cantonese, his leisurely approach to each day.

"It took me months in Hong Kong before I learned how to wind down," Murphy says. "I used to sit with my colleagues in the senior common room for lunch, and after ten minutes, I'd start to twitch. I'd come from a work ethic where I wouldn't normally waste more than ten minutes on lunch. More than ten, that was something I had to adjust to in my new life."

As for his career as a beginning academic, Murphy is enthusiastic about the University of Hong Kong's law school, though he's had to make allowances for cultural differences. In classes, for one thing, the students don't go in for the give and take with their lecturers that Murphy had known in his own school days.

"Part of it is they're too respectful of their teachers in a Confucian sense to raise questions with them," Murphy explains. "And partly—this is amazing when you think of it—the students are taking classes in law in English, which for them is a second language. I have a lot of respect for these young people."

So Murphy is living a life in Hong Kong that seems as close to heaven on earth as a lawyer can attain. Teaching in a society where teachers are esteemed. A month of vacation each Christmas, two months in the summer. Six months paid sabbatical every three years. Side trips as a matter of routine to Thailand, Singapore. A summer safari to Africa in the planning stages. No sweat. No angst. Time to smell the lotus blossoms. And, oh, yeah, there was the invitation to lecture on Western-style litigation at the People's University of China in Beijing.

From the perspective of such bliss, Murphy has formed definite views about the lot of his former colleagues in the law in Toronto, views that aren't likely to thrill the lawyers he left behind in the downtown firms.

"My perception is that too many of them in the big firms are unhappy people," he says. "There are a small number who live for the law, a few who are megalomaniacs who love the power. Many of the others, I think, feel trapped and won't admit it. Some are just reeling around like punch-drunk fighters."

How does Murphy's breakaway from the traditional downtown lawyer's role to an unconventional career on the other side of the world go over with his former mates in the Toronto law factories?

Murphy's expression tightens just a trifle. "When I come back to the city for visits, I don't like to walk through the Commerce Court concourse, right below where I used to work, because I see too many faces I know. I stop to chat, and it gets awkward. The subject of what I've done comes up, and I know, underneath it all, the light talk, the banter, I know many of these people are unhappy. My being there, just passing through from Hong Kong, that rubs it in."

★    ★    ★

John Zinn hasn't the air of a man who's trapped. Or unhappy. Or punch-drunk. And the exercise of power, I judge, comes far down his personal list of pleasures. Probably it's right off the list.

Zinn practises tax law with Davies Ward and Beck. It has eighty lawyers and occupies three floors high up in First Canadian Place on King Street. Zinn and I sit at a table in the window of his office late on a September afternoon, talking, drinking soda water, the sun sinking behind the SkyDome still bright and warm. Zinn is tall, lean, and balding. There's a stillness about him. He's what New Age people call centred.

He grew up in Hanover, a town of five thousand in southwest Ontario, and he enrolled in law school after only two years of commerce and finance at the University of Toronto. The law school accepted students with that minimal education—it still does today—as long as they had good marks in the two undergraduate years, scored high in the LSATs, and otherwise showed promise. Zinn was nineteen years old at the time. He's not sure why he rushed into law. It was a very nineteen-year-old thing to do.

"Ignorance is bliss," he says. "I didn't know what was ahead of me."

The best marks in the class were ahead of him. In the first-year Christmas exams, Zinn stood first. In January, after the marks came out, the dean, Marty Friedland, stopped Zinn in the hall.

"Mr. Zinn, isn't it?" Friedland asked.

"Yes, sir."

"Come into my office, if you don't mind."

The two sat across from one another at Friedland's desk.

"Would you be interested in working as my student this summer, Mr. Zinn?" Friedland said. "Researching cases and materials in criminal law, that kind of thing."

"Oh, thanks, but I've already got a summer job lined up," Zinn blurted, still a nineteen-year-old and none too worldly, not grasping that an honour was being dangled before him. "At the liquor store in Port Elgin."

"Well, Mr. Zinn," Friedland said, patient since this naive kid was after all the top student in the class, "the job I'm offering you is at least as interesting as stacking boxes in a liquor store."

Zinn wised up and took Friedland's job.

Zinn remembers one other significant conversation in first year. It came when the marks were posted after the final exams. Zinn again ranked first. Rob Prichard was second.

"Zinn," Prichard said to him, "I'll be gunning for you."

Two years later, at the graduation of the class of '75, Prichard stood first, Zinn second.

"Rob gunned me," Zinn says in his office. The gunning doesn't seem to have damaged his ego.

"After graduation," Zinn says, "I saw that my classmates were anxious to practise law. They'd been in school a long time. But I was young and hadn't had as much school as they had. I *liked* school. I wanted more. I determined in my own mind that Harvard was the best for me. I applied there, and only there, to the LLM program, and I got in."

Note the verb, "determined." It's Zinn's favourite. While he was at Harvard, the dean of the law school at the University of Western Ontario offered him a teaching job. Zinn says, "I looked at the offer from all sides and determined teaching was a delightful idea." After a few years of teaching, still only twenty-seven, he thought of switching careers. "I determined that, if I ever wanted to try the practice of law, I should resign from Western, not just take a sabbatical because it would be so easy to return to the comfort of Western if I happened to hit a difficult period in practice." He determined Davies Ward and Beck was the best firm for him since it was relatively small and presented a chance to work at both corporate securities and tax law. Later, he determined he would concentrate on tax. And so on. Is it because Zinn is so analytical and methodical that he seems centred? Or is it the other way around, his essential centredness opens him to analysis and method? I'm not sure.

In his office, Zinn talks more about his career. About the year in the early 1980s when he went on loan from his firm to serve on a blue-ribbon panel in Ottawa looking at tax changes for the Minister of Finance. About a year in England in the early 1990s tending to a large real estate development for a client. About his personal life—he's a bachelor, lives in a condo on the lake front, keeps a sailboat at Ontario Place, owns a part interest in two Blue Jays season tickets.

As Zinn's conversation begins to wind down, I try Dave Murphy's notion on him, the view that lawyers in downtown firms may be desperate souls. Zinn doesn't get it. Unhappy? Trapped? Huh?

"I consider myself very fortunate," he says finally. "I'm happy to be in a firm like the one I'm in."

★    ★    ★

Is it my imagination or do I seem to be meeting more than a few big-firm lawyers who have qualities like John Zinn's? Focused, low-key, something cool running through their veins? It isn't my imagination. John Hunter is that way, and so is his wife, Rebecca Winesanker, though, strictly speaking, she isn't a big-firm lawyer. She works for the federal government doing immigration law.

Hunter and Winesanker are one of the two couples who met in the class of '75 and married. (The other is Rob Prichard and Ann Wilson.) They live in Vancouver, in a part of West Point Grey that, on the early November Saturday I come calling, is green and tranquil and neighbourly, many of the front porches still decorated with ingeniously carved Halloween pumpkins. Hunter is a tall, good-looking, straight-arrow guy. Winesanker is dark, petite, and lovely. Both seem utterly content with the hand they've dealt themselves in law and in life.

In conversation, they parcel out biography in short self-effacing takes. John is from Toronto, did an undergraduate degree at Yale, post-grad work at the London School of Economics (where he ran across Dave Murphy from time to time), and enrolled in law at Toronto because, from his teenaged years, he knew litigation was his future. Rebecca started out in Toronto, did much of her growing up in Fort Worth, Texas, went to Oberlin College in Ohio, and on to Toronto Law. John felt impatient at law school, suffering a minor case of study burnout after Yale and LSE. He joined a study group where, he says, "We played a lot of bridge." He threw himself into moot court, looking ahead to that litigation career, and won prizes as a mooter. Rebecca was more keen on studies. She worked on the *Law Review*, and in the summer after first year, a professor, Steve Waddams, hired her to research a book he was writing. John and Rebecca started dating in the last months of first year. By third year, they were living as dons in a residence at U of T's New College. They kicked around Europe for five weeks that summer, and got married in May 1976, just before they began to practise in British Columbia.

Why British Columbia?

It was John's idea. He has Norwegian blood on his mother's side, travelled in Norway during his LSE years, and wanted some of the Norse way of life in his own. The ocean, mountains, a more sedate pace.

"People at the law school thought it was a questionable thing for us to come out here," John says. "U of T Law has an enormous aura of Toronto about it, and anyone who leaves—I had an offer to join a big Toronto firm with an excellent litigation department—is perceived as stepping away from a quality practice."

"At the same time," Rebecca says, "the atmosphere out here wasn't completely welcoming in the legal community. The law firms gave obvious preference to people from the UBC law school."

If it was a nervous beginning, the signs now are only of success and of work that engages them, Rebecca at the Department of Justice, John at Davis and Company, a firm of one hundred lawyers, one of the big four in Vancouver. John is already Davis's senior litigator. He's been busy in court the past couple of years on behalf of one major client, MacMillan Bloedel, fighting the environmentalists and Indian land claimants.

"Oh, yes," he says with equanimity, "I'm on the side that gets the lousy press. But that's changing. People are starting to focus on the loss of jobs that'll result if MacMillan Bloedel has to cut back."

Placid. That's how it seems around John and Rebecca. Three kids. Rebecca's on the board of the Friends of Chamber Music. John teaches an appellate advocacy course at the UBC law school and is a board member of the Vancouver Academy of Music.

"Life is pleasant out here," John says.

Who's to argue?

★   ★   ★

John Whyte is another member of a big downtown firm, in Toronto, whose personality seems securely wrapped. He's Dave Murphy's former sparring partner from the lunches at Ed's Warehouse. He looks like Murphy, the rugged, leading-man type. His firm, Strathy, Archibald, has about 250 lawyers, and in his fifteen years there, Whyte has progressed from real estate to banking and financial, finally zeroing in on insolvency law. He acts for creditors who are trying to wedge the best possible deal out of companies that have gone bankrupt. It's a dicey area of law. Whyte is undoubtedly very good at it. He has an intricate mind. He speaks about law school and the legal profession in *aperçus* that have an edge to them.

For example: "The practice of law has a jock mentality. A lot of athletes are attracted to it. Maybe it's the competitive carry-over."

And: "I had a BA and an MA in philosophy and economics with a strong Marxist-Leninist side. To shift from that to law was a wrenching experience. You couldn't fake it in law the way you could in philosophy."

And: "Why did I go into law? It didn't look like there were many openings around Toronto for a Hegelian philosopher."

More: "The first couple of weeks at law school are the biggest shock. In arts, you're presented with certain principles and you're free to challenge them. In law, you're presented with principles that make up the social, economic, and legal framework by which we live. These are rules. Lawyers don't challenge rules. They work with them. For me, at that point in law school, things closed in, and it got very claustrophobic."

And more: "What's mind-boggling about law is that there's so much of it. So many statutes, so many rules and regulations, so many details. You have to learn the details. But they aren't important. What's important is the way you think about the concepts that drive the details, so that you can cope with the changes that inevitably come when the legislators and bureaucrats revise the statutes and rules and regulations for the one hundredth time."

How does Whyte regard his old friend jumping ship, Dave Murphy's leap from the downtown Toronto firm to the Asian law school?

"A legal mind like Dave's," Whyte says, "it was almost a shame to waste it on a law firm. Now he's sharing it with young people. I think what he's done is great."

If that's another *aperçu*, it's one without an edge.

On a fantastic Indian summer Sunday morning—the leaves blazing orange and yellow, the sun warm on my back—I walk north a few blocks from my house to see Paul Morrison. He lives on one of the streets behind Casa Loma, a neighbourhood of stone houses and towering trees. Paul Morrison has two things on his mind this morning, a hockey tournament and a trial.

The hockey tournament, coming up the following weekend, is to raise money for the Toronto General Hospital. A bunch of companies—Dominion Securities, Mutual Life, Morrison's law firm, McCarthy Tetrault, several others—kick in five thousand dollars each for the privilege of entering teams of their own employees in the tournament. It'll be Morrison's first time on skates in ten years. He used to play top-calibre hockey. He was on the senior team at St. Michael's College in high school, and his years at the University of Pennsylvania, studying economics, were on a hockey scholarship. He played left wing. I figure he would have been a plugger, solid along the boards, hard to knock off the puck. Morrison is built low to the ground, a short but powerful guy. In his senior year, he thinks he got about a dozen goals and maybe fifteen assists, which is more than respectable in the Ivy League. John Whyte seems to have a point about athletes being attracted to the law.

The trial on Paul Morrison's mind sounds grim. It's a medical malpractice case, and Morrison, whose field is civil litigation, is representing the doctor. In 1984, the doctor, an allergy specialist, treated a twelve-year-old boy who had suffered an asthma attack. The doctor prescribed a variety of drugs. A few days later, a full-scale seizure hit the boy. He seemed to weather it, but after a couple of years, a series of smaller seizures, five or six a year, put him in a state where he was brain damaged, a diagnosed epileptic, unable to work, barely capable of looking after himself. The allegation against the doctor, Morrison's client, is that the drugs he prescribed brought on the seizures, that if he had monitored the boy's blood levels, he'd have caught the trouble in time to prevent the damage.

"A case like this one is intellectually demanding," Morrison says. "It takes hours and hours just to understand all the medical procedures. I've been working on the case here at home for the last two weeks. I need the concentrated time away from the office and the distractions down there to make sure everything is clear in my head. I've set aside four weeks for the trial. I'm not sure even that's enough."

Cases like this one are also emotionally demanding. About a third of Morrison's trial work is on medical malpractice suits. McCarthy Tetrault acts for the Canadian Medical Protective Association, and when one of its member doctors gets sued in Ontario, Morrison is often the guy who conducts the defence. He recalls one case that haunted him.

"A woman in her fifties was the plaintiff," Morrison says. "She went to the hospital, doctors thought she'd had an aneurysm in her head. They ran a catheter through her groin and up her arterial system. They injected a dye along the arteries to the brain. That was to locate the aneurysm. The dye turned out to be toxic. It left the woman paralyzed. A quadriplegic.

That was in 1980. She sued the doctors. There were very tough legal and evidentiary issues. We went to trial in 1987, and it lasted six weeks. Every day, every minute of the six weeks, the woman was in court, sitting there in her wheelchair. I know how it wore me down to see her in that wheelchair every day. What must it have done to her? She lost the trial and died a year later. I often wondered if it was the case that kept her alive that long."

Morrison and I are drinking coffee in the kitchen. Before he and his wife bought the place, the former owner ran it as a rooming house. The day the Morrisons moved in, fourteen boarders moved out. The Morrisons invested much time and good taste in making over the house. The kitchen is white and shiny and has a high counter down the centre that's great for eating and family communing.

Morrison talks about the logistics of working at McCarthy Tetrault. It's the biggest law firm in Canada, more than five hundred lawyers, head office on six floors of the Toronto-Dominion Centre downtown, other offices in Vancouver, Calgary, Ottawa, Montreal, Quebec City, Hong Kong, and both Londons, England and Ontario. When Morrison joined the litigation department in the late 1970s, it had a dozen lawyers. Now it numbers fifty. McCarthys was always a good litigation firm, with such masters as the legend, John Robinette (now retired), John Brook (long gone to the Ontario Court of Appeal), Doug Laidlaw (killed in his prime in a freak accident on the Gardiner Expressway), and George Finlayson (also Ontario Court of Appeal, more recently than Brook.) Now it's good *and* big. That means problems in logistics.

"Just directing traffic demands a lot of my attention," Morrison says. "Making sure the work gets spread around evenly to the junior litigators, that they have a variety of cases, and that they work with all the different senior people, things I never dreamed I'd be doing when I got into litigation. Keeping people happy."

The way Morrison explains it, there's a mini bureaucracy within the litigation department that controls the action. Cases can arrive at the department in a slew of ways. Some come because a client specifically wants one of McCarthy Tetrault's stars to handle the case, Tom Heinzman or Ian Binnie or Alan Lenczner or—*ta da*—Paul Morrison. Some are sent over from the firm's mammoth corporate department when a client develops litigious problems. Some cases walk in off the street. The first person in the litigation department who checks over a case, no matter how it arrives, is likely to be a law clerk. Suppose it's an unannounced off-the-street case. The law clerk will assess its nature, the amount of money at stake, the kind of law involved, the case lists of the lawyers in the department, and decide who's best and who's available to take on the case. So goes life in today's world of prime-time litigation.

"Oh, yeah," Morrison says, "it's a long way from the days when a lawyer would see a client, open a file, and get ready for court. We have teams of litigators now. I'm a team leader, and part of the job is an ongoing review of all the cases. What stage are we at? How are we doing? Is everybody satisfied? Not just the clients, but the *lawyers*. It's hectic, the organizational work all by itself."

Morrison's wife drifts in and out of the kitchen as he and I talk. Her name is Janet.

"Don't forget to tell about your honorary membership in the Vagabonds," she tells Morrison.

"Is that Vagabonds as in the big hairy guys on the Harley-Davidsons?" I ask.

"Those guys," Morrison says, and tells the story.

It seems the Vagabonds were planning a party for a July 1 weekend on property they owned in Tiny Township near Midland, Ontario. Not an intimate cocktail party, but a mammoth winging of a celebration. The Vagabond property covered one hundred acres, and bikers and their old ladies on the Vagabond guest list were vroom-vrooming in from all points across North America. When Tiny Township's elected officials caught wind of the planned extravaganza a week or so before the big event, they went to court and got an injunction to restrain the party on the strength of a by-law that prohibited circuses without a licence. The Vagabonds had no licence. They sure as hell were going to put on a circus in the non-specific definition of the word. Somehow or other, the Vagabonds found their way to Paul Morrison's office.

"I moved in court to strike out the by-law," Morrison says. "I argued the by-law was bad because it left the discretion to use it on an individualized basis. It didn't define when certain things could be done or not done. The judge agreed with me. He struck down the by-law and dissolved the injunction. This happened two days before the party was scheduled. People all over the continent had already been on the road for days heading to the big party. It was a very close thing."

"For that," I say, "the Vagabonds made you an honorary member?"

"They even invited me to the party. They said they'd ride me up to Tiny Township in the sidecar of a bike. I respectfully declined."

"How did the party go?"

"Without any problems for people in the township, apparently," Morrison says. "That case, acting for the Vagabonds, was a lot less stress than acting for doctors in malpractice suits."

★  ★  ★

Randy Echlin is a big, bouncy man who wears his enthusiasms for all to see. For instance, baseball.

He has four Blue Jays season tickets in his name. Two are several rows above first base. The other two are at the edge of the Blue Jays dugout, vintage territory, across the aisle from the row set aside for the team's executives, wives, and visiting bigwigs. Echlin's had season tickets since the Jays came to town in 1977. There are eighty-one home games, not counting play-offs. Echlin rarely misses a game, counting play-offs.

*Is* Randy Echlin a baseball fan?

In the contest to name the new stadium, Echlin and some fellow lawyer fans hit on the winner. SkyDome. So did about ten thousand other entrants in the contest. The person who won the grand prize—a pair of season tickets—was chosen by lucky draw. Echlin didn't get lucky. But it was Echlin who successfully lobbied Canada Post to issue a special Canadian baseball stamp.

And further:

In the spring of 1991, Echlin won a lawsuit. The people who owned the company on the losing side also owned the Buffalo Bisons triple-A baseball team. Echlin worked an arrangement with the opposing counsel. "What I want," Echlin said, "is a chance in batting practice against a Buffalo pitcher." Done, said the counsel, who was aware of Echlin's mania. Echlin went into training. He practised his swing against a pitching machine. He practised catching fly balls in the outfield. He watched his diet. On the evening of August 22, 1991, at Rich Stadium in Buffalo, a Bison pitcher named Scott Little went to the mound in the pre-game warm-up. Echlin waited at the plate. His big moment, Robert Redford in *The Natural*. How did he do?

"Well, not bad," Echlin says, looking fairly satisfied with himself. "I made contact with about eight-five percent of the pitches. But most of them were infield grounders or Texas leaguers. I couldn't yank one like Cecil Fielder.

"But shagging flies, oh, my," he says, holding the sides of his head and not looking even fairly satisfied. "They hit probably twenty balls to me in the outfield. You want to know how many I caught? None. A big zero."

Echlin has other enthusiasms. Family. In his office at Borden and Elliott in Toronto (two hundred lawyers, an emphasis on insurance work), among the baseball collectables and memorabilia, there's a fetching colour photograph of Echlin, his wife, and two little kids, Libby and Robbie, taken at the Club Med in St. Lucia.

And, enthusiasmwise, there's the field of law he practises, employment law, the firing of employees, how the employees can fight back, how the employers can handle the firing with style and avoid employee revenge, how the courts view all the shenanigans. Employment law is a recently developed area, not more than fifteen years old. Echlin, early into the field, is one of its pre-eminent practitioners. He loves it. He lectures about it at the University of Toronto's Woodsworth College. He gives seminars in it to business people. He has put together a case book on it. He's nuts about employment law.

And when he describes some of his employment law cases to me, the sad and crazy things he's seen and heard, *I* get excited. It's contagious. Echlin's voice encourages the contagion. Its sound is mellow, the way an announcer's voice is on MOR radio, but Echlin talks very quickly. The effect is like Lorne Greene on speed.

Here are some of the things Echlin tells me:

"Most firings happen in May or June. That's because the decision-makers want to have the summer free of worrying about the employees they're going to let go. The procrastinators fire in September. Some do it at the end of the calendar year, November or December. I'm forever telling employers, do *not* fire before Christmas. I acted for one executive who got bounced at four o'clock on December 24. He worked for an American-based company, and a vice president flew up to Toronto on a visit and decided to fire the guy while he was in town. He told the executive there was a cab waiting for him downstairs, and he was sent home to his wife and kids sitting by the Christmas tree with no job. When we went to trial, the judge took note of the date, and I got a lot more compensation for the guy purely because of the cruel timing. So when I'm advising employers, I say, put an embargo on firing from November 15 to December 31. One employer took my advice and waited until January 5 to fire one of his executives. The executive sued. I was acting for the employer, and when we got to the stage in the case where we were having the examination of the parties at discovery, it became painfully clear that the decision to fire the guy had been made back in mid-November. He leaned across the table and said to me, 'Mr. Echlin, you let me run up my MasterCard over Christmas.' There are no easy answers.

"I intentionally keep my practice fifty-fifty, half employee, half employer. I act for each side at different times in different cases. It isn't like labour law where a lawyer acts for unions all the time or management all the time. An employer will come to me in advance and ask, how do I fire this man? I say, fire him as if you were firing your best friend. Check and make sure you're not firing the guy on the anniversary of an important date in his life, a death in the family or something. A neighbour of mine owned a radio station, and he fired a disc jockey on the DJ's birthday. The DJ was hurt and furious and went after the station for all it was worth. I said to my neighbour, either you've got inadequate personnel files or somebody forgot to look. Another time, a boss fired a senior employee not knowing that, that night, the employee was having the company's top twenty clients and their spouses over for dinner at his house. The employee played it very discreetly. Didn't say a word about the firing. That helped him when it came to settlement time.

"An employee who's been fired goes through four stages. First stage, anger. Why have they done this to me? My standard initial interview involves letting the guy ventilate his rage. He talks about giving his life to the company, working nights, taking files home on weekends. Second stage, denial. I ask the guy, have you told your wife? Lots of executives can't bring themselves to do that. They get up in the morning, put on the suit, go downtown, walk around, see a movie, head home. Denial. They don't want the wife to know, the neighbours. Of course, sometimes the neighbours can't help finding out because the first thing the employer does is yank the guy's company car. What I try to do is get the guy into relocation counselling fast. Put his act back together. Third stage is negotiation. No matter what the company's first offer to a fired executive is, no matter how generous, he usually wants me to take a run at the company. He'll show them what a mistake they made firing him. Once past that, we're into the fourth stage. Resolution.

"The best time to fire is midday, midweek. You fire the guy at noon, it means his fellow employees are out at lunch and he doesn't have the humiliation of facing them. Midweek is best because the guy can get on faster with straightening himself out. But employers still love to fire people on Friday. That's the peak period, four o'clock Friday afternoon, call the guy in, tell him he isn't cutting it and to clear out his desk. What that means is there's a rush hour in my office on Monday mornings from nine to eleven, calls from people who've been fired at four on Friday. They've had the weekend to knock back a few drinks, shed some tears, and phone around to their buddies for the name of a good employment lawyer. Nine o'clock Monday morning, my phone starts ringing. It doesn't matter, I'm in here by six most days anyway."

Six o'clock in the morning? That's when Echlin starts his workday?

Here, I think, is the guy to spring Dave Murphy's thesis on, about downtown lawyers being unhappy workaholics and so on and so forth.

"I disagree with Dave Murphy one hundred percent," Echlin says, and goes on to say much more. His talk falls into an on-the-one-hand-this, on-the-other-hand-that format.

On the one hand:

"The practice of law has changed radically in the past fifteen years. There used to be long-existing client loyalties to firms. Now corporate clients shop around for legal expertise, and law firms have to get into the marketing game to hold old clients and attract new ones. It's a tougher world. Big firms are staggering under enormous overheads. Client demands are increasing exponentially. The fax machine has made lawyers' lives miserable. Clients expect you to act on their faxes immediately. Some clients phone me about a fax sheet before it's made its way from our firm's central fax room to my office. That room gets four thousand faxes a day. But lawyers are in a service industry, and clients don't appreciate it when you're slow responding to faxes or returning phone calls. Clients, fees, everything else, the pressures brought to bear on each individual lawyer in a big firm are huge."

On the other hand:

"Downtown firms are not for everybody, not for Dave Murphy, obviously. I'm cognizant of the stress, and I find ways to combat it. In the summer, I walk over to the SkyDome at the end of the day and turn the world off for a couple of hours. When the winter's bleakest, end of February, beginning of March, I go down to Dunedin. Spring training in Florida. I'm with my Blue Jays. I'm stress-free."

Summing up:

"I strap myself into a heart attack chair every day. I know it. The pressures I go under to produce and to keep my clients happy, my partners happy, are ridiculous. But"—Echlin bounces in his chair and throws his arms in the air—"I love being a downtown lawyer."

# CHAPTER FIVE

## *The Judge*

MY HEART SINKS.

"The only reason I'm talking to you," Brent Knazan has just said to me, "is because I've already lost a lot of anonymity by becoming a judge."

Oh, *terrific*. I'm in the first minute of my first conversation with someone who shapes up, from everything I've heard about him, as one of the exceptional members of the class, and he's telling me he's a reluctant interview subject.

"Don't miss Brent Knazan," Rob Prichard has instructed me. "He's having a fabulous career."

"The left wing of the class?" Leslie Yager has said. "Brent *was* the left wing."

What nobody mentioned is that Knazan is also a man who is very tight about his privacy. He isn't making a show of truculence in letting me know this feeling. He seems to qualify as the least truculent of people, and everything about his looks and manner—the benevolent eyes, the soft voice, the funny little breath of laughter that comes at the end of sentences—makes me warm to the guy. It's just that he's drawn this line around his career and family and life. It's a line that doesn't leave much room for revelation.

"Would you like coffee?" he asks.

"Oh, yeah, great, thanks," I say. (Do I sound over-anxious? God, *yes*.)

We're in Knazan's judge's chambers on the third floor of

Toronto's Old City Hall. The window faces into the courtyard, and the view takes in turrets and peaked roofs, the elaborate mouldings and much of the rest of the weird and charming Richardsonian-Romanesque style that architect E.J. Lennox put into the building a century earlier. Inside the chambers, which are really just another cramped office with a false ceiling, the decor is enlivened by a little kid's art work.

"My daughter's," Knazan says.

He brews excellent coffee from a setup behind his desk, serves it in china cups and saucers, and tiptoes into his autobiography.

Knazan grew up in Winnipeg's north end. He studied economics and mathematics at the University of Manitoba, and formed the notion—from where, he's not sure or isn't saying—that he'd try law at the University of Toronto.

"If you ask me what I remember about the academic work at law school," he says, "the answer is not much. But the legal aid clinic, *that* I remember."

No wonder. He began contributing hours to the clinic during first year. He worked full-time there during the next two summers. He was one of only two students ever to do his articles at the clinic. After that, the practice of allowing clinic articling was cancelled on the grounds that a student didn't get sufficiently varied experience at a place catering to poor-people clients.

Knazan tells a legal aid clinic story. One evening, the clinic dispatched him to a meeting in a small store at the corner of Robert and Sussex streets, not far from the law school. It was a meeting of Spanish-speaking women, women from Spain, from Latin and South America, refugees from right-wing regimes, from the coup in Uruguay and, later, from the Pinochet takeover in Chile. These women had problems. Problems with immigration papers, with jobs, with landlords, with welfare, with men. What they didn't have was a lawyer or much English. Knazan, still a first-year student, hardly knew a whole lot of law and even less Spanish. But he had the heart. He enlisted himself in the women's cause. He'd pick up the law and some of the language at the same time.

"Working for the legal aid clinic," Knazan says, "completely directed the course of my life."

It isn't until later that I understand the meaning of what Knazan's telling me; the man *can* be elliptic in defence of his privacy. I gather that the sort of law he was drawn to at the clinic—immigration work, some criminal—was what he later practised, and that the contact with the Spanish-speaking women and with the countries they fled became a fascination that has lasted to the present. There's also something about a woman named Nancy Goodman. Knazan is scrupulous in pointing out that others from the law school involved themselves with the Spanish-speaking women. One of them, he says, was Nancy Goodman. Nancy Goodman entered the law school in 1973, took a year off to travel in Africa, returned, and graduated with the class of '77. Nancy Goodman practises immigration law today.

"Right," I say. "Who, um, is Nancy Goodman, exactly?"

Knazan smiles the smile I'm getting to recognize, somewhere between enigmatic and seraphic. "The mother of my daughter," he says.

Oh, of course, wife and husband, Nancy Goodman and Brent Knazan.

After Knazan's call to the bar, he headed for Mexico City where he studied Spanish for five months at a language institute. He travelled farther south for five more months, all the way down to Chile and Argentina. Back in Toronto, he practised immigration law with an emphasis on Spanish-speaking clients, then slid into criminal work, and for three years he did labour law at the firm of his classmate and fellow Winnipegger Mike Mitchell.

"My whole career," he says, "kept its focus on Latin America."

This brings us to the spring of 1990 when Knazan decided for his own private reasons to apply for a position on the Ontario Provincial Court (Criminal Division) in Metropolitan Toronto. It's the court where all the minor and many of the major crimes are tried. It's a busy court, inundated with cases, swamped, overloaded. It used to be a court that got little respect from the criminal counsel who appeared before it. Many of its judges were tired lawyers looking for a soft spot to wind down their careers, people with drinking problems, borderline nutcases. All of this had changed by the time Brent Knazan applied. Well, *most* of it had changed. The courts remain places with crushing case loads. But nutcases are no longer on the premises.

Ian Scott and Peter Russell are the two men largely responsible for the provincial court reforms. Scott, as Ontario's attorney general for much of the 1980s, took it as a personal mandate to upgrade the calibre and change the type of judge sitting on the court. Peter Russell is a political scientist at the University of Toronto who is—this is his phrase—a courtroom junkie.

In 1988, Scott set Russell up as chair of a new body called the Judicial Appointments Advisory Committee. The committee's principal duty is to pass judgement on the lawyers who apply to become provincial court judges. What's trailblazing about the committee, apart from its very existence, is its make-up. Besides Russell, who still chairs it, the committee includes just one judge, a mere two lawyers, and a dozen lay persons of both sexes and of varied races, backgrounds, and points of view. A group, you would conclude, that is loaded for bear. In the committee's first year of operation, twenty-eight applicants got provincial court appointments, and among the twenty-eight, the average age was forty-two, compared to mid-fifties for previous appointees; nine were women, one was black, and many were lawyers who had records of work among minorities and disadvantaged people.

"What was it like for you?" I ask Knazan. "Going before the advisory committee?"

"An amazing experience," he says. "First of all, you're putting your whole person in front of strangers. Which is hard. But also the lay people asking me questions were so good at it that I don't think I really knew what I was going through. They were very well trained. They were trying to find out—I realize this now—if I would be rude on the bench, if I'd be short-tempered, if I could express myself clearly, if I could think about substantive questions. The interview was not like anything I could possibly have prepared for."

Knazan must have impressed the committee—not to mention the attorney general and the judicial council, a body composed of senior judges, who also had to approve him—because on July 13, 1990, he was told the job was his. Two months later, he was a judge sitting in provincial court.

"Finding people guilty or innocent," I ask, "is that a tough thing to do?"

Here comes that smile again.

"Sit in court one day," Knazan says. "It might help with the answer to your question."

The policewoman tells me to have a nice day. This is after she's run a metal detector over my clothes, emptied my shoulder bag, and passed me through the barrier inside the front door. I'm entering the Provincial Court Building at 1000 Finch Avenue in North York. It isn't a courthouse that a movie director would pick as the setting for *To Kill a Mockingbird* or even *The Bonfire of the Vanities*. This building is long, low, and windowless, designed in the style of Contemporary Warehouse.

Knazan is assigned to Courtroom 302. Medium-sized, off-brown walls, recessed fluorescent lighting, not an oppressive room, neutral perhaps. Knazan, sitting in front of the Canadian and Ontario flags behind his raised perch, has on striped trousers, white collar and dickey, black gown, a bright red sash running from his left shoulder to his right hip. The people charged with crimes are summoned to justice before him.

An Oriental kid in a white shirt and balloony pants charged with shoplifting a shirt, not in his size, worth seventy-nine dollars, from a mall clothing store.

A man in droopy jeans, wearing a mean scowl that looks permanent, charged with waving a knife at a woman in an argument over the use of the laundry room in a house where both had apartments.

A stylish young guy, gold ring in his left ear, up on a charge of possession of a semiautomatic .22 calibre handgun.

A black dude dressed in leather, posed in a slouch that screams *attitude*, charged with possession of cocaine.

A Wendell Clarke lookalike, charged with blowing over the limit on a breathalyzer. He says all he did was play some darts and drink two and a half Tall Boys at an O'Toole's Roadhouse.

An older black guy who looks like he's coming down from a colossal hangover—he turns out to be a crack addict—charged with assaulting his girlfriend when he threw a ring of keys at her and opened a cut over her eye.

Knazan, absorbing these squalid little dramas, seems imperturbable, forbearing. He takes notes of everything that the accused people, their lawyers, the Crown attorney tell him. He makes one or two rulings on legal points. He asks few questions—it's a good thing the courtroom is extensively miked because his voice really is soft—but the questions are exactly right. (What *is* a Tall Boy? It's a bottle or can of beer that holds a few ounces more than the normal bottle or can.) Sometimes Knazan gives the impression he's almost as much social worker as judge. He's dispensing justice, but there's nothing peremptory about it. His justice is patient and thoughtful and fair.

Me, listening to the cases, I'm getting a headache. Where's it coming from? The stuffy, no-window courtroom? I don't think so. I think it's mostly from the strain of paying attention to the cases, making my own notes, looking for nuances. Nothing especially complicated has happened, just a bunch of routine crimes. But attention has to be paid to these people, the Oriental kid who shoplifted (he says he wanted the shirt to give his father for Christmas), the crack addict, the Tall Boy drinker. They have a lot on the line. They're in *court*. Physical proximity has something to do with my headache, too. The accused people have been standing and sitting a few feet from my seat. This is not a distanced courtroom on television. This is live and real. It can give a person a headache. I wonder if it's the kind of pressure that Knazan—who, unlike me, is involved in the fates of these people—thinks about.

Knazan calls a recess. He and I have coffee in one of the rooms off the corridor behind the courtrooms. I mention my headache and my theory about its source.

"Uh-huh," he says. "Well, sitting on the bench is an experience that's hard to convey to anyone who hasn't gone through it. You are completely alone on the bench. The public scrutiny is fantastic. Every word you say is being transcribed by the court reporter and listened to by the lawyers and accused, and you want to get it right. A wrong decision in criminal law might mean somebody being wrongly jailed. That bothers me. One *hour* of someone wrongly jailed twists my stomach. So it's high pressure, highly charged. At the end of a day, any day, in court, even when it isn't one major case you're hearing, even when the cases might look unimportant to other people, you can feel totally drained."

The report, people tell me. Ask Brent about the *report*. Before I ask, I do some research. Knazan's report is a demonstration that his involvement in minority rights operates on an international scale. It's the report of a trial in El Salvador. When I ask, Knazan doesn't talk much about the trial, but he allows me to make a photocopy of his report. "The answers to all your questions are in there," he says. The trial the report covers in absorbing detail turns out to be, I discover, one of the most dramatic and significant in any country in recent years.

Here's the background:

Alfredo "Freddie" Cristiani is the president of El Salvador. He's a member of the ARENA party, which was founded by a man named Roberto D'Aubuisson and is bankrolled by El Salvador's millionaire coffee growers. D'Aubuisson, who died of cancer in February 1992, was cashiered from his country's army in 1979, but he had such slippery charm and political savvy that he oiled his way to power at the head of the new ARENA party. D'Aubuisson had a couple of other strengths going for him.

One was the backing of the Reagan administration, which was nervous that El Salvador's left-wing opposition with its supporters among the country's peasants, its teachers, union organizers, and church leaders would displace the right-wing D'Aubuisson regime. Another convincing source of D'Aubuisson's authority came from the death squads.

D'Aubuisson didn't invent the concept of the death squad, but he appears to have brought it to a fine, cruel perfection. Between 1979 and 1985, when D'Aubuisson was consolidating his position, the death squads, composed of Salvadoran soldiers and security officers, murdered forty thousand people who were considered D'Aubuisson opponents. Some deaths made the front pages of North American newspapers: the three American nuns raped and murdered in December 1980, Archbishop Oscar Romero assassinated a few months earlier. Most of the forty thousand died without much notice outside El Salvador. D'Aubuisson would appear on television denouncing labour leaders, opposition politicians, and a few days later, their bodies would turn up in one of the dumping grounds around the country.

The opposition to the D'Aubuisson regime within El Salvador collected itself under the Farabundo Marti National Liberation Front. It was a coalition of many groups and claimed wide popularity throughout the country. On November 11, 1989, the FMLN, growing nervier after victories in the long-running civil war against the government and the military, took an armed run at the capital city of San Salvador. The attack was so successful that, for a time, at least, the FMLN controlled many of the city's neighbourhoods.

One area it didn't penetrate was the part of the city where the Salvadoran military maintained its school, the *Escuela Militar*, and other army installations. Inside this military zone was one institution that was decidedly non-military, the University of Central America. The university had a sprawling campus, many buildings, walkways, grassy spaces. In a section of one building, six Jesuit priests who taught at the university lived with their cook and the cook's fifteen-year-old daughter, whose name was Celina Ramos. Father Ignacio Ellacuria was the most famous of the priests, known as a learned theologian and philosopher, but, more to the point, known as an advocate of a settlement of differences between the government and the FMLN.

In the early morning of November 16, 1989, Father Ellacuria was shot to death. Not just Father Ellacuria. The other five Jesuits were killed, too. So was the cook. So was fifteen-year-old Celina.

This was too much. Even for the American administration, the murder of the seven people was too much. Someone had to take responsibility for such a shocking crime. That was the message that the United States—and many other countries—impressed on President Freddie Cristiani. At the scene of the murders, there had been an effort to dress up the deaths as part of the FMLN attack on San Salvador. Someone had scrawled "The FMLN executed the enemy spies" across a sign near the bodies, and the murder weapon was an AK-47, a gun the FMLN favoured. But nobody swallowed the feeble attempt at a frame-up, and President Cristiani set in motion an investigation.

How the names of nine members of the Salvadoran army surfaced fairly quickly as the accused murderers—within two months—is a story too tangled to tell here. It's enough to say that when the man assigned to the case, Judge Ricardo Zamora of the Fourth Criminal Court of El Salvador, got to work in January 1990, he had in his possession the confessions of seven soldiers. Four of the soldiers admitted they had done the shooting that killed the victims. All seven named the same man as the mastermind behind the operation. He was Colonel Guillermo Benavides, who happened to be the head of the *Escuela Militar*, the military school. Colonel Benavides didn't confess to anything. The second most senior officer, Lieutenant Yussy Mendoza, confessed, sort of. He was the officer in command of the operation from the *Escuela Militar* on the fateful early morning, but he said he didn't really know what was planned. In any event, nine men, including Benavides and Mendoza, were charged with the murders.

First, a word about the confessions. They were not made directly to Judge Ricardo Zamora. They were given, in accordance with convoluted provisions in the Salvadoran Criminal Code, to two independent witnesses, and were deemed to be valid as long as the following conditions were met: the confessions were made within seventy-two hours of the confessors' arrest, no coercion was involved, and the independent witnesses later testified before Judge Zamora to what they heard. Who were these witnesses? The question seems to be irrelevant under Salvadoran law. The witnesses were never required to show up at a public trial. All that counted was that they testified to the confessions at an earlier, non-public stage presided over by Judge Zamora.

The point is that Judge Zamora acted as a kind of clearing house of information. He heard the reports of the confessions, he examined witnesses, he perused documents, he weighed evidence. All of this took place in a series of proceedings, with prosecution and defence lawyers present, that were part of the overall trial process. The proceedings have names; they're called the instruction phase of the trial and the proof stage. At them, Zamora compiled a written record, deciding which testimony was to be included, which documents, and which statements. That written record would be presented to the jury when the trial reached its final, and public stage, the *vista publica*.

At last, the *vista publica* was scheduled, mid-September 1991, and for that event, twenty international organizations sent representatives to observe the show. The idea behind the observers' presence was to keep pressure on El Salvador's judicial and political systems, to increase the chances that the trial would be conducted according to law (even if Salvadoran law might strike some observers as occasionally eccentric). A Canadian organization flew in one observer. The organization was the International Centre for Human Rights and Democratic Development. The federal government established the centre in the late 1980s, headquarters in Montreal, with a mandate to study the state of human rights around the world, and to lobby for more of them in countries where they seem in short supply.

Given its unwieldy name, the centre is called by those Canadians who know of its existence (not many) as "the Broadbent group," after the man who heads it, Ed Broadbent. For the El Salvador assignment, Broadbent and his staff decided the observer would have to be someone who had a grasp on the criminal law and was fluent in Spanish. One name sprang to mind.

Brent Knazan's.

Knazan arrived in San Salvador on September 26 and made his way to the courtroom at three o'clock, just as the substantive part of the *vista publica* was hitting high gear. Right away, he could hardly help noticing that, by the standards of his own courtroom back home, the Salvadoran setup had a few quirks.

The jury: the five jurors and one alternate were concealed behind a barrier, which made them visible to no one except Judge Zamora, his assistants, and the various counsel. This piece of secrecy didn't entirely surprise Knazan. "Hiding the jury," he later wrote in his twenty-five-page report of the trial (lucidly and in some passages gracefully written, by the way), "highlighted the power of the Salvadoran military and the danger for those who crossed it." If the jurors' identities were known and if they came down with the "wrong" verdict, their bodies might turn up in one of those dumping grounds.

The accused: the eight army men (one soldier had gone AWOL and was tried *in absentia*) sat in a row, their backs to the judge and other court officials, facing into the body of the courtroom towards the spectators and the TV cameras that broadcast the *vista publica* to the country. Knazan thought this curious arrangement was unfair to the accused. "It meant they couldn't see the proceedings." But on balance, he decided, "It didn't affect the result of the trial."

The trial's structure: "The Salvador judicial procedure is not well-equipped to deal with a lengthy trial," Knazan wrote. That's putting it mildly. On one day, September 27, the court was in session for sixteen hours. On another day—the trial consumed only five days—the session ended at midnight. In fact, Salvadoran law doesn't normally allow for an adjournment of more than five hours in a jury trial. In El Salvador, it almost seems, justice favours the side whose lawyer is most skilled at keeping the jury from dozing off.

The nature of the trial: it did not consist of witnesses testifying, of the play of lawyers examining and cross-examining, all the clash familiar to Canadian courtrooms. It consisted of readings. Interminable readings, repetitive readings, readings that, even if it were Anthony Hopkins speaking the words, would still be guaranteed to lull an audience into a torpor.

Consider, as an example of the readings, the confessions. Each of the confessions of each of the seven soldiers was read aloud by one of Judge Zamora's assistants not once, not twice, but three times. The first was the statement of the accused soldier himself; the second and third were the statements of the witnesses who heard the confessions. Three verbatim statements of each soldier's confession. Twenty-one statements in total.

"The readings of the statements were tiresome, almost boring," Knazan reported. "The near-monotone recitation of the statements in the voice of the judge's assistant, who of course was not even present when the statements were given, could have slightly dulled the ear and mind to what was being read— an explicit and horrific description of planned, cold-blooded executions given by people who were there and either observed or committed the killings."

On the one hand, Knazan thinks, the repetition, dulling or not, must have had the effect of impressing the facts of the confessions firmly on the jurors' minds. On the other hand, something about the confessions came across to Knazan—and possibly to the jurors—as fishy. "The striking feature of the confessions was their similarity in style and content. This may have suggested to the jury that they were not honest statements and led the jury to reject them."

There were bits and pieces of other evidence—a statement that the scrawled writing on the sign near the bodies pinning the blame on the FMLN resembled the handwriting of two of the accused—but the real drama came with the jury addresses by the various lawyers.

Emotion was the key element in the addresses. Some lawyers—there were five prosecutors, four defence counsel, and all nine delivered orations—touched on helpful pieces of evidence. One prosecutor, for example, pointed out that on the night of the murders the university was so ringed by Salvadoran military that no unit could have penetrated it without the authorization of the commander, namely Colonel Guillermo Benavides. Hence, it stood to reason that the killers must have had at the very least the colonel's blessing. But often, the lawyers on both sides chose emotion over sense, theatre over argument.

One prosecutor seized a court exhibit in his hands. The exhibit was a machine gun. He turned to the television cameras, raised the gun over his head, and—*wham!*—he banged the machine gun on the floor.

He raised it again.

*Wham!*

"I call on God and the Fatherland for a conviction," he screamed.

*Wham!*

The defence lawyers tossed politics into the mix of their jury statements. Politics and chauvinism, racism and military ideology, and, most threatening for the jurors, the possibility of danger to their own lives.

"This is not a trial for justice," the first defence counsel said. "This is a show to see if the United States Congress will or will not give El Salvador aid."

That was a clever point—the only reason the government wanted a conviction was to satisfy the American foreigners who might make the conviction a condition of further aid.

And the first defence counsel went at the foreign issue from another angle, pointing out that five of the murdered priests were born in Spain.

"El Salvador has carried the yoke of the Spanish conquest

since the time of Columbus," he thundered at the jury. "I ask you to finally free El Salvador from that yoke."

The families of the accused soldiers rose in the courtroom and cheered.

At the moment when another defence counsel was launched on his performance, the sound of singing, loud and insistent, came from the street outside the courtroom. Knazan didn't recognize the song. Someone told him it was El Salvador's national anthem. Then a bugle blew. No one had to tell Knazan what the tune was. It was "Taps," the song played over military funerals. Did anybody in the courtroom miss the point? Just in case, the bugler blew "Taps" a second time.

Knazan wrote in his notebook, "If I were a juror, I would feel intimidated."

Yet another defence lawyer ended his declarations with a line that seemed curious to Knazan. "I ask God's blessing for the jurors," the lawyer said, "and I wish them a safe return home." Later, outside the courtroom, a Salvadoran lawyer explained the significance of the words. "In this country, where we are accustomed to disappearances at the hands of the authorities," the lawyer said, "that was a fairly explicit threat."

At five o'clock on September 28, counsel finished their speeches. The case was in the jury's hands. To find a verdict of guilty under Salvadoran law, the jurors had to hold an "innermost conviction" that each accused was guilty as charged. What's more, the jury did not have to be unanimous in its decisions. A simple majority was good enough to convict. Very quickly, by ten-thirty that night, the jury found its innermost conviction and its simple majorities.

Judge Zamora read the jury's decisions in court.

Colonel Guillermo Benavides: on all eight murder charges, guilty.

Lieutenant Yussy Mendoza: on seven of the murder charges, not guilty. On the charge of the murder of fifteen-year-old Celina Ramos, guilty.

The other seven soldiers, including those who confessed to the killings: on all eight murder charges, not guilty.

"The verdict of the jury," Knazan wrote, "was bizarre and contradictory."

But that observation didn't prevent him from explaining in logical and persuasive terms why the verdict was also—his term—"not unreasonable."

Colonel Benavides?

His conviction is the most easily accounted for, though, bearing in mind the threats and intimidation during the trial, it must have taken a tremendous act of courage by the jurors to find him guilty. "It is most likely," Knazan wrote, "that the jury was convinced by the argument that the murders could not have occurred without Benavides's approval, if not his planning."

Lieutenant Mendoza?

This is tougher. Why acquit him in the deaths of the priests and of the cook, but convict him of the murder of the cook's daughter? Knazan reasons that the jury's starting point was the knowledge that Mendoza was the officer in charge of the operation from the *Escuela Militar* on the night of the murders. From there, Knazan postulates, "The jury may have wanted to say that Lieutenant Mendoza's responsibility was less than the Colonel's and chose the murder of the most sympathetic victim as representative."

The acquittal of the seven soldiers on all charges?

Here we come up against the most seemingly implausible decision by the jurors. These guys *confessed*. They said they were present at the murders, that some of them actually pulled the trigger on the victims.

"I conclude that the acquittals were not unreasonable," Knazan wrote, "because the jury was entitled to reject the confessions."

In his report, Knazan devotes a couple of pages to the proposition that, "Confessions are unreliable and have been the source of many injustices." Bear in mind this is a *judge* making the point that confessions, supposedly the most solid piece of evidence against an accused person, aren't necessarily to be trusted.

What about the Guildford Four in England? Knazan asks the

question. The Guildford Four were Irishmen who served long terms in an English prison until it came to light in 1991 that the confessions that were the basis of their convictions had been concocted by the cops.

Or, closer to home: "The morning after my return to Canada, October 1, an article appeared in a Toronto newspaper about a case in Winnipeg. The prosecutor withdrew a charge against a young Canadian native man who had confessed to murder, after jail records showed that the man was in jail on the day of the murder."

In the case of the seven Salvadoran soldiers, Knazan mentions that he learned from lawyers in San Salvador that juries in the country generally mistrust statements that come to them from sources other than direct testimony. "There have been established cases of confessions extracted by torture," Knazan wrote, "sometimes by the military."

Knazan stops far short of saying that this is what happened here, that the confessions, or some of them, were made under a form of duress. You'll recall, though, that Knazan took note of the suspicious "similarity in style and content" of all the confessions. Knazan also speculates briefly on other motivations for acquittal, which may have occurred to the jurors, that the seven soldiers, whatever they did on the night of the killings, thought they were performing their duty, that they had no choice except to follow orders.

But in the end, it was enough for Knazan to write on the last page of his report that, "A mistrust of confession evidence . . . is healthy and should be encouraged not only while the military have a major role in governing El Salvador but in any legal system under any form of government."


Knazan wrote his report of the trial at the end of October 1991. I read it five months later. And reread it, and read it a third time. That's how gripping it is as a piece of judicial and political history. But something occurred to me. What happened to the two men who were convicted? Did Colonel Benavides and

Lieutenant Mendoza somehow get off the hook? Did Freddie Cristiani's government rig something to win them probation? Knazan's report mentions nothing about sentencing.

I phone Knazan at home and ask him.

"The sentencing only happened last month," he says. "The maximum. Judge Zamora gave both of them thirty years."

For a moment, I think Knazan may expand a little more on his experiences in San Salvador. What was it *like* at such a dramatic trial?

"Take care," Knazan says to me in his soft voice.

He's gone.

# CHAPTER SIX

## *The Women*

HARRIET LEWIS has a chipped tooth halfway back on the upper right. It looks sexy. She has a lot of frizzy brown hair and a throaty voice like Debra Winger's. It sounds like a seventy-eight rpm record playing on an old phonograph, rushed sometimes, syllables getting skipped now and then.

"The women of my generation who went into law," she says, "we didn't feel we were going to get respect unless we had something that gave us respect. Maybe we didn't respect ourselves enough. Whatever, we thought we needed something besides our personalities and brains to get recognition, and law seemed a good way to accomplish that. Law is so structured that you could just fit into it, and if you did, a lot of good things would follow. That was the theory anyway, and it turned out to be true. We got good jobs, and we got control over our lives, and we got respect."

Lewis and I are talking on an autumn Saturday morning in her kitchen. The house is quiet. Lewis's husband, Eldon Bennett, also a lawyer, has taken their sons, Daniel and Sammy, seven and five, to hockey practice. The house is in the Annex section of Toronto, a residential neighbourhood close to the downtown core, five subway stops away. The Annex has a lot of three-storey brick houses and tall trees, and a ferocious ratepayers' association that keeps developers' hands off the houses and the trees. Lewis's house is across from a small park whose main feature, for a reason no one can recall, is a bust of Jean Sibelius.

"Besides all that, the control and everything," Lewis goes on, "I never wanted to give up the female things. I wanted nice clothes and to have a husband and children and give dinner parties. Most of the women of my generation felt the same way. We thought we could get away with it, that we could have a great job and not surrender the other women-type things. Little did we know about all the aggravation that would go with the situation."

"Aggravation?" I ask. "Like what?"

"Oh, like nothing a man could imagine." Lewis gives her wonderfully infectious laugh. "When I think of most of the 1980s when I was working in a small law firm and having babies, what I remember is being totally exhausted practically all of the time. Sammy was born at ten to eight in the morning, and at ten-thirty, I got a phone call from my office wanting to know about one of my files. I perfectly understood why they called. It was a small firm, and I happened to be the only person who had the answer to the question. But those years, my God, there was work and babies and a busy husband and stress and strain, and I was unhappy and depressed and I didn't think Eldon and I were getting any quality of life for the investment we were putting in."

There's a happy ending to the story—since October 1988, Lewis has been the legal counsel at York University, a job she finds, by comparison with her past working life, practically stress-free—but the beginning to the story reaches back to Medicine Hat, Alberta. Lewis was born there and got out at the first opportunity. "My parents brought me up to leave Medicine Hat and experience the world," Lewis says. "I celebrated my eighteenth birthday on the train to Toronto."

She enrolled at York University, wrote an undergraduate thesis on Sylvia Plath in the years before writing about Sylvia Plath became a major industry, took an MA in English, and, in 1969, married Eldon Bennett, a political science student. The couple lived a year in North Carolina, where Bennett worked on a graduate degree at Duke University, and another eight months in Grenoble, France, when Bennett got a travel grant to study

French Marxist philosophy. Back in Toronto, Lewis made the decision about looking for direction and structure. She enrolled in law school.

So did her husband. Eldon Bennett's career gets staggeringly complicated at this point. A week after classes began at law school, York University's Atkinson College offered him a job lecturing in the evenings. He took it. By night, he taught a full load of courses. By day, he prepared for the courses and showed up from time to time at law school. He passed the first-year law exams. Halfway through second year, he dropped out to write his PhD thesis, *Marxist Revisionism and the Crisis in Western Sociology*. He and Lewis lived in a cottage on Wards Island, one of the lovely islands that ring the Toronto harbour. Bennett kept up repairs on the plumbing and electricity in the cottage, which was of the basic sort, and played hockey on the island lagoon. Somewhere in there he wrote a textbook. In September 1974, he resumed law school, and two years later he got his LLB from the University of Toronto and his PhD from York University. Today he practises commercial litigation at Aird and Berlis, an old, established downtown Toronto firm. He and Lewis didn't move out of the cottage on Wards Island and into the three-storey house in the Annex until 1986.

"Some parts of law school I reacted badly to," Lewis says, picking up the story in her kitchen. "In first year, Marty Friedland gave us a talk about how these were the most important years of our life and how hard we would have to work to pass the exams in the spring. He said, since the year he himself entered law school, he had never been able to enjoy spring. Well, you know, out in the back of the law school, there was this blanket of blue dewdrops growing in the spring. They were beautiful, and I thought, God, I'm going to enjoy this, I don't care *what* Marty Friedland says."

At graduate school, Lewis had scored straight As. In law school, she was a B student. The drop in marks may say something about her determination not to miss spring or her desire to be both a career person and a traditional woman. Or maybe she was just getting ennuied out on all that schooling.

After graduation, she found her niche practising mainly family law with Raymond and Honsberger, a firm that consisted of Lewis and three men.

"In a small firm, you have to make immediate decisions," she says, explaining what was tough and what was fun and what was both about Raymond and Honsberger. "You have to fight hard because your clients are real people paying real money. You have to learn to stand by your decisions and clean up your mistakes. It's like living in the trenches. But I loved the hands-on part of the work. Meeting people is what interests me. Doing corporate-commercial law in a big firm, which I experienced briefly, you don't in fact *see* many people. In a small firm, there's much more of a family feeling. One part of me hated to leave Raymond and Honsberger when the time came, but the other part of me was completely weary."

At York, where Lewis is the first ever university counsel, she touches myriad legal bases. Advising the university on legislative changes that affect it. Drawing contracts and leases. Assisting on student disciplinary matters.

"There's only one stress in the job," Lewis says. "People at universities don't make decisions right away. They want to write a paper and have meetings and confer and *then* decide. I'm learning to be more patient with that. But, the big thing, I'm home by five-thirty, and there's no more, like it used to be in private practice, waking up at three every morning worrying about some poor beleaguered client."

From the kitchen, I hear the front door open. The gang is back from hockey. Sammy, the five-year-old, is decked out in complete hockey uniform, minus the skates. The shoulder pads make him as wide as he is high. Eldon Bennett is tall, slim, and youthful looking. He and Lewis get to reminiscing about law school days.

"When you walked into the library," Bennett says, "you used to smell something you'd never smelled before. It was the smell of fear, all the students who were afraid they couldn't cut it at law school."

"And everybody's legs jiggled under the library tables,"

Lewis says. "If you could just hook up all those jiggling legs, you'd have a real power source."

"Exams were a tense time," Bennett says.

"Yeah," Lewis says. "There was the day you smoked a cigarette just before an exam."

"What's surprising about that?" I ask.

Lewis answers. "Eldon had never smoked."

"Remember the property exam at Christmas in first year?" Bennett says to Lewis.

"The teachers told us the Christmas exams didn't count," Lewis tells me. "They were practice exams. So we thought, well, okay, *practice*, that means we can take them or not take them. That wasn't what the teachers meant at all. They meant we should bear down. We were supposed to bear down on *everything*. Anyway, the night before the Christmas property exam, we had plans to see the Chinese acrobats who were on tour, and we weren't going to pass that up. So we went out to dinner with friends and saw the Chinese acrobats, who were wonderful, and when we took the ferry over to our place on the island, eleven o'clock at night, Eldon said, let's write the property exam tomorrow. Of course, since he hadn't been to classes, he didn't know much about property. We sat up in bed and I read him my notes. Next day, we wrote the exam. I got forty-nine out of a hundred. Eldon got forty-seven."

"From the marks," Bennett says to me, "it was obvious Harriet taught me everything she knew about property."

"Yeah," Lewis says, "I was a great teacher but a lousy student."

She gets up and pours more of the powerful coffee she's brewed.

"The women at law school were more interesting than the men," she says. "The men just wanted to be lawyers. The women wanted more. The point, I think, is we were more worldly than the guys."

She drinks some of the coffee.

"Also, though, we were *girls*," she says. "We used to go over to the Courtyard Café and eat gooey desserts and talk about

everything except law. And there was this student who transferred into the school in second year, Paula Stark, she became
our role model. She actually shopped at Creed's and Holt
Renfrew. Every day we used to hold our breath to see what she
would wear next."

Lewis laughs.

"Leslie Yager and Catherine Catton and me," she says, "the
three of us used to run at Hart House for exercise, round and
round the oval track."

"That doesn't seem like much fun," I say.

"Sure it was. We'd pick out the best pair of male buns on the
track and chase behind them for twenty minutes."

Lewis laughs again. It's really a terrific laugh.

*     *     *

Maybe Harriet Lewis is on to something. Maybe the women in
the class of '75 *were* more interesting as students than the men.

If so, the explanation begins with numbers. There were more
women students in that year's class than in any previous year in
the law school's history. The class of 1972, the one that began
three years earlier, was the first to graduate more than ten
women. By contrast, the class of 1975 started with twenty-
seven women in first year. Of those twenty-seven, five dropped
out during first year or at the end of it. But another twelve
women joined the class in second year and stayed, which means
that an impressive total of thirty-four female students—
impressive by earlier standards—graduated in the spring of
1975. That doesn't mean the class produced thirty-four women
lawyers; almost a quarter of the female graduates chose not to
get into the profession. Laurie Christianson, academically
bright, from a science background, married a doctor, had a baby
immediately after her third-year final exams, and never cracked
another case book. And she wasn't an exception.

One woman who dropped out at the end of first year—a
student who nevertheless helps support the thesis that the
women were more interesting than the men—was Fredericka
Rotter. Everybody from the class remembers Freddie Rotter.

"She was the best at breaking the ice," Howard Feldman says. "We'd be having some conservative lecture, and all of a sudden, Freddie would start talking about the real world beyond law, about poverty, about left-wing politics. And the class, or the part of it that wasn't too uptight, would go on a whole different tangent of thought."

"Freddie was strong and afraid of nothing," Mike Mitchell says. "A lot of people in first year who didn't have the nerve or awareness to raise the issues she raised thought she was a complete idiot. Not only that, but an *extreme* idiot. They'd groan when she started to ask questions. But that didn't stop her. I remember Freddie as a very determined, brave person."

Rotter passed her first-year exams, then dropped out. But not for good. She took a year off to live and work in Israel, returned to the law school, and graduated with the class of 1976. She articled with a labour law firm, practised some law, and married a Toronto doctor named Phil Berger, who has a large AIDS practice. Rotter still holds strong opinions and doesn't mind expressing them.

There were ways, often wrenching and unasked-for ways, that other women were separate and distinct, sometimes from the men *and* from the other women. One woman came into law on the rebound from a divorce. Another woman, married, lost her husband to suicide partway through law school. Both graduated with the class and today have solid careers in law. In the matter of politics, proportionately more women lined up to the left of centre, and proportionately more women worked nights and weekends for the law school's legal aid clinic. Does this mean the women students were generally more activist and caring than the men? The evidence leans that way.

All of which isn't to suggest that many women didn't slot themselves into the straight-ahead grind that consumed most male students. They did—but, even here, often with a difference. Take Gladys Pardu. She was only nineteen when she entered law after two years of undergraduate arts. She was married to a dental student, and the couple lived in student housing. A woman classmate in law remembers Pardu as a nose-to-the-books type, but amazingly generous. "I used to go to their apartment," the classmate says. "Gladys's husband would make dinner while she helped me with my studying. We'd eat and get back to the cases. I probably wouldn't have made it through law without her help." Pardu graduated, practised civil litigation in Sault Ste. Marie, and in the summer of 1991 took an appointment to the Ontario Court of Justice.

Were the women of the class of '75 feminists?

Not, it seems, in a radical, acting-out sense. They came to the law school too late to be considered pioneers. Other women had blazed the trail into law years earlier. Still, the women of '75 were in a minority in the class, and for that reason alone, they needed more nerve than the men, more resolve. But on the question of women's liberation, Harriet Lewis reflects the view of the class's female members.

"We weren't raging feminists," she says. "But we knew we needed to do something like law to get anywhere in the world. We were determined. We expected to compete with the guys."

In the competition with the guys, did the women encounter sexism at the school?

It appears not, though they ran into plenty in the world of law beyond school. In classes, in the library, in study groups, around the halls, women and men seem to have operated on a basis of mutual respect, and sexism rarely, if ever, surfaced. Even Derek Mendes da Costa, the staff member generally regarded as the most male chauvinist of the profs, had cut out his practice of "Ladies' Day," the classes where, as announced, he would ask questions only of the female students in the room. And when I canvassed the women for memories of sexist incidents, nobody could come up with anything threatening or even annoying.

"Well, there was the time I was carrying the books through the school," Rebecca Winesanker recalls.

Winesanker was staggering under a load of case books one day. She came to a closed door. A male student opened it for her.

"If you think those books are heavy to carry," the male student said to Winesanker, a touch of smirk in his voice, "you should try reading them."

"I *have* read them," Winesanker answered.

It's Harriet Lewis again who probably best sums up the sexism question in the class of '75.

"There was never any put-down of the women by the guys," she says. "If anything, since the women were more mature than the men, they might have been scared of us."

★    ★    ★

On the telephone, Leslie Yager says to meet her for lunch at the Victoria Hotel.

Oh, really, the *Victoria?*

I remember the place from the 1960s when I worked for the old *Canadian Magazine.* It had offices in a building on lower Yonge Street next door to the Victoria. The hotel, built around the turn of the century, had fallen on hard times and suffered from a status just a cut above fleabag. But it served ninety-cent martinis and fat cheeseburgers, and the people from the *Canadian,* whose standards weren't fussy, became lunchtime regulars.

I show up for the appointment with Leslie Yager and hardly recognize the Victoria. It has a grey and pink colour scheme in the lobby, chicken paillard and cappuccino on the menu, Sinatra tapes on the sound system, and a marketing manager who thinks up doozy ideas for attracting clientele to the new renovated, upscale Victoria. The marketing manager is Leslie Yager.

"This is tons more fun than law," she says at lunch. "You should hear what I did in here on Queen Victoria's birthday. This was great, honestly. We put on an Empire Dinner. Twelve courses, and each one was from a different part of the old British Empire. There was a bagpiper to lead people in, and one of the waitresses was dressed up in a Queen Mother outfit, and I got a woman who was a guest with her dogs in a room upstairs to make an entrance holding the dogs on a long leash. The dining room was packed. Sold out. No empty seats. *Really.*"

Yager is a lively, pretty woman. She has brown hair and wears glasses and is unfailingly chipper. But she's no pushover, and one subject she eventually gets to with much heat is the episodes in her law career when men in the profession displayed macho insensitivity.

First, though, she sketches the route that took her to law school, from her home in Chicago to a couple of years at Oberlin, the liberal arts college in Ohio ("I got gassed twice there in anti-Vietnam War demonstrations"), to an English course at the University of Toronto, and into law.

"I was disappointed in first-year law," she says. "I thought it would be about ideals. It wasn't. It was about rules. You know, 'Here's this rule, now apply it to that situation.' I just wondered, where are the ideals?"

For Yager, who placed herself on the political left in those days, the answer was that the ideals were over in the school's legal clinic where students could work with indigent clients on such matters as landlord and tenant squabbles, minor criminal offences, family law blow-ups. A small core of the class devoted much time to the clinic—Rob Prichard, Ellen Murray, Brent Knazan, Murray Rankin—and Yager was one of the most passionately involved. Another clinic regular has told me that, "almost single-handed and with fantastic dedication," Yager set up a series of clinics to assist injured workers in pursuing their claims for compensation.

All of which, being a leftie, an activist, an idealist, made Yager a very unlikely person to seek a career at the conservative, establishment downtown Toronto firm of Cassels, Brock and Kelly. Still, needing a job and looking for security, Yager joined the firm's real estate department in 1981 and found male chauvinism alive and discouraging.

"I was pregnant with my first daughter when I started with Cassels, Brock," she says during lunch at the Victoria. "Just to show you the kind of atmosphere I sensed in the office, I was terrified about showing my pregnancy. Some people there took the approach I shouldn't be *seen* by anybody like a client."

"Sexism, you think?" I ask, just to be absolutely sure I'm on the right wavelength.

"Tell me about it," Yager says. "Someone once said to me the reason they didn't like me at the firm was that I was never available to work after hours. How did they *know* I wasn't available? Nobody ever *asked* me. They just made the assumption because I was a woman and a mother."

"Other women at the firm had things happen, too? Or was it just you?"

Yager shakes her head. "There was a hockey pool at the office. Listen to this, a *woman* won it. It was no fluke. The pool took skill, and the woman happened to know a lot about hockey. But the guy holding the pool money would not give it to her because she was a woman. She was so pissed off, I kid you not, she was going to sue. It became very ugly until finally the guy paid up."

"Any more? Did things get worse?"

"For me, yeah. My second baby, another daughter by the way, started to come one day at the office. The place went insane. I could hear one of the senior partners screaming at the receptionist, 'Get her out of here!' Meaning me, get me out of there."

"The baby wasn't born in the waiting room or anything?"

"I was at the hospital in plenty of time, no problem. But I never went back to Cassels, Brock."

"You quit? Or were fired?"

"Some of both," Yager says. "A person from the office said to me, 'We'd like you to leave, you'd like to leave, so don't bother returning.' It was a miserable three years."

After Cassels, Brock, Yager worked as in-house counsel for a young developer. Next, she ran the riding office for Ian Scott when he was Ontario's attorney general. ("He was a fabulous guy, plus I liked riding around in his limo.") Then she handled the intricacies of a building project in Toronto's Chinatown. And finally she was hired on as the Victoria's marketing manager by a group of lawyers who bought the hotel.

"You want to know why this job beats law?" she asks me. "Creativity. There's very little creativity in law, at least the kind of law I've done. Here, in *this* job, at the Victoria, I'm on my own to think up all kinds of ideas. Within reason, within our budget, but, honestly, this is *fun*."

Yager talks more about the gimmicks she's cooked up to promote the hotel. She's funny and entertaining and smart, and at the end of lunch, she picks up the bill.

★     ★     ★

Ellen Murray has a record for taking stands and doing the right thing, both from a leftish slant. After she got a sociology degree at the University of Toronto, she spent two years working as an organizer for the Company of Young Canadians. At law school, she assumed a leadership role around the legal clinic because she had an aura about her.

"Maturity," Rob Prichard tells me. "Ellen was outstanding because she was more mature than the rest of us about her politics."

Murray, I decide, may be just the person to shed some light on the extent and intensity of the left-wing political feeling in the class of '75, especially among the women. We meet in her office on the second floor of a nice old downtown Toronto building over a restaurant called Friar and Firkin. Murray has even features, good facial bones, and a thoughtful way of speaking. She practises with another woman, concentrating almost entirely on family law. The office staff includes a resident dog. He's an affable little mutt named Bingo.

Did politics have anything to do with Murray's decision to study law?

None.

"I went to law school because I thought it would be useful," she says. "I didn't go to get an education about politics or social issues. I already had ideas about them. I wanted to learn plain old black-letter law."

What about politics *at* law school?

"In those years," Murray says, "you have to remember there was plenty of change in society in general, and a little of it permeated U of T Law. There was some progressive political thought among the students. But that was a tough nut to crack, taking time to think about social change at a law school. The class had a lot more young Tories and young Liberals than young Socialists."

There's a scratching noise from the other side of the closed door to Murray's office. She gets up and opens the door. Bingo makes an entrance, tongue out, tail wagging. Murray shuts the door and strokes Bingo's head.

"It's all relative, anyway, the idea of politics at the school," she says. "I might have been on the left. Might've been a bit of an NDPer. I still am. But, I mean, look at me, I'm middle class and a professional. I'm not a flaming radical. You don't *go* to law school if you're a flaming radical."

Still, the sense of Murray as a highly principled person comes through when she describes the process that led her to practise family law. Before she settled on it, she did several years of immigration work, twelve months of criminal law, and a touch of corporate law. Eventually, family law won out.

"Most of the time in a family practice," she says, "what I'm doing for the clients is important to them. In commercial litigation, after I'd done a little of it, I realized the result wasn't *that* important to the client, not in a fundamental way. In criminal law, I didn't like the people I had to deal with. Whether it was the clients or the police, I was usually involved with antisocial young men. The up side to family law—the down side can be that it's emotionally charged—is that I know I'm helping people."

Bingo scratches on the door. He wants out. Murray obliges.

She talks some more about her life and her career. She's married to a man who teaches urban studies at York University. They have no kids. She works about sixty hours a week, which represents a large reduction from the load she once carried. She used to do prosecutions for abused women who laid private complaints against their abusing husbands. Crown attorneys refused to prosecute such cases. "Making the problem worse by taking it to court," they would tell the women. "Wasting the court's time," was another line. If an abused woman was brave enough to press on, Murray assumed the role of prosecutor, preparing the witnesses, presenting the case for conviction to a judge in court. These days, Murray says, prosecutors no longer refuse to handle such cases, though the police remain a problem. When they investigate complaints of a husband beating a wife, they decline to lay charges in more than half the cases. "Just making the problem worse," the cops tell the women, and leave them to lay private complaints. Win some, Murray says, lose some.

As she talks, Murray circles back to the question of political thought at law school. It seems to be on her mind to place it in perspective, and she does.

"People from my age group lived in a golden era," she says. "Times were prosperous, and you had the luxury of worrying about what you could do to find yourself. You didn't have to worry about what you could do to earn a living. That was already taken care of. You could practise law or choose from other options. Today, people at law school have to concern themselves about finding a job and making an income. We were the privileged group."

The conversation is over. Murray opens the door. I go out. Bingo passes me on the way in.

★　　★　　★

What's intriguing in talking to Diane Harris about the position of female lawyers vis-à-vis male lawyers is that it doesn't seem to have occurred to her that there *is* a position. Men lawyers? Women lawyers? What's the difference? It's just all us lawyers moving paper, stroking clients, earning fees.

When Harris speaks, everything is in motion. Her mobile face signals punch lines. Her hands float and flutter. Her words come fast. So do the laughs that serve as punctuation marks. She's the kind of person who would be dynamite at a dinner party. She's not bad one-on-one in her office. She works at Aird and Berlis, the ninety-lawyer firm where Harriet Lewis's husband, Eldon Bennett, also practises. Harris's specialty is doing deals for developers. There's a Matisse reproduction on the wall of her office. It's serene. But the desk, which is a clutter of files, documents, and letters, is probably more in tune with Harris's style.

She starts by telling me her reaction to the first months of law school, and right away it's clear that any division between the men and the women, any ghettoization of the female students, isn't an issue.

"What I liked best in the first months was the small class I was in. It was torts, just the fourteen or fifteen of us, and that was where I got friendly with people right away. Paul Morrison. Rob Prichard. Paul Lindsay. Rob had this place near the law school, and a bunch of us used to sit around there talking, having fun, not studying. At least I wasn't studying. After I wrote the Christmas exams, I really freaked out because I got terrible marks. I was used to being the smart person in whatever school I was at, class valedictorian in high school, an incredible scholarship at York University, like that. So I asked Rob how he did, expecting he got Cs and Ds like I got. Instead he rattled off all these As. I could have strangled him. I had assumed he wasn't studying, either. I mean, all of us were hanging around and doing nothing *together*. But it turned out he *was* studying. He could do it from one in the morning till five and get by on two hours' sleep. He's lucky I didn't throttle him. But after that experience, I turned it around as far as work and studying went."

Harris takes a quick breath.

"Third year was my best year. That was because by then we'd stopped taking courses that were about theory and concepts. The *concept* of contracts, the *concept* of property, I could never visualize what those things meant in real life. But in third year, I took courses like securities law and corporate finance and tax law, and I did great. Now we were talking about the real world. I'm a person, like, give me a real situation with some problems and I'll identify the problems and find solutions. But theory? Forget it."

Without a pause, Harris zigs back to the social life around the school.

"As an adult today, I miss the hanging out I did with all those people, the other students, men and women. As women, we were a minority in the class, but we weren't an oddity. If the staff treated us differently, if *anyone* treated us differently, I didn't notice. There were quite a few law school couples, people dating back and forth. At Christmas of first year, I met the man I eventually lived with and married, Gord Fox. Gord was a year ahead of me, class of 1974. He does corporate-commercial work at Goodman and Carr now, and we have one son. I met him that Christmas, and after that, I spent a lot of time with two other women who were in the '74 class and were dating law guys, too. We used to have endless cups of coffee and talk about our boyfriends. I miss that life today."

Another zig and zag, and Harris is on to her practice at Aird and Berlis.

"We act for the medium-level developers. Not the giants, the Bramaleas, the Tridels, more medium than that. We do everything from helping them with financing to arranging joint ventures. In the mid- and late 1980s, there were a lot of joint ventures because it seemed the developers didn't want to go it alone in big deals. They wanted partners, which dictated the kind of work I did. Joint ventures, partnership agreements, borrowing money. In those years, it was running from one big deal to the next big deal. I was going crazy, working ridiculous hours. But my adrenaline was pumping so fast I didn't have time to realize I might have been on the verge of a nervous breakdown."

"Things have changed?" I ask.

"Definitely. In the economy of the early 1990s, it's different because the banks aren't lending and people are just trying to stay alive. It's a whole different practice. My clients have these projects, and they're not starting up, not because they aren't good projects but because the market's gone soft. So I work with them and their lenders to restructure loans and rearrange financing. It's crisis management I do now."

"Over the years," I ask, "how have your clients liked you?"

Right away, I realize I've asked the wrong question. In my mind, I was thinking, how do the developer clients, who are overwhelmingly male, react to Harris, who isn't? But with Harris, the only question that would occur to her is, how has she reacted to the clients? The second question is, in fact, the one she answers.

"The thing I've always liked about my clients is they're very diverse. All kinds of types. Some are a complete delight, and they become friends in the sense that after a deal, I go out to dinner with them, and you know what?"

"What?"

"I actually enjoy hanging out with them."

★    ★    ★

Everyone in the class takes the same line about Jean Fraser. Jeannie, they say, has climbed higher in the law than any other woman from the class. Fraser wouldn't indulge in such blowing of her own horn. She's an authentically modest person. Besides, she seems too caught up in the thrill of her practice to bother dwelling on the status it might bring her.

Fraser focuses on securities law at very close to the top level at Blake, Cassels and Graydon. It's the firm, a century and a half old, numbering about 350 lawyers, that ranks two or three in the country for quality and quantity of corporate lawyering. (It's also the firm that Fraser's classmate, Dave Murphy, bailed out of in favour of a teaching job in Hong Kong.) Fraser has been rising steadily through the Blake, Cassels ranks since, fresh from law school, she articled there.

"Being a woman was more an advantage than a disadvantage when I came to Blake's," she tells me one summer morning in her office. "In those years, the late 1970s, the bigger firms wanted to be seen to be interested in hiring women lawyers. They didn't necessarily *want* the women, but they realized to be *recognized* as wanting them was somehow important. I was lucky enough to be hired in that atmosphere."

"You're still here," I say, "and getting more senior."

"The interesting part today," Fraser says, "is whether women lawyers, now that they're in here, are going to break through and go further. Whether they're going to become active members of corporate boards. Whether they're going to be fully accepted as the number one lawyer on a major client account. I still don't know how all of that is going to shake down."

"Well," I say, "but it must be exciting to be one of the few women to have got where you are in corporate law."

"No," Fraser answers. "I'll tell you what I do find exciting. It's when I go to meetings where the lawyers and the accountants and the business people in the room are more than half women. That happens fairly frequently these days. It happens a lot more at meetings I go to in New York. The Americans are way ahead of us. But I still meet those situations sometimes in Toronto."

Jean Fraser is a slender, athletic-looking woman. She wears her brown hair cut short. She has a firm handshake and a direct gaze. Her way of speaking is no-nonsense, but there always seems to be a smile playing somewhere behind the words. The smile breaks through in a series of laughs when she describes the convoluted route that took her to law school.

"I started at the University of Toronto thinking I was going to be a doctor," she says. "As it turned out, the university changed my mind for me. I went into a four-year honours course called Biology and Medicine, which prepared you for meds and gave you a science degree on the way by. Well, two things happened. One was that in second year, we took a course in anatomy, the basic stuff a doctor has to know about where a muscle originates and where it ends, that sort of thing. The memory work in this course was crushingly boring. That was one thing. The other thing was that I found my interest in having fun was higher than my interest in memorizing anatomy. So my career as a doctor went out the window. I switched to a course in general science, and when I got my degree, I went to work for some quasi-academics who had moved into the business of computer consulting. Of course, computers were in the Model-T stage at the time. But never mind that. The point I realized in the two or three years I worked for this group was that it was going to be a lot easier for me as a woman to get on in the world if I had a professional credential. It didn't matter what it was, an engineering degree, a law degree, whatever; if I had it, it would be hard for people to argue that I wasn't employable. So I chose law. I applied to every law school in the province of Ontario. I heard from all of them except the University of Toronto, and all of them turned me down, probably because I had such mediocre marks in my unfortunate career as a science undergrad. As for the U of T Law School, I decided the reason they hadn't contacted me was that they thought I was such a crummy applicant they weren't going to waste a stamp on me. By that stage, late in the summer of 1972, I'd sold all my worldly goods and bought a one-way ticket to England with the man to whom I am now married. We were going to knock around Europe for a couple of years. But I got a phone call on the Thursday before Labour Day from the U of T Law School asking if I was still interested in enrolling. I've never known why they asked me. Maybe they were trying to increase their female quota. Anyway, my future husband said maybe I should take the opportunity while it was offered to me because clearly I wasn't everybody's idea of a strong candidate for law. The result was we didn't go to Europe, I entered law, and once I was in there, I decided I'd better work very, very hard."

She did, and in third year, Fraser found a course that shaped her future. It was a business seminar run by Frank Iacobucci with the assistance of guest lecturers from the senior ranks of downtown corporate practitioners. Only a dozen students took the seminar, and in the course of the year they went through, in simulation, a complete business cycle. They started by forming a sole proprietorship, then a partnership, then incorporated it, financed it, took it public, the entire corporate route in miniature.

"The seminar was the most useful thing I did at law school," Fraser says. "That begs the question whether what you do at law school is supposed to be useful. But it made my day as far as law was concerned."

Iacobucci, impressed by Fraser's performance, recommended her as an articling student at Blake, Cassels and Graydon, and when Fraser checked in for work, her timing was fluky but fortuitous. Fluky? She arrived at Blake, Cassels on the Tuesday after Labour Day rather than back in June when all the other eager-beaver students showed up. Fortuitous? She was plunked into the corporate-commercial rotation at the moment a major deal was on the boil.

"It was the *Toronto Star*'s takeover bid for Harlequin Books," Fraser says. "This involved a public bid plus private agreements with the various major shareholders. In something big like that, all an articling student contributes is an ability to comprehend the English language. My job was to proofread prospectuses for hours on end over several weeks. But the Blake's lawyers on the deal were very generous about including me in the meetings and everything else that was going on. This was an exciting, fast-moving transaction, and to me, it was like eating peanuts. I just didn't want to stop."

And Fraser didn't. She worked, learned, moved up in responsibility, made herself expert in securities law, until today, as a woman in an area of practice that has been traditionally a strictly male preserve, she's close to facing the last hurdles.

"Clients are, generally speaking, happy to have women on their files as the number two, three, or four lawyer," she explains. "But not every client is happy to have a woman as the number one lawyer. For myself, I've never encountered rejection, and I'm the senior person on several files, so I may be anticipating rejection where none will come. But I'm still concerned about the situation down the road. For one thing, the real stamp of approval for a corporate lawyer is to get placed on a public board of directors, and I sure don't see many women on those boards. I'm not on any myself, but I wouldn't expect to be, not yet, not for a few years, when I have seniority. When that time comes, well, we'll see what we see."

Whatever happens, Fraser has paid a price to get where she is, the same price a male corporate lawyer pays plus several dollars more.

She says, "It's pretty hard for women to compete with our male colleagues *and* juggle all the other balls."

A working husband, for example, and kids and a lively

domestic scene. Fraser's husband is in the investment business. They have three children ranging from early teens to beginning grade school. And the household includes a full-time nanny and a cleaning-cooking person who comes in two and a half days a week.

Fraser talks about her juggling act, about the hours she grinds out at Blake, Cassels, about the shortage of holidays over the years. There isn't a hint of regret in her voice, but as she analyzes her position as lawyer-wife-mother-major-domo, at the end of the conversation in her office, she arrives at a point that, in terms of haute feminism, presents something close to a contradiction.

"What I notice now," Fraser says, "is that younger women coming into law have far less inclination to do the sort of thing women like me have done, keeping a career and a family going at the same time. The younger women are saying, we know it can be done, it has been done, but why? They want arrangements from law firms to work part-time in the years when their children are young. In my day, we women wouldn't have expected such concessions. Or even dreamed of them. We just hoped nobody would notice when we were pregnant and that the pregnancy would fly by as fast as possible."

"How do you account for the change?" I ask.

"Easy," Fraser answers. "Women are more confident now about what the world owes them."

"So that could mean in the fifteen years since the women from your law class have entered the profession, a revolution has arrived and departed?"

Fraser smiles. "Could be."

# CHAPTER SEVEN

## *The Scion*

ON THE SHELVES of the credenza in Brent Belzberg's office, there's a ceramic running shoe, a framed blow-up of the cartoon of Belzberg that appeared on the front page of the *Financial Times* on April 22, 1991, and a new hardcover book. The book is *Circles of Power* by the business writer James Fleming. Belzberg picks up the book and shows it to me.

"The guy who wrote this sent it over a couple of days ago," he says. "It's about Conrad Black, the Reichmanns, all kinds of people like that. There's stuff on me in there, a few pages."

"Well, hey, look at that," I say, pointing to the book's subtitle. *The Most Influential People in Canada.* "Putting you in there, is he serious?"

(Wait a minute, I think, what am I *doing*? Making fun of a major league businessman, a company chairman, in his own office?)

"You know it!" Belzberg's laugh almost explodes. "The kind of year I've had, jeez, that's *influential*?"

(It must be okay—he's making fun of *himself*.)

"Anybody I'm influencing," Belzberg says, "they better look out for themselves."


In a nutshell (though how do you squeeze six billion dollars' worth of trouble into a nutshell?), Brent Belzberg's task at the period I call on him, mid-December 1991, is to reorder, maybe dismantle, his family's business as painlessly as possible. By the time he's finished, even the company's name will have vanished. No longer First City Financial Corp., but something that sounds like an English suburban housing estate, Harrowston Corp. Worse, where once the senior Belzbergs—Brent's father, Hyman, and his uncles, Sam and Bill—owned eighty percent of the outfit, their ownership share will plunge to around fifteen percent. No need to hold tag days for the Belzbergs—they have other sources of wealth—but it's a long tumble from the glory days. Those were the 1980s, when First City Financial, on a roll, showed assets on the books of $6 billion, and in 1989, for example, rated as the fifth most profitable Canadian company in the financial services field with revenues of $970 million. But here's the catch—it *was* the 1980s, and as with the empires of many other big shooters in North America (with names like T. Boone Pickens, Carl Icahn, Saul Steinberg), First City's fortunes, guided by Sam Belzberg, were largely built on junk bonds and greenmail. When those dangerous devices and iffy tactics came unravelled in the late 1980s (and some of the people who cooked them up—Michael Milken, Ivan Boesky—started to go to jail), First City was at the mercy of its creditors and bondholders. And there wasn't much mercy to go around. At that point, in the late winter of 1991, Sam slipped out of the picture—or was pushed—and Brent was handed the job of either rescuing First City or cutting it back. Some choice. Why Brent? Because he's smart—and because he has his ethics on straight. It can also be said of Brent Belzberg what isn't said of your average businessperson but what Trevor Eyton once said of John Tory, Brent's hero and prime influence: "He doesn't have a mean bone in his body."


Belzberg is tall and slim (newly slim, it turns out, from long daily runs). He's balding on top, black hair curling at the sides and back. He has a long face, heavy eyebrows, and a little kid's smile. On the morning we talk, he's wearing a white shirt, a tie that looks like he knotted it in the dark, and charcoal grey suit pants. The jacket is nowhere in sight. His office is on the top floor, the nineteenth, of the new First City Trust building at the southeast corner of Richmond and Yonge streets in Toronto. The office itself is nothing special, medium-sized, a desk with a bit of paper clutter, an arrangement of sofa, two armchairs, and a coffee table against one wall. Belzberg fetches two cups of coffee, and we talk about his background. When he talks, he does a lot of hitching his leg over the arm of the chair, a lot of laughing, a lot of "yeah, yeahs" and "jeezes" at the beginnings and endings of sentences. A business writer has described Belzberg to me as "a rec room kind of guy." That hits it on the mark.

Brent Stanley Belzberg was born in Calgary on January 1, 1951, son of Hyman and Jenny. He had two grandfathers who were monumental figures in his life, both named Abraham. Abraham Belzberg was the one who got the family business under way, accumulating a ragtag of small properties, interests in trailer parks, laundromat operations. When Brent was a little kid, Grandfather Belzberg used to pick him up early on Saturday mornings and drive the boy around in his Caddie to collect rents and check on houses he might buy or sell. Brent's first exposure to capitalism. The other Abraham, the maternal grandfather, Abraham Lapvin, was huge physically and in heart. He weighed close to three hundred pounds, probably not much of it fat since he was a farmer. Grandfather Lapvin had a habit of bringing strangers home to dinner. These weren't people Lapvin invited for their glamorous presence or their sparkling reminiscences of life on the Rialto. These were people down on their luck, beggars, drifters, grateful for a square meal and a friendly table. Brent's first exposure to generosity.

Brent grew up in the Mont Royal section of Calgary—prosperous, but not the most tony address in town—went to public schools, and as a teenager, sold part-time on the floor of his father's furniture store. He earned excellent commissions, enough to pay his way through first-year university. He chose Queen's.

Why Queen's?

"Nobody in my family had gone to a university," Belzberg

says. "A buddy of mine from Calgary was going to Queen's, so I thought, okay, I'll choose that one, too."

You think that sounds naive? Listen to this:

"I got there, to Queen's, and they said, what's your major? I didn't know what a major was. Well, all right, they said, what'd you do best in at high school? English. Okay, they said, your major's English. I took English for two weeks, then I switched to business courses and got a commerce degree."

After Queen's, he applied to two institutions of even higher learning, Harvard Business School and the University of Toronto Law School ("I figured they were the best"). He left for a summer trip in Europe where he decided to forget about Harvard and Toronto. He took a job at a merchant bank in London, England. Towards the end of August, a guy he'd roomed with at Queen's, Mike De Rubeis, phoned him from Canada.

"Why don't you go into law?" De Rubeis asked.

"I don't know, I think I'll just work here for a year anyway."

"What're you doing at this merchant bank?"

"Right now? Accounting, I'm doing accounting."

"*Accounting!* Listen, Brent, law school starts in two days. Why don't you fly over here and see how you like it, and if you don't like law, you can go back to your, Jesus, *accounting.*"

Belzberg put in the day at the merchant bank thinking over De Rubeis's idea. It was boring, the accounting. He went out to Heathrow, no luggage, only the clothes he was wearing, and flew to Toronto. Law seemed okay, and he stayed.

(Mike De Rubeis took his first-year law at the University of Western Ontario, transferred in second year to Belzberg's class at Toronto, and is today a crackerjack Toronto criminal lawyer and still Brent's good buddy. Guys close to Brent are, interchangeably, "buddies" and "comrades.")

"I never had a burning desire to be a lawyer," Belzberg says, in the department of it-seems-to-go-without-saying. "I was young, twenty-one, a really young twenty-one, and law was a way of postponing a decision about what I was going to do in my life."

And, a young twenty-one, he broke in slowly at law school. He remembers one classmate who, not aware of the impact he was having on Belzberg, threw a scare into him. This was Phil Siller, a guy who, though Belzberg may not have known it at the time, had a PhD in mathematics from the University of Minnesota. All Belzberg knew was that the Siller guy seemed a fantastically, frighteningly mature person.

"In class, he asked all these questions, raised esoteric points," Belzberg says. "He was only three or four years older than me, but it might as well have been a century. I felt pretty intimidated. I thought, oh, my God, I better get out of here fast."

Instead of getting out, he took the only other alternative. He buckled down.

"I went to the library every day and worked harder and memorized more. I was sort of conned by the people who were smarter than I was. So they worked hard? I'd work harder and memorize more. It was silly."

Calling the grind "silly" comes in retrospect. At school, Belzberg had no perspective that reached past the next case he thought he had to memorize. Now, these days, he's developed a piece of wisdom about the study of law. He's been forced to develop the wisdom. People keep asking him for some.

"The children of people I know in business, friends, they come to me for advice about whether they should go into law. What am I, an old man already, I should have all the answers? Anyway, I tell them, people talk about the study of law. But it isn't the *study* of law. It isn't like going to a technical school where you learn a trade. I see law more as a philosophy course. You go to law school to learn a way of thinking, a way of analyzing things.

"It's different from medical school. If you're a doctor and a patient comes to your office, you have to say, oh, oh, the appendix looks terrible, it's gotta come out. You don't have to act that fast in law. In law, you can think about the problem, analyze it, plan a solution.

"I think the best advice, when you read law, is really *read* law. Sit back and read everything like you'd read a novel. Read each case for the principles, for the ratios, for whatever you can derive from it, so that at the end of the year if you have one statement about each case you've studied, then you've succeeded. But if somebody asks you, what do you know about the term 'consideration' in the law of contracts and you give him fifty cases and all the principles that are in them, then you've failed."

During our conversation in Belzberg's office, his mind is on a shuttle between past and present. One sentence, it's at law school in the 1970s, the next sentence, it's at First City Financial, December 1991. Perfectly understandable, because right outside the door of his office, as he's talking with me, there are people punching up computers, talking to Zurich, moving paper, negotiating over hundreds of millions of dollars of debt. And Brent Belzberg is the boss of the people with the computers and telephones and paper.

All of which makes it brave and charming and grim when he drops in thoughts such as:

"Now, at last, I actually can read law like I'm reading a novel. I pick up a case sometimes and read it, and I love it. I don't *need* to read law. I got lawyers to do that. I walk down the hall and all I see are lawyers. I got *rooms* full of lawyers."

To Belzberg's classmates at law school, he was a really nice guy. Note, not a really nice *rich* guy. The Belzberg family empire, though it was confined mostly to western Canada in the mid 1970s, was worth a few millions, and in second and third years in law, Belzberg had an apartment in the ManuLife Centre, which is a fairly pricey place for a student to hang his hat. But for a long time, nobody at school much associated Brent, schmoozing, laughing, hanging out, with large money. When Leslie Yager found out, she suggested marriage, just kidding. Jim Blacklock's reaction was probably typical: "Brent was terrific to be around, intelligent and funny, just natural, and then somebody told me he was as rich as Croesus. I never would have guessed." Ask Belzberg how he remembers Blacklock, and he says, "With unbelievable fondness." It was like that, lots of buddies together, and it still would be today if

Belzberg didn't happen to have this mountain on his back. "I used to have lunch now and then with people from the class. Jeannie Fraser, she's a fantastic lady. Phil Siller, who became a good friend. Other people. Now, the only time I see anybody is if I have the time to go to a school fund-raiser. I miss the comradeship from law school."

In the first two summers of his law school years, Belzberg went home to Calgary and worked in a small firm that specialized in labour law. The firm didn't act for management. It represented unions. Belzberg says he loved those summers.

"I thought labour law was what I wanted to do when I graduated."

Belzberg laughs.

"But it didn't work out that way."

It wasn't likely, a scion of a nouveau capitalist family doing the bidding of the workers. And anyway, in the second semester of third year, Belzberg got turned on totally by a special study group on commercial law. It was, he recalls, a highly intensive course, it called for the writing of a minutely researched paper on a corporate law subject, it brought in guest lecturers from the corporate-commercial departments of the big firms, it put business law in brilliant focus.

Belzberg, at the end of third year, went downtown to article with Tory, Tory, DesLauriers and Binnington.

The Tory firm was founded by J.S.D. Tory, who was a traditional corporate lawyer. And then some. And then a great deal more. He was clever, intuitive, flamboyant, well-connected in business circles and in Ottawa, a grand dresser, an eloquent speaker, an appreciator of the pleasures of life, a highly visible fellow. He put together a great little law firm, though much of its strength depended on his impressive presence. When he fell ill, his twin sons, Jim and John, were very young lawyers in the firm, not yet thirty. They were also quite unlike the old man except in brains, guys with calm voices and a lifelong aversion to spotlights. They'd been top students at the University of Toronto Law School right after Dean Cecil Wright took it over, class of '52 (Wright and Tory Senior were close friends), and after J.S.D. died, the Tory boys set about rebuilding the firm almost exclusively with U of T law grads. Bill DesLauriers came from Toronto, and Art Binnington, and Trevor Eyton (who stayed at Tory's until 1979, when he left to run Brascan), and plenty of others. Taking the lead from Jim and John at the top, the firm won clients and made its reputation on a pair of the usual attributes—hard work and intelligence—and on one that was not so usual—a kind of perpetually youthful élan.

The Tory firm struck Belzberg, when he got there, as an articling student's paradise.

"The spirit was just incredible," he says. "Besides me, there were four or five other people articling from our class, Bruce Barker, Marilyn Pilkington, John Loosemore, and we did everything together. We worked really hard until ten at night and then we went out for something to eat or drink. Socially we did a lot of stuff, and it was so much fun, that year, I couldn't believe it."

As he reminisces about articling at the Tory firm, Belzberg does another shuttle in time, something from then, 1976, meshing with something from now, 1991.

"I tell the people at Tory's today the best thing they ever did was hire me as an articling student. I always used to pride myself that the reason they hired me was because they thought I was a smart guy, not because they thought they were going to get any legal work out of me or my family. Okay, in the years since I came into First City, I've never given them any legal work, not until this year. But this year, oh, my God, I'm really making up for it. This year, I'm the biggest client they've got. That's *true!* What an awful year I'm having, you wouldn't believe it. Or you probably do believe it if you read the financial sections of the newspapers. My God!"

As an articling student, Belzberg did the usual rotation, a couple of months in tax, a couple in corporate, in litigation, and so on. He succeeded in ducking out of the two months in real estate, which struck him as dull. Litigation caught his fancy. The litigation department at the Tory firm had come as a kind of afterthought. At first, whenever something went wrong with a deal, a lawsuit loomed, the Tory brothers retained outside counsel. But by the mid 1970s, the firm had its own in-house gang. Lorne Morphy, Sheila Block, Charles Scott—they and their associates and juniors matched up with any of the big firms' litigation departments.

One day, Belzberg the student accompanied Morphy to an examination for discovery. Morphy was going to question under oath a party on the other side of the case. The case, as Belzberg recalls, was a sure loser for Morphy. The lawyer representing the opponent was a partner from Osler, Hoskin and Harcourt. Morphy and Belzberg entered the room where the examination was to be held. The Osler, Hoskin lawyer sneezed.

"What's this?" Morphy snapped. "Have you got a *cold*?"

"Yes, as a matter of fact, I do."

"A cold! How dare you come to this discovery with a cold and threaten the health of everyone in the room!"

"Well, it isn't that bad . . ."

"I'm not staying two seconds in here with you coughing and sneezing and spreading your damned infections!"

Morphy snatched up his papers and slammed out.

"I'm left standing there with my briefcase," Belzberg says, "and I'm thinking, I can't *believe* Morphy did that. But afterwards I realized he was trying whatever he could, right or wrong, to get an edge. You have to be aggressive to be a litigator. I wasn't sure I had that kind of aggressiveness in me."

The clincher for Belzberg, the incident that convinced him he wasn't a litigator in the making, was even more bizarre than the sneezing episode. It happened in Provincial Court in Toronto's Old City Hall.

"All I had to do," Belzberg says, "was ask a judge to set a date when one of the firm's senior lawyers could appear and argue the case. Just a few words, that's all I had to say, but I prepared for about two days."

Belzberg showed up in court on the appointed morning and stood in the line of students and lawyers waiting to make their pitches. The judge's name was Maurice Charles, known in the legal profession as, charitably, unorthodox. Belzberg's turn came. He opened his mouth to speak the prepared sentences.

"Are you chewing gum?" Judge Charles demanded, his voice raised almost to a shout.

"Chewing gum?" said Belzberg, who wasn't. "Me, Your Honour? No, I'm not. . . ."

"You're chewing gum in my court!"

"I'm not chewing gum, Your Honour."

"Don't lie to me!"

"I'll show you, Your Honour, there's no gum. . . ."

"Get out of my courtroom!"

Belzberg left.

"After that," he says, "I told myself I was never going into a court for the rest of my life. So far I haven't."

Tory, Tory hired Belzberg to stay on as a junior lawyer. He did securities work, handled part of the firm's Wood Gundy account, did some commercial law, some public issues, gradually moving to more sophisticated files. He felt in his element.

"I loved the people at Tory's," he says. "There were about thirty lawyers, and I knew everybody. I knew their wives, knew the names of their children. It was a fantastic place. It wasn't elite in terms of being better than everybody else. But it was elite in terms of being a true group. I felt so special to be there."

Halfway through his second year at the firm, Belzberg was moved to one client, the Thomson organization. Lord Thomson of Fleet, newspapers, department stores, hundreds of millions of dollars. Thomson was in the process of transferring its operations from England to Canada. That required myriad legal chores. In one year, Belzberg flew round trip, Toronto to London to Toronto, thirteen times. The chiefs on the job were John Tory (who had left the Tory firm to run the nuts and bolts—*some* nuts and bolts—of the Thomson organization) and Bill Des-

Lauriers. And the association with those two, up close for a year, had a long-term effect, probably lifetime, on Belzberg.

"They're the two most important developing influences for me, John and Bill," he says. "Their patience, their intelligence, their discipline, all of those, but most of all, their ethics. You have to go at things the moral way or else forget it. Those two guys are real comrades."

In August 1979, Belzberg, rather troubled, went into Jim Tory's office. Jim Tory was the most senior of the firm's senior partners.

"Do you think I could have a sabbatical?" Belzberg asked.

"Well, sure."

"I know I've only been here two and a half years and I'm not even a partner, but I'd really appreciate it if you'd think about a sabbatical. Sabbatical probably isn't even the right term. . . ."

"Where is it you're going on this sabbatical or whatever it is?"

"My family's bugging me to join their business. I don't know, it hadn't entered my mind I'd do something like that. I'm not sure I want to."

"Brent, come back here any time you want," Jim Tory said. "Just let us know."

In truth, it wasn't the family who was pressuring Brent to come into First City. It was Uncle Sam Belzberg.

"My father wasn't that involved in the running of the business," Belzberg says. "And I thought I was going to have a good career as a lawyer at Tory's, which is why I asked for the sabbatical even though I probably knew I'd never be back. Anyway, Sam kept pushing. So I agreed."

In the late summer of 1979, Belzberg moved from Toronto to Vancouver, where First City and the family businesses then had their headquarters. He moved, but what was he getting into?

Abraham Belzberg emigrated from Poland to Calgary in 1919 and started the family on the road to financial glory by buying and selling a few properties around town and by opening a used furniture store called Cristy's. Abraham had three sons— Hyman, followed three years later by Sam, then, after five years, Bill—and the three, working for the most part as equal partners, though assuming different roles, picked up where the old man left off in building the First City empire.

Hyman is the stay-at-home brother, still living in Calgary, still running the furniture business. He's an affable, obliging, down-to-earth man. "My dad was kind of the anchor, especially at the beginning," Brent says. "He came up with the money from the store when it was needed for other businesses."

Bill Belzberg is the Los Angeles brother. He moved there in the summer of 1976 to run FarWest Financial Corp, a business owned jointly by the three Belzbergs but without ties to First City. The FarWest operation flourished at first. It included FarWest Savings and Loan, a thrift bank that was said to have accumulated one of the largest portfolios of junk bonds in the S and L industry. Like many S and Ls of the 1980s, like many junk bond dealers, FarWest Savings and Loan went deep into the toilet in the 1990s, and in January 1991, United States regulators stepped in and wrenched FarWest S and L from the Belzbergs. Junk bonds are a recurring bad news theme in the later Belzberg saga.

Sam Belzberg is the Vancouver brother. He bought a sleek glass and steel house in the Shaughnessy Heights neighbourhood in 1977. He put together an art collection that is long on the best Canadian painters: Town, Bush, Snow, Colville. He did good works in the international Jewish community such as the Simon Wiesenthal Centre for Holocaust Studies, and the Dystonia Medical Research Foundation (dystonia being a neurological disease that particularly strikes Ashkenazi Jews). And he presided over the family business, consulting his brothers, sharing with them, but essentially taking the lead in aggression and direction.

The Belzberg financial universe, under Sam for the most part, came together from scratch to hundreds of millions in two and a half decades. It began in the 1950s with warehouses and apartment buildings in Calgary, escalating in the 1960s to shopping centres and other commercial developments. It included a trust company, City Savings and Trust (later First City Trust), incorporated in 1962. But it was another Belzberg company, Western Realty, that provided the immediate wherewithal for the family's great financial leaps forward. Western Realty, sixty-two percent owned by the Belzbergs, the rest by private investors, housed the vast array of real estate that the brothers accumulated over the years. In 1973, the Belzbergs negotiated a sale of their sixty-two percent in Western to an English consortium for $12 a share. This gave the Belzbergs a war chest to operate with, though the sale cheesed off Western's minority shareholders, since, cut out of the Belzberg deal, they had to settle for the market price of their stock, $7.50 a share.

Sam targeted eastern Canada for expansion. First City was a very big fish in a small pond, close to the largest financial institution in western Canada, but why not think bigger fish in lakes and seas? In 1981, Sam went after Canada Permanent Mortgage Corporation in Toronto, 126 years old, solid, established. Management at Canada Permanent reacted with horror at the prospect of a Belzberg takeover. Canada Permanent— eastern, establishment, WASP—in the hands of people who were western, Jewish, outsiders, *arrivistes*? Never.

Canada Permanent went looking for another purchaser who would buy the company and head off Sam Belzberg. They found the white knight in San Francisco, a company called Genstar in the real estate, financial services, and construction businesses. Genstar charged to the defence, scooping up thirty-nine percent of Canada Permanent stock in quick order. Sam decided to back off and give up on Canada Permanent. One consolation, the Belzbergs realized a profit of $5.5 million in the sale of their Canada Permanent stock, but the whole poisonous experience—with anti-Semitism in the air—hardly made Sam feel welcome among the powerful and credentialed of Canadian commerce.

If not Canada, how about the United States?

The Belzbergs had made a few incursions into the United

States in the 1970s. They invested in a Cleveland venture capital company; a Denver real estate outfit; in a tool company, Skil; and an advertising agency, J. Walter Thompson. The Belzbergs had also, almost as an afterthought, bought themselves a small stake in Bache, the New York investment house, and it was Bache that Sam decided to get serious about. He had his reasons. Since he had become increasingly interested in financial services as a moneymaker, Sam reckoned he needed the kind of distribution system that a company like Bache, with its stockbroker facilities, would provide. And in addition, Bache, one hundred years old in 1979, the eighth-largest investment house in the United States, represented an entrée for Sam into the respectable, big-time American business community.

Bache's management reacted to the prospect of Sam Belzberg in the picture, a possible majority shareholder, on Bache's board, exactly the way Canada Permanent reacted in Canada. Look out, the barbarian is at the gate! Bache appealed for a white knight and came up with Prudential Insurance. Sam had scooped up twenty-one percent of the Bache stock. But Prudential, dripping cash, outspent him. It offered thirty-two dollars a share for Bache's outstanding stock, a total outlay, in the end, of $385 million. Once again, Sam elected to retreat in the face of rejection by the business establishment. But once again, while there was nothing in the Bache venture to soothe Sam's *amour-propre*, money eased the pain. Thirty-two dollars a share was about fifteen dollars per share more than the Belzbergs had paid. When Sam walked, he carried along a $40 million profit.


What happened when Sam Belzberg accepted big money to leave Bache alone later acquired a name. Greenmail. The word describes the process whereby an investor, usually a little guy (relatively speaking) and invariably an outsider, threatens to take over a large company and ultimately accepts a handsome payment to call off the takeover and vanish. Two points to consider, though: greenmail as a descriptive and as a practice didn't have its widest currency as early as 1981; and Sam wasn't engaging in greenmail with Bache because he genuinely wanted into the firm and wasn't making his bid simply to weasel a cash settlement out of Bache. But greenmail's period and the Belzberg place in it were just around the corner.

Something else the Belzbergs got into, an entity that often accompanied greenmail as Butch Cassidy accompanied the Sundance Kid, were junk bonds. These were bonds issued on behalf of small or medium-sized companies. The companies couldn't get the attention of conventional investment bankers, who shunned them because of their lack of stature, because they were often already highly leveraged, because they might lack a credit history. But if the mainstream bankers refused to issue bonds for these little guys, the little guys found one saviour in a trader named Michael Milken at the investment firm, Drexel Burnham Lambert. Milken underwrote bonds for the orphan outfits, plenty of bonds, $50 million worth if that's what the orphan thought he wanted, $100 million. The bonds, it goes without saying, were low-security and high-yield to the investors, and they came to be called, in a term that Milken coined in an inadvertent moment, junk bonds.

The two concepts—junk bonds and greenmail—came together most actively and ultimately most disastrously in the person of Milken. He was a Californian. (Though Drexel Burnham's principal offices were on Wall Street, Milken's personal department was in Century City on the west coast.) He was a guy who gave fresh meaning to the noun workaholic—his business day began at 4:15 a.m. and lasted until nine or ten at night. He was a rich man—in a five-year period through the mid-1980s, his pay topped $1 billion—who didn't care much about money, not to spend on himself, anyway; he lived in an unpretentious house in a neighbourhood, Encino, which was barely above middle class. And he was a frightening combination of visionary and megalomaniac.

Milken was by definition an outsider to the established investment community, and he gathered around him, as purchasers for his junk bonds, as principals in buy-out raids on large corporations, other men, risk-takers, entrepreneurs, who likewise found themselves on the wrong side of the window, on the outside looking in. Some of their names? Carl Icahn, T. Boone Pickens, Ron Perelman, Saul Steinberg, and Sam Belzberg, who, as we have seen, experienced more than his fill of elitist putdowns.

Carl Icahn began business life as a New York stockbroker but had too much breadth for the small time. He was a shrewd, stubborn, analytical, intense negotiator. In 1979, operating with not much in the way of capital, he bought a 9.5 share of a copier company called Saxon Industries. When Saxon, fearing an Icahn takeover, bought him out at a $2 million profit, Icahn was in the greenmail game, to become arguably its master (though, again, it wasn't called greenmail yet; something more polite, "buyback at a premium," was the phrase of choice).

Icahn didn't use Michael Milken's junk bonds to finance the Saxon raid. But when Icahn declared a tender offer of $8.1 billion for the giant Phillips Petroleum in 1985, Milken raised $1.5 billion for Icahn in forty-eight hours, all junk bonds. Phillips beat off Icahn, rewarding him with a trading profit of $52.5 million. Greenmail with a vengeance, and by 1985, that's what everybody was calling it.

How did the Belzbergs figure in all of this?

Prominently.

They bought $287.5 million of Michael Milken's junk bonds in support of the Icahn assault on Phillips. The Belzbergs also declared themselves in when T. Boone Pickens made his greenmail run at Texas Gulf in 1984. And they bought more junk to back a very little guy named Ron Perelman and his supermarket chain Pantry Pride in the 1985 shot at knocking off the mighty Revlon, Inc. Not greenmail this time, because Perelman actually captured his prey. It was a junk bond raid that succeeded in putting the little guy in the chairman's office at Revlon.

Within the Michael Milken coterie, everyone hung together, all these men who were perceived by America's entrenched business leaders as parvenus (though the iconoclastic Icahn was in and out of the Milken group as it suited him). They backed one another's hostile takeover bids, they bought one another's junk bonds. The Belzbergs, Ivan Boesky, and Saul Steinberg shared in one of Milken's personal, very special investment partnerships, Reliance Capital Group LP. And everybody in the gang flocked to Beverly Hills in the mid-1980s for the annual four-day jamboree hosted by Milken and Drexel Burnham. A combination of business seminar, blow-out party, and exercise in investment uplift, these gatherings acquired a name—the Predators' Ball.

The Belzbergs were plenty active in their own greenmail forays, usually financed by Milken's junk bonds. The targets included a California forest products company called Potlach Corp (1985), a Chicago building materials and manufacturing firm, USG Corp (1986), and Lear Siegler, the aerospace manufacturer (1986). In each case, the Belzbergs bought minor positions in the targeted companies and accepted profitable payments to vamoose.

Then there was the Belzberg bid for Armstrong Industries. It came in 1989, and it wasn't greenmail, it wasn't junk bonds, it wasn't profits. It was big trouble. Armstrong had been manufacturing furniture, flooring tile, and building products for 130 years, head office in the peaceable Pennsylvania Dutch town of Lancaster, population sixty thousand, of whom five thousand worked at the Armstrong plant. The Belzbergs liked the looks of Armstrong as the object of a takeover. What wasn't to like? Two and a half billion in sales in 1989, $188 million in profits, $70 million in cash on hand, lots of divisions in the company, which a new owner could split off and sell at a profit.

When the Belzbergs commenced their leveraged buy-out try for Armstrong, it was almost a foreshadowing of the plot to Norman Jewison's 1991 movie *Other People's Money*. Charmingly rapacious takeover artist (Danny Devito) sets sights for folksy little town's only industry run by crusty but kindly boss (Gregory Peck). In real life, Sam Belzberg had the Danny Devito role, and Armstrong's chairman, William Adams, stood in for Gregory Peck. A major difference, though, was that Adams, unlike Peck, played dirty. There were nasty little tricks, like hiring a private eye to dig up any scandal that might be lurking in the Belzberg past. And there were larger transgressions, like lobbying the Pennsylvania legislature to pass a bill that included some terribly dubious provisions; for example, anyone who puts his hands on twenty percent of a company's voting shares and then sells them within eighteen months must turn over his profits to the company in question. The result was that William Adams and Armstrong Industries beat the Belzbergs into a withdrawal at a loss to the Belzbergs of $17 million.

The Belzbergs didn't use junk bonds to finance the failed Armstrong takeover. That was because junk bonds had fallen into partial disrepute and because Michael Milken had fallen into a disrepute that wasn't at all partial. It was total. After two years of fighting government allegations of hanky-panky, Milken pleaded guilty on April 19, 1990, to six felony counts of securities fraud, mail fraud, and income tax evasion. He drew a ten-year prison sentence. And what of Drexel Burnham? In early 1990, it filed for bankruptcy. Talk about the clock striking twelve at the ball.

If the Armstrong $17 million had represented the only loss for the Belzbergs, they would still have been laughing. But it didn't, and they weren't. In general, the economic and investment climate heading into the 1990s had turned bleak. The markets were hardly so munificent as in the mid-1980s, and the businesses that made worthwhile marks for leveraged buy-outs were few to nonexistent. In particular, the Belzbergs, as with most heavy dealers in junk bonds, were reeling under the junk bond debt that had financed all the greenmail and other activity. A junk bond dealer was a little like a man carrying a tray of drinks that are close to overflowing; in order to keep them from spilling, he must rush forward at an ever speedier clip, and if he slows down or, worse, trips, he's going to get all wet. The Belzbergs, holding all their junk, were soaking in debt.

Or, as Connie Bruck wrote in her absorbing account of Drexel Burnham, *The Predators' Ball*, apropos of two leveraged buy-out artists, "They reached the stratosphere of American industry not by years of work in building companies and creating products, but by putting what little they had on the line, rolling the dice—and issuing mountains of debt. Thanks to Milken the magician, these mountains can simply be moved from one place to another. Not surprisingly, some critical observers . . . decried the creation of such empires as being 'achieved with mirrors.'"

Or, as Brent Belzberg himself asked when he went on the board of First City Financial early in 1990 and realized first-hand the extent of the company's indebtedness, "What happens if we can't roll the debt?"

"You can always roll the debt," the old hands answered him. Not in the 1990s, you couldn't.

There were other debts besides those from junk dealings, notably $305 million of First City bonds held by investors in Switzerland. First City's assets, on the other hand, were largely in unfinished real estate, a commodity that wasn't worth much as a fluid investment in the 1990s. Nor were things bright over at First City Trust. Trust companies are supposed to make money the steady, conservative way, by investing in mortgages, bonds, some stocks, by building consumer deposits. But First City in the 1980s had been nervier. Its management, which seems to have been short on long-term strategy, bet the house on speculative investments, on speculative stocks and speculative real estate. At first, in the flourishing mid-1980s, the securities investments yielded profits—the trust company's *only* profits—but coming up to the 1990s, trading took a nose dive. Everything in the Belzberg empire was drenched in red ink.

All of which raises the question, where, all this time, during the frenzy of the 1980s, the highs and lows, where was Brent Belzberg?

In the late summer of 1979, Brent moved from Toronto and the Tory law firm to Vancouver and First City. He was instantly miserable.

"I was in a new city," he tells me in his office. "I'd only been married a few months [to the former Lynn Rosen], and we couldn't find a place to live. The most important person practically in my life, my grandfather Lapvin, had just died. I was used to working in a law firm, which is like working in a cocoon. You're protected by your comrades. You never have to make a decision all by yourself because there's always somebody to share the decision with. In Vancouver, I was alone in the cold, cruel world. Put all those pressures together in a package, I'm telling you it was the worst."

Belzberg laughs—and does another of his shuttles in time.

"Of course, looking at it today," he says, "what I went through then seems like nothing compared to what I've gone through in this last terrible year."

In Vancouver, he was put in charge of real estate operations. This was the guy, remember, who had skipped the real estate rotation when he was a student at Tory, Tory. This was a lawyer who'd never handled so much as a simple house purchase. But, beginning with a semi-fluky incident, he came up smelling of roses in real estate.

A man came to the Belzbergs, to First City, with a property to sell. He was ushered into Brent's office. The property was directly across from Vancouver's City Hall on Broadway Avenue. Brent put down a $100,000 deposit and drew up an option agreement while he looked into the deal.

He hired an architect, and he and the architect visited the zoning department at City Hall.

"What can I build on this parcel of land?" Brent asked.

"It's zoned for a hotel," the man in the zoning department answered.

"Okay, I'll build a hotel."

Belzberg and the architect dropped in on City Hall's planning department.

"You can't build a hotel on that land," a planner told Belzberg.

"Why not?"

"Because, look, you build a big hotel there, it's going to block the City Hall's view to the north, to the mountains and the water."

"Well, what do you want me to do about it?"

"We don't want you to build on it, that's all," the planner said.

"Okay, if you won't let me build on it," Belzberg said, "I guess you're going to have to buy it from me."

The problem was kicked upstairs at City Hall.

"How much do you want for the property?" someone upstairs asked Belzberg.

He named a figure that would produce a profit for First City of $1 million or so. City Hall went for the deal.

"All of a sudden," Belzberg says, "people around the office thought I was this great flipper of land, a developer, a guy who knew what he was doing."

Sam Belzberg decided he had just the job for Brent, the newly revealed real estate genius. In 1979, the senior Belzbergs had bought real estate companies in Boston, in Denver, in Toronto, and two in California. It looked like a swell bargain at the time. The Belzbergs didn't want to run the companies, just own them under the umbrella of an outfit called First City Development Corp. They'd leave the managing to the people who were already in place. But by 1980, interest rates were soaring to twenty percent and beyond. The real estate companies began to look like not such a swell bargain. There was no cash flow from the companies, and the debts incurred in purchasing them were approaching the horrendous level. What the Belzbergs needed was someone close to home who would impose order on the chaos and get the family's money out of the companies. Brent got the call.

"This I didn't need," he says. "I'm about thirty years old, and I've now got seven hundred people reporting to me and a billion dollars of real estate in a twenty-two–percent-interest climate and no cash flow and no ability to develop anything and no money."

Added to the general turmoil was a particular item that was a real pain in the neck for Brent. None of the properties were in

Vancouver. They were in—he can still tick them off from memory—Boston, Philadelphia, Chicago, Miami, Fort Lauderdale, Dallas, Houston, Los Angeles, San Francisco, Seattle, Montreal, Toronto, and Boise, Idaho. In Vancouver were his wife, their new home, and their new baby (the first of three children, Bram David, Kate Sonia, Zachary William). Brent had to leave wife, baby, and house behind while he hit the road to tend the far-flung properties. Get on the plane Sunday afternoon, make three or four stops, return Thursday night, put in a couple of days at the home office.

"I always say," Belzberg says, "I never lived in Vancouver. My wife lived there and my kids grew up there."

Despite his lack of regular presence in the city, many young Jewish people around Vancouver remember Brent Belzberg for one special reason. He and a friend organized a small speakers' group that was designed to bring into colloquy young Jewish business people, doctors, lawyers.

"There's a real lack of Jewish identity in Vancouver," Belzberg says. "Marriage of Jews to non-Jews is around seventy percent, so the Jewish community is effectively disappearing."

As a partial solution, or at least as a response, Belzberg and his friend got monthly gatherings under way for young Jewish people who weren't otherwise interacting. They met in the First City boardroom, fifteen or twenty people, listened to speakers on a variety of topics, usually related to Judaism, and entered into general discussions.

"The point was to get the people together," Belzberg says.

David Cohen attended some of the sessions. Cohen was a classmate of Belzberg in U of T law. He's a professor at the UBC law school, a guy whose brilliance is so out-front he seems almost wired, and he remembers Belzberg's boardroom seminars with admiration.

"No one else I knew of was making that kind of commitment," Cohen says. "But Brent, who already had about a million things on his plate, cared enough to do it."

(Belzberg, for his part, remembers Cohen's wife with gratitude. Her name is Gloria, and she's a doctor. "On one of my trips, I got some awful virus," Belzberg says. "I came home and couldn't move out of bed. My GP was on vacation, and Gloria was doing a locum for him. She got me to the hospital. Jeez, she cured me." What are classmates' spouses for?)

After four years on the road, Belzberg steered First City Development clear of disaster. Interest rates were dropping, real estate values were up, the market had some stability. Sam Belzberg rewarded Brent by handing him another load of potential grief. Sam and a partner had done a number of complicated mortgages. The partner, who was the managerial half of the team, departed. The mortgages looked shaky. Brent, said Sam, please clean this up. Brent was back on planes for another year.

"Finally," Belzberg says, "I told my wife, I'm not gonna do this one day longer. We moved back to Toronto, and I started a merchant bank over on King Street with a couple of other guys."

The year was 1986, the merchant bank was First City Capital Markets. But inevitably, what with one thing and another, chiefly the perilously high-flying state of First City Financial Corp. and its subsidiaries, Brent was persuaded or coaxed or cajoled, or felt concerned enough, to get back in the Belzberg mainstream. In mid 1988, he became vice president of First City Trustco, which used First City Trust as its operating unit, and the following summer, 1989, he took the jobs of president and CEO of First City Trust. (Both companies were run from Toronto.)

At these stages, Brent could not have been unaware of the course that Sam Belzberg had pursued for First City Financial through the previous decade, couldn't have helped being nervous of the consequences, couldn't have avoided losing a little sleep.

The way he explains his position and attitude, looking back at the wreckage from the vantage point of December 1991 (that's a *vantage point?*), is like this:

"I did know the problems First City Financial had, but

nobody listened to me for a very long time. They all thought I was just some silly over-concerned lawyer, that I made a big issue out of everything. Nobody listened to me. So finally one day I just pushed all the phones and called everybody and said I'm leaving if you don't let me put things on a different format. After that, the board asked me to do it. But it was too late. The place was a mess."

In March 1991, Brent took over from Sam as president of First City Financial. Sam stayed on as chairman. It was a gruesome muddle that Brent contemplated.

"You're talking about refinancing a few hundred millions of U.S. junk bond debts," he told Jennifer Wells of the *Financial Times* in April 1991. "You're talking about refinancing a few hundred millions of Swiss debt in markets that don't exist."

(He also underlined to Wells in the same interview, just in case anyone doubted it, that, "It's no secret on the Street that I didn't participate in the greenmail activities and wasn't comfortable with them.")

Brent started in, trimming back staff, closing branch offices, cutting overhead, unloading much of the stock and bond portfolio, paying off some bank loans, and, most urgently, appealing to creditors for a restructuring of those awesome debts. All the while, though, he had to glance over his shoulder at Sam in the chairman's chair.

A Toronto lawyer, not with the Tory firm, told me of a phone conversation he had with Brent in the spring of 1991.

"The way it sounds to me," the lawyer said to Brent after a few minutes of commiseration over First City and its troubles, "you're thinking Sam should be out of there. That's what's on your mind."

A moment of silence came from Brent's end.

"You're probably right," Brent said at last.

At First City's annual shareholders' meeting on June 17, 1991, it was announced that Sam was stepping down as chairman. Brent was stepping up and taking the president's job with him.

"Nobody was forced out," Brent told reporters after the meeting.

Things got worse at First City, the avalanche that had been building from years past. First City Industries, an American subsidiary, defaulted on $97 million (U.S.) in debentures, which had been used in a 1984 buy-out of a Connecticut brass button and lock company called Scoville Inc. Stock in First City, which sold at twelve dollars a share in December 1989, was at ninety cents in June 1991, if anybody was buying. The Bank of Nova Scotia had to be dealt with; it led a group of eight banks that were sitting on a $100 million demand credit line. There was more, lots more. There were the bondholders in Switzerland, about four thousand of them, many of them senior citizens who weren't entirely clear on the nature of the investment they were venturing into when they bought First City bonds. What they had *in toto* was $305 million in bonds, which matured between 1992 and 1995. Some of the bonds were dual currency with the principal payable in U.S. dollars and the interest in Swiss francs; on others, both principal and interest were payable in Swiss francs. That made for investor confusion, but the bottom line was that, in any form, any old way, First City didn't have a dream of meeting a maturity date of 1992 to 1995.

Brent Belzberg proposed a trade-off. The Swiss investors would relinquish their $305 million in bonds in return for $100 million in bonds, maturing at the end of the decade, in a successor company to First City called Harrowston, plus eighty percent of that company's common stock. The Swiss agreed, okay, sure, *anything*. It seemed the best chance they had of coming out whole.

"Let me assure you that obtaining [the Swiss] approval wasn't easy," Brent told a meeting of First City shareholders called in Toronto on November 11, 1991, to approve the arrangement. "They weren't interested in hearing about alternatives that didn't give them one hundred percent of their money back. To have to stand up and tell four thousand bondholders that they haven't got what they thought they got was a very hard thing for me to do. I really feel bad for them."

First City's shareholders voted 99.9 percent to okay the deal with the Swiss. The vote bought time, and it also diluted the share of the three senior Belzbergs, Hyman, Sam, and Bill, in what had been First City Financial, to fifteen percent of whatever survived.

Diluted?

Liquidated might be more like it.

I ask Brent in his office in mid-December 1991, "Will all of this be easing up on you soon? All this coping with the mess?"

"Oh, yeah, yeah," he says. "It's almost over. I don't think there'll be much left in the companies when I'm finished. But I have a few comrades, and I'll go out on my own with them and start again."

Here we are in the last stretch of the Belzberg drama and nowhere near a happy ending. But there are two more points to make about Brent Belzberg, one anecdote and one quote.

First, the anecdote. The ceramic running shoe on the credenza shelf in his office isn't without meaning. In the fall of 1990, Belzberg took up running. "I needed *something* to relieve the tension," he says. Others in his office were runners, David Sutin, First City's executive vice president, John Bradlow, head of First City's capital markets division. Brent ran with them, he ran alone, he ran at odd hours, six in the morning through the downtown streets, or late at night. "I couldn't do something like play tennis because, the life I lead, it's impossible to schedule things with other people," he says. "But running, it doesn't depend on anyone else." So he ran, and something amazing happened.

"You go out and you run twenty minutes at the beginning," Belzberg says. "Then you run thirty minutes. You keep pushing it, and all of a sudden, without noticing, you've run an hour and a half, which is, like, twelve miles. Then you think, if I ran twelve miles, maybe I can run a marathon."

A marathon? Come *on*. Twenty-six miles?

In the autumn of 1991, Belzberg and his First City associates entered the New York City Marathon.

"I didn't think I'd finish. I'm no jock. But the spirit was fantastic, and the other guys I was running with, my comrades, they were going to do the whole marathon, so I had to finish. And I did it, the entire thing. It was one of the great experiences."

Forty-one years old, and twelve months after he takes up running, he completes a marathon, you know Brent Belzberg is a guy for the long haul.

The quote is a reprise of a subject Belzberg touched on earlier in the time I talked to him when he was summing up his legal experience.

"There were things about practising law," he says, "that I think really helped me in the sense of what's right and the way things should be done in ethical terms. But I think I was like that even before I went into law. I was always a guy who thought you should line yourself up with what's right."

# CHAPTER EIGHT

## The Neighbourhood Lawyers

HERE'S AN ENCOUNTER from Colin Wright's past, as Wright told it to me:

Wright thought he might try a career as an investigative reporter. It was the mid-1970s. Watergate was in the air. Woodward and Bernstein were the by-lines of the moment, two guys on the staff of the *Washington Post* bringing down a corrupt administration. Wright was drawn to the excitement and integrity of investigative journalism. He got a reporter's job at the *Globe and Mail* in the summers between his years at law school. He wrote stories that tried to pry the lids off doubtful issues. After his call to the bar in the spring of 1977, he was back at the *Globe*. He figured his legal training made a perfect fit for a future in investigative reporting. He explained his ideas one day in July to a *Globe* senior editor.

"Well, the best investigative guy we've got on the paper is Gerry," the editor said to Wright. "You agree with that?"

"I admire Gerry tremendously."

"Okay," the editor said, "visualize the following situation. There's a scandal we're trying to get at, a real dirty mess that needs to be exposed. We know one guy's at the heart of it, a businessman, and you go around to this businessman's office. He's out for a few minutes, but his secretary shows you into the guy's office. You're alone in there, right in the man's inner sanctum, papers on his desk, the drawers unlocked, all that. What do you do?"

"Well," Wright said, "I suppose I sit in the chair and wait for the fellow to come back to his office."

"Exactly," the editor said. "You, with your lawyer's background, you know it's not proper to fool around in a man's office. Hell, it might not even be legal."

"Yes."

"Now me, if I was in the same position, waiting in this guy's office, I might get up and look at the papers on his desk, sniff around a little, see what I could learn."

"You might?"

"Sure," the editor said. "But Gerry, put *him* in the same situation, alone in the office of this guy who he knows has the material to break open a great story, Gerry would run around the office and he'd scoop up every loose piece of paper, search every drawer, grab every document, and he'd be out of there like a bandit."

"He would?"

"And that's the difference between you and Gerry," the editor said. "You've got too much legal training in you to be a top investigative reporter like Gerry."

That summer, the summer of 1977, Colin Wright went back to his home town, Gananoque, Ontario, and began to practise law. He's still there, still practising.


It was Marty Friedland's idea that I should make a point of calling on a few people like Colin Wright, members of the class of '75 who practise in small towns or in defined communities within larger centres, people who have set up shop on their own or with one or two partners, lawyers who, for whatever reason—Colin Wright's motivation *was* unique—chose small over big.

"Are they happier than the people who joined the downtown firms?" Friedland said to me. "I'd be interested to know the differences in their lives today. Are they glad they made the choices they did? Or envious of the lawyers who went downtown?"

Starting out on the Friedland mission, the only fact I was certain of was that the small-community lawyers were in the minority. The largest group from the class had entered established firms that already numbered anywhere from three or four lawyers to a hundred or so. The next biggest bunch branched out of the practice of law into business or academia or a specialized area where their legal training came in more or less handy. That left the last group, the smallest, the neighbourhood lawyers, and after Marty Friedland pointed me in their direction, I was as curious about them as he was.

Was there a personality factor at work among them? A kink in their thinking that took them out on their own? Did they tend to be loners in law school? Was there something special, even especially weird, that drove them? Were they less ambitious than their brothers and sisters in the Toronto bank towers? Or maybe *more* ambitious?

I set out to look for some answers.


Gananoque, population 5,200, lies about twenty kilometres east of Kingston, and it's situated directly opposite and at the midway point of the Thousand Islands. The geographical position is crucial to Gananoque's economy. The Thousand Islands—in fact, there are closer to seventeen hundred islands, but "the Seventeen Hundred Islands" doesn't have the same euphonious ring as "the Thousand Islands"—are a huge draw to summer visitors, and most of Gananoque is geared to cash in on the seasonal tourist trade. In the winter, as I was told by Debbie, the nice young woman who runs the only bookstore in town, "We roll up the sidewalks and doze off."

One thing about tourism, it doesn't do much for a town's beauty. When I arrive in Gananoque to call on Colin Wright, I take a walk to check out the local landmarks. It's a short walk. The town hall is a lovely old Georgian house that once belonged to a lumber baron named Charles McDonald. There's a fine stone bandstand, 135 years old, and the former Victoria

Hotel has been converted into the Gananoque Museum, which is full of everything you might want to know about Charles McDonald and other luminaries. That seems to exhaust the list of architectural highlights.

Except for the house at 280 King Street. It's a gracefully sturdy building, constructed of limestone from Kingston in the front and Gananoque sandstone on the sides and rear. A man named James Robinson put it up in 1856 and ran a dry goods and grocery store out of the ground floor. The house stayed in the Robinson family until 1968, when a lawyer named Ronald MacFarlane bought it for an office. He took in one partner, Harry Clarke, in 1969, and another, Colin Wright, in 1977. MacFarlane was appointed to the Ontario bench in 1984, and the other two carry on as Clarke and Wright in the fine old Robinson house.

"Oh, yes, tourism is responsible for the way the town looks today," Colin Wright says after we settle in his small office on the second floor. "We've got some beautiful turn-of-the-century buildings along the west end of King, quite lavish metalwork on them, but it's covered in layers of garish paint now. It's a shame really. But none of this has actually affected the local people in the way they talk and think. Gananoque's really quite isolated, you know. Maybe we're one of the last bastions for idiosyncratic people."

Wright has on a short-sleeved striped sport shirt, no tie, and casual green pants that need a press. He's a tall, slim, pleasant man. His hair is thick and has been completely white for twenty years.

"I grew up in Gananoque," he says. "My father died when I was nine, and since I was the youngest by far of five children, my mother thought a boys' boarding school was a good idea. She sent me to Ridley College. It wasn't a good idea. I found it a very narrowing experience to be constantly in the company of people who all came from the same background."

Over Wright's head, a large framed poster hangs on the wall, a photograph of a foot bridge over a river, an eight-man crew sculling on the water, a lovely building in mist in the background. The photograph is of Champlain College at Trent University in Peterborough.

"My years at Trent, now they *were* excellent," Wright says.

He stands up from his chair and points to the photograph in the poster. "That's my college, Champlain. I helped build the retaining wall along the river just about here." His finger lands lightly on a spot in the mist. "A group of us students did that as part of our physical contribution to the university. And right at this point"—he runs his finger softly over the water under the footbridge—"I went swimming one day with the president of the university. Man named Tom Symons. A great fellow. Loved swimming."

Wright moves back a step to get a better perspective on the photograph.

"I studied history at Trent," he says, his back to me. "I was very keen on it. All of it. The place, the life, the classes."

Wright sits down and clears his throat.

After Trent, Wright took an MA in history at Carleton University in Ottawa and helped the historian Denis Smith organize John Diefenbaker's papers. He married, and he and his new wife spent part of a year in a town in northeast France teaching English. In the late summer of 1972, the Wrights headed for Toronto, she to write a doctoral thesis on an aspect of Thomas Hardy, he to enter the University of Toronto Law School. As educational experiences go for Wright, law school seems to belong in the middle, not nearly so elevating as Trent, not quite so stultifying as Ridley.

"I admired my law teachers quite extravagantly," he tells me. "But they were talking a language I could only respect. I couldn't engage in it. I don't think I ever did engage in it during law school. I just saw the teachers as extremely talented actors. I didn't start to grow fond of law until I got out of school."

He stops and thinks about what he's said.

"Maybe I should go back to law school."

He looks at his watch. It's about three-thirty. "Remind me I must stop by the house at four. I want to roll the pastry for the quiche." He looks at me. "You will stay to supper?"

"Uh, yes, thanks very much," I answer. *Roll the pastry?*

"One reason I've grown increasingly fond of the law," Wright continues, "is that it's the most civilized way of settling disputes. The work I do is mainly civil litigation, and again and again I've seen the same thing happen, clients enter into cases wanting to take knives to one another and the courts have managed to calm and control them. I can really only think of one of my cases where I thought the judge made a big mistake. It was a custody matter, and in my opinion, the judge chose the wrong parent to give the kids to. He chose the mother. The mother wanted to be *chosen*, but she didn't really want the *kids*. The father ended up raising them anyway, which means that even though the judge was wrong, everything worked out for the best."

At four, we get into Wright's aging Volvo station wagon and drive to his house, west on King Street, two stoplights and a couple of turns. It takes three minutes. The house is old, elegant, and nearing the end of an extensive renovation. We walk straight through to the kitchen. It's enormous, about the size of a Four Seasons executive kitchen, but the floor is unfinished, and there are other signs that the carpenters haven't completed their sawing and hammering.

Wright's wife is sitting at a big wooden table in the middle of the kitchen chopping vegetables on a board. Her name is Lynn. She has black hair, a full figure, a good face that sometimes wears a sardonic look. Lynn, as it turns out, is a generous-hearted woman, but she isn't inclined to suffer fools or foolish thinking gladly. It also turns out that Lynn isn't the Thomas Hardy scholar. Lynn, who runs the Department of Immigration office in Kingston, is Wright's third wife—number two was a lawyer—but she and Wright have been together ten years and have two young sons, Wright's only children.

"The renovations have been going on for three years," Lynn says to me. "Can you believe that? Three *years*?"

"There're only three workmen," Wright says. He's taking a rolling pin to a fat ball of dough on the counter.

"Portuguese," Lynn says. "All named Manuel."

"Only one is really a Manuel."

"But we *call* them all Manuel."

"That's true."

"They don't seem to mind."

"Yes," Wright says, "but they hardly speak any English."

"The real Manuel does."

"The other two."

"Hardly any at all."

"Any what?" Wright asks, looking up from his dough.

"Any *English*. The two don't speak *any* English."

Lynn hands me a beer. Wright drapes a flat sheet of dough over a deep tin plate. I drink the beer and listen to the delightfully daffy conversation. It seems entirely natural *chez* Wright.

"We bought the house from three spinsters," Lynn says.

"They were reputed to have kept fifty cats here," Wright says.

"I believe it," Lynn says.

"Yes," Wright says. "If you happen to sniff at the wrong moment you can still catch the odour of cat urine."

He trims the edge of dough off the plate and announces that he and I are going to drive to the cottage. The cottage? I have visions of an hour in the Volvo. It's more like five minutes. We go west through a suburban neighbourhood and down a dirt road toward the St. Lawrence. The road is silent and runs between tall trees.

"Years ago, my parents bought fifty acres out here," Wright tells me. "This is where I've always come, ever since I was a little boy. I feel more attached to the cottage than any house I've ever lived in."

The cottage is simple and small, just one bedroom. It's perfectly placed, under the trees a few clear yards from the water. There are boats pulled up on the shore, a canoe, a sailboat, a medium-sized motorboat. A solid new dock projects over the river in an L-shape.

Wright changes into his bathing suit and dives off the dock. He swims with a vigorous crawl.

"Refreshing," he says, back on the dock.

I mention that I don't know many lawyers in the Toronto-

Dominion Centre who can take a swim a few minutes from the office.

Wright gives it some thought. "I suppose not."

He sounds as if it hasn't occurred to him that he leads a life different from big-city lawyers. I decide it probably hasn't.

The view from the dock is of the nearest clump of the Thousand Islands, less than a kilometre across the water. No boat traffic comes down the channel while we're on the dock. It seems to be off the main tourist route. A man fifty metres away is fishing from a small aluminium punt. He lifts his hand in a lazy wave to Wright.

"Pickerel, I believe," Wright says to me. "I'm not much for fishing. Sailing, though, I enjoy sailing."

The mood on the dock is drowsy. I feel myself on the edge of dozing off.

"I'm not getting rich practising law," Wright says suddenly.

"Oh?"

"I've never figured out the art of billing clients in a small town. And it really is an art. How do you decide what to charge per hour for services to people you've known all your life? Of course, one problem is that in a case, I might have to deal with the same complex legal issues as a lawyer in a big city. But in his case, the amount at stake might be $10 million. In my case, in Gananoque, it'll be more like ten thousand."

Wright changes back into his clothes, and we make a tour of the property. The trees are so high and so closely packed that I can see only patches of sky above the tree tops. But enough sun comes through the leaves to make a soft dappled effect on the ground where we're walking.

"Here's an example of the billing problem," Wright says. "A man I know who owns a motel is being sued by a former employee for responding to a garnishee notice from the employee's wife to deduct money from his wages and send it to her. The employee says the motel owner deducted the money but didn't send it to the wife. He says the motel owner kept it. This all happened five years ago. The motel owner retained me, and it's very time-consuming digging into five-year-old records. The former employee doesn't care. He's on legal aid. The motel owner isn't in a strong financial position himself, but he doesn't qualify for legal aid. Under those circumstances, what do I bill him? Not very much, not when I've known him here in town from years ago."

We drive to the house. The kitchen has the luxurious smell of baking quiche. Wright unscrews the top from a litre bottle of red wine.

"Home-made," he says.

He shows me the label. It's stylishly designed, announcing that the wine comes from the vineyards of Colin Wright. It shows the year, 1990, and the name, Killer Shit.

Wright explains. "There was a big family gathering. I took a few bottles of my wine. It didn't have a name then. My nephew-in-law drank some. He drank quite a bit, as a matter of fact, and he said to me. 'Hey, this is some killer shit.' I came home and had the labels made."

He pours me a generous glass. I try a careful sip. The wine tastes raw and whaps straight into my bloodstream.

"I'm with your nephew-in-law," I say.

Lynn serves the quiche. It's almost two inches high, packed with cheese and eggs, onions and tomato. There are green beans and salad and more of the Killer Shit.

"Another problem practising in a place as small as Gananoque," Wright says, "you often have two clients doing business with one another, and you end up in the middle acting for both in some matter or other, a real estate transaction perhaps. That reminds me, the founder of our firm, Ron MacFarlane, once ran into embarrassment in a two-client situation. One of his clients was selling a substantial piece of the west end of Gananoque to another of his clients. Ron acted for both. The deal came very badly unravelled and the argument over who was at fault went all the way to the Supreme Court of Canada. Chief Justice Laskin wrote in his judgement that it was prudent—I think that was the word, prudent—for a solicitor to act on only one side of a real estate transaction. And that's the definitive judicial statement on the practice of representing both sides in a matter."

Wright hesitates, a glass of wine halfway to his mouth. "I wouldn't say the chief justice's warning is always observed in a small town."

The talk around the table turns general. Wright is a fan of Elmore Leonard novels, of the old English TV series *Fawlty Towers*, and of Peter Gzowski's CBC radio interviews.

"Peter Gzowski went to Ridley," I say.

"Really? Well, maybe the school did something right."

The empty plates are shoved back on the table. Wright fetches a refill of wine. Outside, the night is beginning to close in, and the kitchen catches the last of the light.

"I've grown to like lawyers now," Wright says. "I suppose it's because I've grown more confident myself. I don't feel the enormous waves of self-doubt whenever I enter a courtroom that I used to feel. It's very competitive in a courtroom, you know. Someone has to win and someone has to lose. That thought puts a lawyer on his mettle. But now that I've got confidence in my skills, I've become fonder of the legal profession and of my colleagues and of the institution of law."

Wright is almost in darkness across the table. He drinks more wine from his glass and wipes the back of his hand across his mouth.

"Besides," he says, "I realize whatever I do in a courtroom, whatever happens, it isn't going to bring about the total collapse of the world as I know it."

★   ★   ★

Derek Ball admits he probably wasn't the most dynamic president the Mississauga Kinsmen Club ever elected.

"Nobody'd call me a glad-hander type of person," he tells me. "I'm not great at patting guys on the back and asking, how's business?"

But Ball sucked it up, overcame his anti-gregarious instincts, acted presidential, and went the whole Kinsmen route. Songs, jokes, good works, one of the guys. Ball figured he had no choice. He was a lawyer in a single person practice beating the bushes for clients. He found some in the Kinsmen ranks.

"That's nothing," he says. "There's a guy down the street, a lawyer, he came up here from Nova Scotia and joined a bowling league. It was amazing the clients he got. Every night he bowled, he met someone who was buying a house or getting a divorce or had a son on an impaired driving charge."

Mississauga, where Derek Ball and the guy from Nova Scotia practise law, is the suburban city immediately west of Metro Toronto. As recently as the early 1960s, it was an area of green spaces, dusty roads, and quaint towns. Torontonians went out there for picnics. Three decades and three hundred thousand residents later, Mississauga is a city that's got everything except a specific centre. There are shopping malls and housing developments, all the usual, main streets lined with Burger Kings and auto body shops and Relax Inns, a high-profile woman mayor named Hazel McCallion, and no place that can be called downtown. Torontonians find Mississauga confusing.

"People who come out here from Toronto think they're headed for a foreign country or something," Derek Ball says on the phone when I ask for directions to his office.

Ball doesn't find Mississauga confusing. He grew up in the most upscale of the quaint towns, Oakville. He's practised in Mississauga since his call to the bar, and he lives in a condominium in Mississauga's Meadowvale area.

It isn't as hard as I expect to pick my way to Ball's office. Drive out Dundas Street past Dixie Road, watch for the McDonald's, take the next street on the right. I'm on a cul-de-sac that has a curling rink at the end and the Mississauga School of Music, spelled in English letters and Chinese characters, on one side. On the other side, Ball shares a squat, grey stone building with a bunch of doctors and dentists. He has three secretaries, cramped quarters, and a Kinsmen plaque on the wall.

Derek Ball is a lanky man with sandy hair and a sandy moustache. His looks are attractive in an anonymous way, except for the eyes. They are astonishingly blue. Paul Newman blue. The eyes are what you pay attention to when he speaks. His voice is soft.

"All my clients are out here," he tells me. "The courts and registry office I use are out here. All my business is out here. The only thing I do besides work is play golf, and I play on courses out here. Public courses. What I do, when I come into work, which is early, six-thirty, I might stop at a club south of here, Lakeview, buy a greens ticket and reserve a time for later in the day. I quit work at two in the afternoon and play a round with a couple of other guys. Those are the only days I stop work early. I shoot in the eighties."

What about holidays?

"You kidding? This year, I took a week off, the first time I've done that in three years. I went to Myrtle Beach, South Carolina, and played golf. The trouble is, I'm an idiot for not taking more time off, but I suffer if I do because before I go, I have to work like crazy so that everything's caught up. And then I have to work like crazy when I get back to catch up on what happened while I was playing golf in Myrtle Beach."

Put that way, what, I wonder, is so terrific about the life of a sole practitioner?

Ball explains. "I'm always here, that's true, and there's nobody I can load work off on. It can get stressful, people yelling on the phone, people wanting to know when I'm going to get their work done. That's the bad part. The good part, I'm my own boss."

That still doesn't strike me as exactly a conclusive argument in favour of the sole practitioner's life.

Ball explains some more. It isn't so much the text of what he says that begins to clear up the point. The message is in the subtext. Practising law by himself, Ball gets across, was almost foreordained. It was his fate. Destiny. Kismet. He had no choice.

"I wouldn't have lasted two minutes in a downtown Toronto firm. I couldn't handle that way of working. When I was in first-year law school, I already knew I wouldn't end up in a big firm. I stayed away from the courses in second and third year like securities law and advanced tax law, all the courses you need for big corporate work. That would have been crazy, me studying those subjects. I wasn't going *near* a downtown firm."

From law school, without hesitation, without second thoughts—no need to *think* about it—Ball went on his own in Mississauga. He scraped by at first. He lived with his parents to save expenses. He took pay-by-the-hour jobs as duty counsel at the courthouse in nearby Brampton advising small-time offenders on how to make bail, how to get a trial date, how to plead guilty. He joined the Kinsmen, found clients, established himself as a lawyer with a name in the community.

"I also hope I've been smart enough not to take on stuff I can't handle," Ball says. "The kind of work I do, it's the kind where I don't have to look up much law. Forty percent of it's real estate, ordinary house deals. The companies I incorporate for clients are small companies, and most of the criminal work I do is young offender crimes. And I take simple divorces and separations. One time, I went to a Canadian Bar Association seminar in Toronto on family law, and the lawyers were talking about marriage break-ups where there were issues about cars and a boat and a cottage and a nanny and tax implications for everyone. The kind of divorces I act on in Mississauga, the people don't *have* a boat or a cottage or a nanny or tax implications."

The conversation drifts back to golf.

"I played the Glen Abbey course out here two weeks ago as somebody's guest," Ball says. "I shot a 93, which is good on a championship course like that. I'm used to courses where you can bounce the ball up to the green. You can't do that at Glen Abbey. Make a mistake and you're in a trap or the water."

I ask about the eighteenth, the hole that's shown over and over on TV during the Canadian Open every year, a five-hundred-yard par five with a miniature lake enclosing the green.

"I didn't go for the green," Ball says. "I hit my shot up to the left. You know? Away from the water? Then I chipped up and putted out."

What did Ball score on the hole?

The astonishingly blue eyes flash.

"Par."

Play up the side, go the route away from trouble, putt out for par. Are we talking metaphor here? Has Derek Ball just defined his approach to the practice of law?

\*        \*        \*

Ron Flom knows precisely why he practises alone. No need to look for subtext or mess around with metaphors. Flom deals in black and white.

"I always felt life is too short to be a servant to others," he says to me in his office. "I thought from the time I was quite young that this is where I should be, working for myself. I told myself that unless something changed my mind along the way, that is what I should do. Nothing changed my mind. Articling in a large prestigious law firm, which is what I did, did not change my mind. In fact, it reinforced my thoughts that I should practise alone."

Flom's voice, expanding on his philosophy, is calm and deliberate. The phone on his desk rings. He picks up the receiver and listens for a few seconds.

"One moment, if you don't mind," he says to me. "This is business."

He speaks into the phone. I eavesdrop and give Flom the once over. He has beautifully cut hair, tanned features, very white teeth, and an overbite. He looks dapper in an off-white jacket, white shirt, and dark tie. On the phone, his voice has escalated to the speed and intensity of a jackhammer.

"Listen, there are two ways to handle this. You agree to what's in my last letter or we argue it. We argue in *court*. This is very cut and dried, you follow me? Sign the paper or go to court. Our position is the correct one. I know it, my client knows it, you know it, and I presume your client knows it. Call me back."

Flom hangs up the phone.

"Well, now," he says to me. His voice has come back to ground level, relaxed and soothing. "Where were we?"

"Practising alone. You were talking about the reasons for working by yourself."

"I never had a dependence on anyone else," Flom says. "Not in my educational or professional life, I mean."

He talks about growing up in downtown Toronto, "On the other side of the tracks, so to speak, in a sphere that was essentially one of poverty." He says, as a young man, "I had no money, no influential family, no connections whatsoever."

Beyond Flom's head as he speaks, out the window of his office, a Speedy Muffler King sign blocks out most of the sky. The office is on the second floor of a square red-brick 1920s bank building on Yonge Street above Davisville Avenue. It's an in-between Toronto neighbourhood, too far north to be included in Moore Park, too far south to be called north Toronto. It's middle-class, struggling to be more, to be classier. Flom has been practising in the area from the day he was called to the bar.

"No lawyers in the neighbourhood, lots of residences, a few businesses," he says. "This was the kind of spot I sought out. The office is two blocks from a subway stop. Everybody knows how to find Yonge Street."

"What kind of law do you do?" I ask.

"This is very interesting. In first year at law school, I got the top mark in criminal law. I thought a career as a criminal lawyer might be a good thought, all that Perry Mason manoeuvring. But the entrepreneurial side of my personality asked a few questions. What are you actually going to be doing for a living as a criminal lawyer? I asked myself that question. What types of people are you going to be associating with? And, as a criminal lawyer, are you going to be able to extract yourself from the position of near poverty you find yourself in? The answers didn't provide a promising future. But I must admit that at the beginning I accepted everything that came through my door. This included criminal cases. But as I got into areas of commercial law and real estate, I found the work more to my liking, and I took to the people I was dealing with more than I did to the criminal element."

"You concentrate now on commercial and real estate?"

"Exclusively."

"How's business?"

"Basically excellent. I also handle the litigation personally for my corporate and real estate clients. So when the market is good, we do deals. When the market is bad, we litigate."

Flom expands a little on the life he leads. He takes a holiday every three months, a week at a time. He plays tennis on the courts at the Inn on the Park. He lives about a mile from his office, in Moore Park. He's busy. He's more than content.

The phone rings again. Flom talks into it for a moment. He puts his hand over the mouthpiece and looks up.

"Is there anything more?" he asks me.

I stand to leave.

"Let me put things this way," he says, his hand still covering the mouthpiece. "When I started in law, I saw few lawyers more capable than me. Whether that was true or not, I was of that thinking, perhaps you might say the victim of that thinking. But today, I don't find myself at a disadvantage in abilities when I deal with the lawyers in the big firms downtown."

I open the office door.

"And in private," Flom says, "the downtown lawyers might even agree with my assessment."

⋆    ⋆    ⋆

The summer Wednesday I drive to Barrie for a talk with Jack Armstrong isn't the best day Armstrong has ever known. On the personal front, the youngest of his three sons, a five-year-old, is down in Toronto having a skin graft at the Hospital for Sick Children. And on the professional front, trucking companies all over the country are getting kicked in the teeth by deregulation of the industry and by American competition. Armstrong's practice consists almost exclusively of acting for truckers. Still, despite the blows from both sides, Armstrong seems upbeat. He says he's been this way for a year, ever since he made the decision to move his practice and his home out of Toronto and into the country far up Highway 400 north of the city.

"I'm a small-town person anyway," Armstrong tells me. He is sitting across the desk from me in his Barrie office. "Born and raised in Midale."

"Come again?"

"Never heard of Midale?" Armstrong pretends to be shocked. "Midale's famous. Some people struck oil there in 1956. Lived like the characters in *Dallas*. Not my dad, though. He had a scruffy piece of farmland, and he also ran the general store in town."

"But where *is* Midale?"

"On Highway 39 between Estevan and Weyburn."

"Oh, *Saskatchewan*."

"See, you *have* heard of Midale. In the southeastern part of the province. I played a lot of hockey when I was a kid. Might've been on stream for the pros. But my parents said, no, you're getting an education. I studied political science and economics at the University of Saskatchewan. First time I saw Toronto was four days before law school started in September 1972."

Armstrong taps an unlit pipe against his teeth. He's a big man, with glasses and dark hair. He has a big man's fastidious way of speaking and holding himself. But the fastidiousness, I have the feeling, is spread over steel. Don't mess with this guy.

Armstrong says he didn't have much time to spend on friendships at law school. He had a weekend job stacking beer cases at a Brewers Retail Store, and he carried another job during the week shelving books in the law library. He needed the money. When he wasn't working or studying, he played on the law hockey teams. They provided his social connections. To this day, he gets together with a bunch of old law school guys to play some shinny every Tuesday night.

After law school, he took a position as an in-house counsel at the Ontario Trucking Association. His job was to champion the cause of the association and all its member companies. He argued the truckers' interests before the Ontario Transport Board, before various legislative committees, before the courts, before any group that might chip away at the scope of Ontario truckers' business through deregulation or the expansion of

American trucking companies into Canada. In 1986, Armstrong and another association counsel, Gord Meakins (U of T Law, class of '73), broke off on their own and set up a partnership acting privately for trucking outfits.

"Our clients are the guys with maybe a hundred tractor trailers," Armstrong explains. "The intermediates in the industry, we represent them. Reimar out of Belleville, McKevits out of Thunder Bay, the Network Group who handle a lot of the Toronto–Montreal runs. Those are our kind of people, and as clients, they're great. Very straightforward and damned loyal. Make one screw-up, and they forgive you. But you better not make two. With ordinary corporate clients, it's just one mistake and you're gone."

"What exactly do you do for these trucking companies?" I ask.

"This isn't going to sound terribly sexy, but something like fighting over who gets the rights to transport cornflakes from Toronto to North Bay might mean economic life or death to one of our clients. That's our job as the truckers' lawyer. We appear before the transport board and ask them to open up a client's rights to carry a certain product on a certain route. Or, the other way around, we argue it isn't in the public interest to extend the operating rights of somebody who isn't our client."

Armstrong clicks the empty pipe on his teeth again. "The climate of the industry right now, some of my clients will ultimately go out of business. The third-generation truckers, the ones who don't have any debts and they can afford to park some trucks against the wall and keep their cost level down, they'll hold on. Some of the rest are going to get squeezed. Hell, I may have spent the past fifteen years learning to practise a kind of law that'll soon be redundant."

Armstrong switches topics to something happier, his decision a year earlier to light out for the north. What made the move work in practical terms is that most of Armstrong's clients had their offices north of the city anyway. But Armstrong had much earlier arrived at a social-philosophical rationale for the big shift.

"Lawyers my age, people from our law class, are at a stage where burnout's a possibility," he says. "It was great when we were young and energetic and trying to establish ourselves. But now we—or maybe it's just me—can't do the hours."

And there was something more that motivated Armstrong, something that gets deeper into his own nature.

"I've never been a person for big institutions. Big law firms, big business, big anything, I don't have the discipline or whatever it takes to survive in that environment."

Hence, long overdue as far as Armstrong is concerned, he made over his life. He and his partner, Meakins, closed their Toronto office and reopened in a brick house opposite a pleasant green park in Barrie. Barrie, population 35,000, is an hour's drive north of Toronto, but Armstrong pressed farther north to find his new home, another fifty minutes up the highway to a smaller town, Bracebridge, population 9,000.

"Very low stress," Armstrong says. "We bought a house where you stand at the front window and you're looking at Crown land. Bush and open spaces for twelve miles. You wouldn't believe the quiet."

Armstrong tips back in his chair.

"Here's what it comes down to," he says. "If I want to go fishing, damn it, I go fishing. Hiking, camping, playing golf, I'm out there when I want to be. The golf course is five minutes from my house. Like I told you at the start, I'm a small-town individual. It just took me a long time to get back to what I am."

Armstrong straightens up in his chair.

"A lot of people in Toronto think I'm crazy for what I've done. I smile and let them think I'm crazy."

\* \* \*

At this point, after talking to Colin Wright, Derek Ball, Ron Flom, Jack Armstrong, and two other neighbourhood lawyers, I'm beginning to wonder whether I'm getting at any of the answers to Marty Friedland's original questions about them. Are they happier, less ambitious, more ambitious, weirder than their classmates who joined the large urban firms? Some seem happier, some don't. Definitely the quotient of eccentricity is higher among lawyers who practise alone. Perhaps, though, the questions about the differences that mark off neighbourhood lawyers are irrelevant. Maybe it's a state of mind that counts, a predisposition to go it alone, which almost guarantees that, even in law school days, certain people are destined to practise law in some sort of solitary circumstance.

Colin Wright, for example, describes himself as "a bit of a loner at law school." Two other sole practitioners I speak to use the same word, "loner," to characterize their U of T Law experience.

Wright didn't join a study group.

Neither did Ron Flom or Jack Armstrong.

"I felt like an outsider," Armstrong says. "Maybe it was the cultural shock, a Prairie boy transplanted to the big city. It took me the whole three years of law school just to get adjusted to Toronto and the people."

Derek Ball hung out in first year mainly with a classmate, Colin Jones, whom he'd known since grade two. The pair roomed together on the Danforth, in the east end. "My recollection of first year was I was kind of scared," Ball says. "Colin and I came in to classes, took them, and left. I studied alone and just worked hard to keep up." Later, Ball loosened up and included himself in an informal study group. But the way he speaks of it, the group sounds slightly quirky. "We decided we'd summarize all the courses. The idea was, each person—there were five or six of us—would take a section of a course and boil it down for the others in a written summary. The thing was, one person would come in with an eighty-six page summary, and another person would have his section wrapped up in about half a page."

And then there's Bert Arnold. He falls into the category of neighbourhood lawyer, and he seems, when I talk to him, to have shared the experiences of Wright, Ball, and the others. Essentially a loner, no membership in a study group, a guy who apparently glided through the law school without many people noticing. I mention his name to several of his former classmates, big city people, and the reaction is uniform. Bert *Arnold? Bert Arnold?* You sure he was in *our* class?

Yeah, he was, and for me, he comes to symbolize the quintessential neighbourhood lawyer.

★    ★    ★

Georgetown is forty minutes by car from the centre of Toronto, west on Highway 401, turn north through countryside that has low, rolling hills, many farms, and one humungous new golf course called Lionhead, then west again on Highway 7, which turns into Guelph Street as it enters Georgetown. The outskirts of the town, population 17,000, haven't much distinction, just a stretch of shopping plazas, muffler shops, and Pizza Pizzas. But the old part of town is an exemplar of grace. The houses cling to touches of pioneer Ontario, wooden and antique, Victorian doodads here and there, sheltered in lots of greenery, though when I visit on a late October afternoon, the green is beginning to assume its autumn disguise of red and gold.

Bert Arnold's office, Arnold and Banbury, is fitted into a small and tidy plaza at the southeast end of town. There's a flower shop, a men's clothier, a beauty salon out front, and at the back, besides the law firm, there are two other offices, a dentist's and a developer's. In 1985, Arnold, his law partner, and the developer bought the land, built the plaza, installed themselves, and rented out the rest of the space.

Arnold and I drink Diet Cokes in his office's boardroom. Arnold is a trim, good-looking guy. He dresses in sharp taste and has a relaxed air. He's better than relaxed. The longer we sit talking in the boardroom, the more I realize Arnold is one of the few people in the world, especially in the world of law, who fit that 1960s cliché adjective, laid-back.

Why did Arnold decide to go to law school?

"A friend of mine who was already taking law said I might like it. Strictly as an intellectual thing, he meant. I thought it'd probably be boring myself. A lot of silly rules, stuff like that. But I looked into it and I thought, well, okay."

What did Arnold enjoy at law school?

"I was good at tax. I don't know why. It seemed to belong in some kind of Alice in Wonderland area. But once you got in there and understood the terms, you could come up with the answers within this surreal framework. I liked that."

Arnold grins and lounges in his chair, not the least bit cocky or arrogant or off-putting. Just laid-back.

After law school, Arnold articled at a medium-sized Toronto firm, Robertson, Lane, where he handled mostly mortgage work, which he enjoyed. Robertson, Lane was in the process of breaking up, and the firm invited none of its articling students to stay on as lawyers. Another articling student suggested an idea to Arnold. The other student was Clinton Banbury, a guy from Saskatchewan who'd studied law at Ottawa University, and his idea was that he and Arnold should set up a partnership in Arnold's home town, Georgetown.

Arnold hadn't considered that possibility. He planned to stay on in Toronto. But, hey, why not?

Arnold's roots run deep in Georgetown. His great-grandfather came out from England and started a leather glove business in the town in the late nineteenth century. Arnold's grandfather took over the company and kept it going until he closed down in 1954. Arnold's father stayed on in town working at one of the two local paper mills. That makes Arnold fourth-generation Georgetown.

"How many lawyers were already established in town when you and Banbury opened your office?" I ask Arnold.

"A lot. A couple offices with three lawyers, one with six people. About twenty lawyers altogether, I guess, at least twenty."

"Didn't that worry you? All those lawyers here, it might've been tough to carve out your own spot."

Arnold pauses a second or two. "Never occurred to me."

Then he tells the story of how he got into the specialty he practises today. The story begins about a month after Arnold and Banbury hung out their shingle in the summer of 1977. Arnold was having a cup of coffee in a Georgetown diner. One of the town's larger developers sat down beside him. He had a question for Arnold.

"Listen," he said, "how many severances do you have to have before you've got to put in a plan of subdivision on a piece of property?"

"No limit," Arnold answered without hesitation. "In principle, you can have any number of severances."

"Yeah?" the developer said. "That's interesting. Thanks."

A severance is a consent from a municipal body to divide up a large piece of empty real estate into smaller lots for the purposes of building houses on them. Granting or withholding severances is a way for the municipal body to control land development. The method of turning land into housing lots through a plan of subdivison also requires municipal approval, but it's a longer, more time-consuming procedure.

Two days after the encounter over the cup of coffee, the developer dropped by Arnold's office.

"I've got a strip of land in town I want to buy. I'm gonna put some houses on it. How'd you like to act for me? Negotiate the purchase?"

"Sure thing."

"I'm going down to Florida for a holiday. Take care of it while I'm away, okay?"

"You really want me? I'm just out of school."

"I'll leave you my power of attorney. You just look after the details."

"Huh," Arnold said. "That's a lot of responsibility. Are you alone on this deal, just you doing the purchase and the development?"

"I've got a partner. He'll be around town while I'm gone."

The developer left for Florida, and Arnold called on his partner.

"What do you know about this deal?" Arnold asked him.

"Me?" the partner said. "Absolutely nothing. I've never been in a deal as big as this before."

Arnold went back to his office. He had a power of attorney to act for a developer who wanted to buy a large chunk of George-town land, and he had the developer's partner who would be no help in negotiating the deal and its terms.

Arnold stopped in at the office of the lawyer who was repre-senting the vendors of the property.

"*You're* the lawyer for the purchasers?" the lawyer said. He was Georgetown's senior solicitor, and he was genuinely shocked to find a pup like Arnold on the other side of the deal.

"Looks that way," Arnold said.

He and the senior solicitor spent two weeks in back-and-forth negotiating.

The developer returned from Florida.

"I got two deals for you," Arnold told him. "In one, the purchase is conditional on thirteen severances. The second, at a much lower purchase price, is unconditional."

"I'll take the conditional offer," the developer said. "Sounds like it'll be quicker and cheaper in the long run. Of course, you gotta go get me those severances first."

Arnold went through the process—"very contentious," he remembers—of persuading the local Committee of Adjustment and other municipal bodies to approve the severances on the large piece of property. In the end, everything clicked into place. The severances were granted, the deal closed, the developer built his houses.

"For me," Arnold says in the boardroom of his office, "the rest was all word of mouth. Talk got around that I knew how to handle those kinds of deals. I had a reputation, and I've been doing developers' work ever since."

"Hold on a minute," I say. "It must have taken a lot of nerve for a young guy like you to even say you'd think of handling that first developer's deal."

"Nerve?" Arnold shrugs. "Well, I was interested he picked me. But it didn't take nerve. I mean, the guy left me no choice, the developer. I just cut the best deal I could. I enjoyed the idea of doing it for him."

Hey, why not?

Arnold describes the work he's been doing for the past fifteen years, handling projects of all kinds in the area, housing, commercial, industrial.

"I did the first co-op housing development in Georgetown," he says. "I had to go all the way to the Ontario Municipal Board to get that one approved. There was plenty of opposition from neighbours who thought low-income people were going to move in and drive property values down. But that didn't happen. It turned out to be a model development."

"What's it take to do your kind of work?" I ask. "What skills?"

"Well, apart from knowing the written stuff, things like the official plan, the zoning by-laws, I have to understand what the local policies are, the kind of ideas the planning officials like and don't like, the way they want the town to go. So, for instance, if I get developers coming into my office and they say they want to do a certain project, I can tell them, look, the planning people are never going to give you that. But, I tell the developers, they'll give you this other thing. And the developers'll switch the plans. That's how it works."

"You make it sound simple."

"Mostly it is simple. It's a good type of law to practise in a town like this. Except for the nights."

"What about the nights?"

Arnold grins. "Town councils, Committees of Adjustment, other boards, in small towns they always hold their meetings after dinner. So if I have to get an approval on something or I want to talk to an elected person, I go to the meeting and I sit and wait my turn. I've already got a five o'clock shadow by the time I get there. When I finally leave, I got a midnight shadow."

"That's the only complaint?"

"Basically."

Arnold talks about his life in Georgetown. He has all kinds of social ties around town, though it doesn't sound as if he pushes them. It doesn't sound as if he pushes anything. He has two children, a son in his early teens and a younger daughter. He belongs to the North Halton Golf Club. He bought a piece of land not long ago on the Niagara Escarpment, five minutes outside of Georgetown, 157 acres with a 10-acre lake. He's planning to build a house out there.

"Sounds ideal," I say.

"Not bad."

Arnold sits at an angle in his chair, leaning against one arm, drinking the Diet Coke. Good-looking guy, in control, content, likes the place where he's practising law even if it wasn't his idea to open an office in his own home town fourteen years earlier. Bert Arnold. Neighbourhood lawyer. Laid-back.

# CHAPTER NINE

## *The President*

ROB PRICHARD is saying he's changed his mind about experience. He used to think it was overrated as a prerequisite for the job he holds right now.

"In the balance of credentials," he says, "my view was that if you're a good person, have some energy and intelligence and a willingness to try hard, then as a qualification for the president's position, experience was somewhere down near the bottom of the list."

Prichard leans forward, gives his winner of a smile, and speaks a little more quickly. "Of course, it served me to downplay experience because I didn't *have* any."

He sits back. "But now that I've been here long enough to appreciate the size of the job, the enormous range of this place, the fact that you could be in the office for twenty-five years and not come close to reaching the full dimension of the institution, now I think prior experience in a large-scale job might be kind of useful."

This is a fairly interesting concession when you consider that the man making it, Prichard, is a mere forty-three years old and that, at the time he and I are talking, the spring of 1992, he's approaching the end of his second year as president of the sixth largest university in North America, his alma mater, the University of Toronto. Not only is the place huge in numbers and territory—fifty thousand students, thirteen thousand employees, three major campuses scattered east to west across Metro

Toronto—it's also got financial and other dilemmas that don't look as if they're about to go away soon. Statistics can be tricky, but as best anyone can figure, the pull-backs in provincial funding to universities announced by Bob Rae's government in January 1992 mean that Prichard may have to face cuts in his university's budget of $9.7 million in each of the next four years. And that's just one of Prichard's problems.

"I thought the first two years in the job would be the toughest," Prichard says. "Well, okay, at the end of my first year, we had a dinner for my predecessor as president, George Connell. There were speeches, toasts, all that kind of thing, and finally it was George's turn. He stood up and looked at me. 'Rob', he said, 'people have been telling you this has been a tough year for you. You've had strikes at the university, money difficulties, the government on your back. People say to you it's been a very tough year. Don't believe it. *Every* year is a very tough year.' George is right."

But is Prichard downbeat? Not close to it. Besides being the smartest guy in the law school class of '75, he's the most consistently optimistic, sunny, and positive. He is a tall, erect man, and has pale blue eyes, light brown hair that flops to the right, an overall presence that wins him the same adjective in many of the magazine and newspaper profiles of him that I've read— "Kennedyesque." That's how he looks. How he projects is something more difficult to catch in a comparison. Mr. Micawber with brains maybe, Dr. Pangloss plus a sense of reality, Mr. Deeds going to town and *knowing* he'll triumph. Upbeat? Prichard makes Mary Poppins—Mary Poppins but hold the sugar—seem down at the mouth.

In our conversation, Prichard returns to the subject of experience and tries his best to sound hard-nosed and objective about the presidency.

"Now that I've been in the job long enough to become more experienced," he says, "I'm more effective at it than I was a year ago. But no matter how experienced you get in the job, no matter how much better you get at it, all that does is allow you to take on more things. It's always *more* in the president's office.

There's a never-ending supply of worthy tasks. The job'll stretch you intellectually and emotionally to the very limits of your ability until you're tempted to throw up your hands and say, *no more.*"

I listen to Prichard make this colourful complaint, and I have the feeling he doesn't really mean it. It isn't his last word on the subject. I'm right.

"But you know something?" he says. "I wake up every morning, very early, and I'm excited by whatever I'm going to do that day. I don't have to look at my calendar to see exactly what's on my schedule. I'm excited anyway. Maybe there've been three mornings I haven't felt that way in the time I've been president. Only three. And it's the same thing at night. I stumble into bed, always late, and there might have been five nights when I've said, today it wasn't worth the effort, when I've said the job is too hard, too tiring, too demanding, and I want more time to myself, more time for Ann and the kids. But that's only five nights I've felt the doubts. All the other nights, I've thought to myself, what a *fabulous* job this is!"


John Robert Stobo Prichard was born on January 17, 1949, in London, England.

Stobo?

It's a name that has passed down the maternal side of his father's family. Prichard's father, whose name was John Stobo Prichard, was known to his friends as just plain Stobo. The name is preserved in the middle names of each of Rob Prichard's three kids. It also lives on in the names of Rob's two sisters' children. Stobo is due for a long run.

Prichard's mother and father came from Welsh stock. His mother, Suzanne, was the daughter of Sir Robert Webber, one-time chairman of Reuters news agency. Prichard's father served six years in the military in World War Two. Afterwards, he got on with his medical training in London, completed it with a year at Harvard, then packed off the family for Toronto. Once there, he shaped a most distinguished career as a paediatric neurologist at the Hospital for Sick Children and a teacher at the University of Toronto's Faculty of Medicine.

The Prichards brought up their three children—Rob is two years younger than Jane and a year older than Sarah—in an atmosphere that crossed the Brady Bunch with the Quiz Kids. There was a premium on discussion and education and family. On Sundays, Stobo and Suzanne organized personal sermons at home. The kids were expected to read the relevant Bible passages and contribute their own interpretations. When it came to wrongdoing, everyone convened at a family court to debate the wrongdoer's fate.

It was the sort of upbringing that could turn a kid into a rebel drug dealer or a happy achiever. We know which route Rob went. He wasn't the only one. Jane, the older sister, went off to success and great marks at Swarthmore, a small Quaker liberal-arts college near Philadelphia. She also took a PhD in sociology at Harvard, and is today the head of the University of British Columbia's Department of Social and Educational Studies and an important feminist voice. Top that? Sarah, the youngest Prichard, probably matches it. She's a professor of medicine at McGill and Chief of Service, Department of Medicine, at Montreal's Royal Victoria Hospital.

Compared to these academic hares, Rob began as the turtle of the family. He went to Upper Canada College where, he says, "I was only a moderately good student." Next was engineering at Swarthmore where "I was rapidly becoming a lot less than moderately good." Prichard's original plan was to get an engineering degree, do an MBA, and go into business. The plan came unglued at the first step, the engineering degree. But salvation was at hand. Swarthmore's engineering course divided into sixty percent technical subjects, forty percent arts subjects. "I adored the political science and art history and economics," Prichard says. "But I was not in love with the maths and physics." After a year and a half of this scholastic schizophrenia, Prichard dropped the engineering subjects, piled on more arts, revamped his overall plan in a way that left in the MBA, eliminated the business career, and replaced it with a future in law.

After Swarthmore, which included six months at Pomona College in California on an exchange program, Prichard got his MBA. This was at the University of Chicago's School of Business. Prichard specialized in finance and international business. Then . . . then he hitchhiked around the world.

Well, he didn't hitchhike the *entire* way.

The first leg of the year's journey was by plane from Toronto to Canton, China. In the early 1970s, it was impossible for a humble tourist to gain entry to China. Prichard finessed his way around that restriction. His father had a friend in Kitchener, Ontario, who was in the glove business in a big way and purchased in large quantities from China. He appointed Prichard a special assistant to the president of the glove company. That exalted status got Prichard a visa to China and an assignment at the Canton Trade Fair, where gloves were a feature attraction.

"I knew nothing whatsoever about gloves," Prichard says. "Which made it difficult because I had to visit all kinds of Chinese glove factories. I tried to figure out some way to look like I was knowledgeable, and what I did was smell the gloves. I'd walk through a factory, pick up a glove here and there, and I'd sniff it as if I was this master connoisseur of gloves. After awhile I looked behind me, and the Chinese managers, these extraordinarily polite hosts with a lunatic guest, *they* were smelling the gloves, too."

Checking out of his hotel in Canton, Prichard hooked up in conversation with a Canadian businessman working out of Hong Kong. The businessman ran a company called Market Group Asia, which put Chinese suppliers in touch with American purchasers by way of Canadian middlemen. This was in the period when direct trade between China and the United States was forbidden. The businessman offered Prichard a job at his company. Prichard signed on and lived the life of Riley, Chinese version, in Hong Kong.

"I earned incredible amounts of money in that job," he says. "I ate in fantastic restaurants, the kind that if they had an equivalent in Toronto I could never afford. It wasn't all luxury. I lived in a room in a Chinese schoolteacher's apartment on the Kowloon side. The room had a mattress on the floor, and it was so small I slept on the diagonal. But from that job, months later when I got home, I had more money than I started out with."

Prichard travelled east from Hong Kong. He visited Indonesia and Nepal and Burma and Afghanistan. He went by boat, bus, train, plane, and, oh, yes, he hitchhiked. In Israel, he bought a car, drove it to Greece, and sold it. In Czechoslovakia, he met up with his father. Almost a year had gone by. Time to head home. He'd been accepted at the University of Toronto Law School.

"If I hadn't taken the time to travel when I did, I'd feel itchy today," Prichard says. "But having done it, having seen Nepal and all those fabulous countries, it's made me feel completely comfortable with the prospect that living in Toronto and working at the university is the most fulfilling thing I could ever do."


On the first day of law school, September 1972, the office opened at nine in the morning for registration. Prichard, super keen, got there at eight-thirty. He was the only student present. A line-up of one. Another guy arrived fifteen minutes later. A line-up of two. The other guy was Elliott Belkin, who would turn out to be the class eccentric.

Patrick Boyer, who became Belkin's best friend in the class, thinks Belkin is brilliant. Everyone else talks of Belkin's unusual habits. Coming to school with his head shaved (that was unusual in the early 1970s). Bringing a lecture to a halt with a monologue that may or may not have had a bearing on the subject at hand.

"Elliott was a humorous voice carping from the wilderness," Howard Feldman says, "and most of us felt he should stay there. On the other hand, at moments of extreme boredom, Elliott provided a raucous distraction."

On the morning of registration, stuck with Belkin for fifteen minutes before other students began to straggle in, Prichard remembers he took the brunt of the Belkin eccentricity.

"Elliott was very, ah, forthcoming," Prichard says. "He told me he was from Vancouver and his father owned a packaging business. Later on I learned it was the biggest packaging company in Canada. Within about two minutes of our conversation—actually Elliott was doing all the talking—he told me the reason he was going to law school was that his father had fired him from the packaging company. I'm standing in line listening to this and I'm beginning to think, 'Gee, if *everybody's* like this fellow, have I chosen the right place to spend the next three years?' "

After law school, Elliott Belkin articled with the British Columbia attorney general's office, practised a little law around Vancouver, worked briefly in Patrick Boyer's Ottawa office, drove a cab, dabbled in business ventures, marched to a different drummer. I traced him to a house on Point Roberts, the small chunk of land a few miles south of Vancouver that sticks into the Strait of Georgia and is part of Washington State. In several telephone calls at all hours of the day and night, I didn't get past a message on his answering machine. Patrick Boyer says Belkin is busy sorting out the multimillion-dollar estate his late father left.

Prichard gets a kick out of telling stories from the lighter side of his law-school career. Another neat encounter came in October of first year. There was a trial advocacy program in which teams of two students argued cases against one another, a sort of preparation for the full-scale moot court competitions, pretend trials, which came later. In the trial advocacy program, the arguments were supposed to last no more than a couple of hours. But Prichard and his partner found themselves in a clash with two other students that raged for hours on a Saturday until finally, at five o'clock, the sitting judge, a lawyer from the downtown firm of Weir and Foulds, adjourned the matter to Monday when he hoped all parties would finally wrap things up.

"The main reason it went on so long," Prichard says, "was that a guy from our class on the other side named Simonelis was very determined and incredibly talkative. He absolutely would not shut up. So we went back on the Monday to resume the argument, and there was no Simonelis. He didn't show up for the trial advocacy program. He didn't show up for class. He vanished. He was never seen again, not *ever*, at the law school."

But—let's not kid ourselves—while Prichard has a sharp eye for the funny detail and a wonderfully self-deprecating style of telling a good story, he was launched on serious business at the law school.

"Rob had the whole school cased in about five minutes," Harriet Lewis says.

"Rob dominated the class," Arnie Weinrib says. "He had more depth than the other people."

Certainly the depth was on display in the classroom. Weinrib and the other professors remember his voice as the one they heard most frequently and compellingly in class. But Prichard was also singularly involved in non-classroom activities.

To name one, the legal aid clinic. Prichard—along with Ellen Murray, Brent Knazan, Leslie Yager, and others—looked on work at the clinic as fundamental to his legal education.

"This is how you justify your time becoming a lawyer," Prichard says. "You get into the legal aid program. Maybe for me that feeling came out of my American education. At the time I was an undergraduate down there, you were expected to do something socially responsible. When I was in Chicago getting my MBA, I worked in the black community at a free income tax clinic. That was nothing special. Just something everybody did."

In Toronto, Prichard got into the legal aid clinic in first year, and by second year, he was one of the four directors who ran the clinic. That was a breakthrough because, until then, directors had always been third-year students. Prichard repeated as a director in his third year.

"It was good for me to work in the clinic," Prichard says. Then he slides into one of his characteristic jokes turned on himself. "It was clearly less good for the clients I advised."

Getting involved in the moot court program, another area where Prichard was more industrious than most students, was absolutely central to his future. That's Prichard's story, anyway.

According to him, no matter what Weinrib and the other profs say about the frequency and intelligence of his classroom comments, the act of speaking was close to terrifying for Prichard.

"When I started in law school," he says, "I was practically inarticulate. I found standing up and speaking in front of other people, in front of *two* other people, never mind a whole class, really difficult. I knew I had to overcome it. I knew there weren't many successful lawyers who couldn't actually *speak*."

Prichard fixed on the moot court program as one answer. In second year, there was a compulsory moot court, but there was also the Jessup International Moot Competition, which was voluntary. Prichard volunteered. The Jessup was a big deal. Law schools from across the country competed against one another until a champion was declared. The champ's prize was a trip to Washington, D.C., to square off against teams from law schools around the world.

Each Jessup team—one per law school—was composed of three members. At the University of Toronto Law School's competitions for the team, the three who survived were John Hunter (the man who married Rebecca Winesanker and practises civil litigation in Vancouver), Bruce Barker (today a leading litigator at McMillan Binch in Toronto), and Patrick Boyer (no introduction needed).

Where was Prichard?

"I finished fourth," he says. "As a consolation prize, they named me a researcher for the team. I could help with the law, but I wasn't allowed to open my mouth."

Then, on the eve of the Canadian competitions, with the team members practically packing their bags for the trip to the site of the competitions at Queen's University in Kingston, Patrick Boyer, loaded down with work on the MA he was doing simultaneously with his law degree, busy writing politicians' speeches, burdened with a half dozen other chores, withdrew from the team.

"That meant they were stuck with me," Prichard says. "I was the only other person around, and they had to promote me to a speaking role."

At Queen's, the Toronto team, with Prichard as replacement, emerged as the champs, the group that would represent Canada at the international competition.

"It was John Hunter who won it for us," Prichard says. "He was a spectacularly good mooter. I'll tell you how good—he argued half of each of our briefs, and Bruce Barker and I split the other half."

In Washington, the setup was that all of the teams from within the United States—from Harvard, Yale, and so on—competed against one another. So did the teams representing law schools from around the world. And the final came down to an American team against a team from the rest of the universe.

Did the Toronto team reach the final? Did this team with a superior debater at its head, and in the number three spot a guy who just wanted to learn how to speak effectively on his feet, come out triumphant?

No. Not quite. Close, but no cigar.

The Toronto team finished in second place in the international division, one step away from the finals. Prichard can't remember which country defeated the Toronto guys. All he remembers is that he had a lot of fun in the five days in Washington and that the moot competition was invaluable to his later career.

"That's one of the messages I still give to students when I'm at the law school," Prichard says. "I tell them, whatever you may think of my ability to stand up and speak to you right now, you should know when I arrived at law school, I couldn't put six words together in front of a group. It was the mooting program that taught me to speak in public."

Prichard stops for a smile.

"Of course," he says, "some students may not think I'm all that articulate now."


Prichard says the second best thing that happened to him at law school was joining three classmates in a study group.

The three whom Prichard teamed up with were David

Cohen, Jean Fraser, and Phil Siller. What played a large part in their coming together, and in their success as a group, is that Prichard was in one half of the class and Cohen-Fraser-Siller were in the other half. The halves were for the purposes of teaching in first year. About seventy-five students made up one section, the other seventy-five were in a second section, and while each section took the same subjects, they had different lecturers and different timetables. Section A, for example, took property from Derek Mendes da Costa, section B was taught it by Arnie Weinrib. And so on. Different lecturers, different angles and interpretations and styles.

Bearing that in mind, picture Prichard in a ten-minute break between lectures one morning in late November of first year dropping in at the small cafeteria downstairs in Flavelle House for a quick coffee. Cohen, Fraser, and Siller were sitting at a table chewing over a lecture from one of their profs. They had plenty of time on their hands since their section wasn't scheduled for a lecture in the next hour.

"I listened to the three talking," Prichard recalls, "and I thought, holy mackerel, I can learn a lot from these people."

Prichard passed up his lecture and insinuated himself, in the inimitable, ingratiating Prichard manner, into the conversation.

"I recognized right away," Prichard says, "that they were remarkably able at the kind of legal analysis we were being asked to do at the school."

Before the four rose from the cafeteria table, it was agreed they would meet regularly and get on with the task of organized analysis. And there was no doubt about the identity of the force behind the organizing.

"It was Rob who put it all together," David Cohen says. "Rob put *everything* together in our class."

Who were the other three, besides Prichard, in the small group?

Jean Fraser. We've already met and admired her.

Phil Siller. He was the erudite fellow who threw an unintentional scare into Brent Belzberg. Siller came from New York City. Howard Feldman knows Siller in two capacities, as a classmate and as the person who, along with Siller's second wife, introduced Feldman to the woman he married. "Phil went to Hebrew school in New York," Feldman says. "Like all of us in Hebrew school everywhere, he hid a secret book under his Hebrew text. With us, it was *Playboy*. With Phil, it was Immanuel Kant." Siller took a PhD in mathematics at the University of Minnesota and proceeded to law school in Toronto, where he struck the other students as a most worldly chap. "Phil seemed not only older," Howard Feldman says, "but beyond the general neuroses that afflicted the rest of us."

David Cohen. He was the baby of the group, twenty-one years old and mystified by the study of law in the early months of first year. He grew up in Ottawa, the son of a small businessman, and took a good science degree at McGill. He wanted to do more work in physiological psychology, but a short period of graduate study at Dalhousie, "an awful program," switched him off. He decided to take a crack at law. That turned out to be, initially anyway, trouble. "I was a scientist. I was used to having a hypothesis and then developing an experiment to test the hypothesis and having methods to apply to see if the experiment supported the hypothesis. But in law, there was no data or hypothesis or method of testing it. I didn't know what to look for or think about in the literature."

The group got into a rhythm of regular meetings. Some were held at Prichard's place. Some were held in a seminar room off the solarium in Falconer House, the building north of Flavelle House, which the law school took over as an annex.

"Boxes of pizza used to be delivered through the window at Falconer House at three in the morning," Jean Fraser remembers.

As the meetings continued, as a magical chemistry developed among the four—"Other people were invited to join us, people with fantastic marks," Cohen says, "but they could never seem to feel the connection the four of us had"—the role of each fell into place.

"Cohen and I were the honest plodders," Fraser says. "We went to class and made notes, we briefed our cases, we'd have summaries of summaries that we brought to the group meetings."

Prichard made no notes?

"Great notes from class, yes, he made those," Fraser says. "But he'd show up at study group with absolutely virgin case books. He hadn't cracked them."

"Jeannie," Prichard says, "says she came to group meetings and knew the most and I knew the least, and by the end of the sessions she had been generous enough to transfer what she knew to me."

"About Rob's virgin case books," Fraser says, "I remember years later when he started teaching at the law school, he said to me, 'You know, some of these cases are pretty interesting.' It was the first time he'd read them."

But in the group, Prichard displayed other talents.

"He could put things together," Cohen says. "Rob could take six or seven pieces of paper and bring them into one. He could take one thing and go around it from all 360 degrees and see it clearly from every single angle."

And Siller?

"Phil would become really interested in certain aspects of things we were studying," Fraser says. "He'd read material and run the subject into the ground. Other things bored him. He wouldn't touch them."

Here's how Fraser sums up the normal pattern of meetings: "David and I would take Prichard and Siller through each course with our summaries. Then they'd step in and analyze and synthesize and drag David and me forward. It worked extremely well. More than that, it was fun."

More even than that, as time went on, the group got positively scientific in their tactics.

For instance, consider the approach they took after the first-year Christmas exams. "We wanted to determine what the difference was between an A and a B," Cohen says. "Why does a teacher assign an A to one person's exam paper and a B to another person's? We went over and over our own exam results, trying to get into the teachers' heads, trying to calculate the difference. The idea was that in the next exams, we'd know how to write As."

And then there was the devilishly clever—and scientific— notion of breaking down each course into quarters for the purposes of study. "Each person was responsible for preparing a set of notes on the material in a course for one of its quarters," Cohen explains. "The point was to go way beyond the lectures, to read other articles, get new material and see all the problems. Each person did that, put together a summary for his or her quarter, Xeroxed the summary, handed out copies to the other people, and taught it as if we were in a class. Here's the key—not once, in all the years, for all the quarters in all the subjects, not once did a person come unprepared. The dedication was fantastic."

"On one level, it wasn't terribly intellectual," Prichard says of the quarters method. "It was pragmatic, born out of the fact that each of us faced a hurdle we had to get over—the exams."

What put an extra spin on the group's studies was that, as noted, Prichard came from one section of the class and Fraser-Cohen-Siller from the other section.

"Maybe that benefited me more than the other three," Prichard says. "It meant, for example, if I had Dick Shibley for civil procedure, they had Ian Scott, and I was getting the insight they got from Scott. But maybe it evened out. Maybe all of us got the richness of our different teaching associations."

"The way we went at our studies," David Cohen says, "the organization, the methods, the approach, it put us so far ahead of everybody else in the class it was almost unfair."

Two final points remain on the subject of the study group.

One is that it became the only other group, apart from the Feldman-Baker-Blacklock-Mitchell-Saltsman alliance, to stick together for the entire three years of law school.

The second point is that an agreement was made some time in the spring of first year that the person who got the highest marks in the group on each year's final exams would treat the other three plus companions to dinner in a smart restaurant. After the first-year exams, Prichard picked up the tab for a dinner for eight at a French restaurant that used to be on Charles Street called La Chaumière. It almost destroyed his bank account. The decision was made that henceforth those who got reasonably good marks—namely everybody—would contribute to the year-end dinners.

Who made the decision about the change in payment?

"Rob," Cohen says.

After law school, Jean Fraser has shaped a marvellous career in corporate-commercial law. David Cohen teaches law at the University of British Columbia. Phil Siller works for the largest land developer in the world. His voice, you may have noticed, is absent from these pages. That's because he was the only person in the class who declined to be interviewed for the book. It's my fault. I made the mistake of contacting him at a time, March 1992, when his employer had hit a rocky patch, and Siller was occupied with crisis management. Siller is senior vice president and special counsel at Olympia and York.

Prichard spotted Ann Wilson on the first day of law school. Not just spotted her.

"I felt an immediate and strong reaction to Ann," he says.

This was across the lounge in the law school basement. She was the small, attractive blonde.

"My immediate and strong reaction was not reciprocal on Ann's part," Prichard says.

He got himself introduced to her and progressed as far as a casual-friendship stage. He formed plans to push the friendship past the casual stage.

The plans cracked up one morning in the first autumn. Prichard was walking to school from an apartment he rented nearby in the Annex neighbourhood. He saw Ann Wilson up ahead with a man Prichard knew was Stephen Grant. Grant was two years senior at the school, class of '73, a tall, handsome, big-man-on-campus type. Prichard picked up the pace, closed in on the couple from behind, and was setting himself to deliver a gallant greeting.

"What'll we have for dinner tonight?" he heard Grant ask her.

*Damn*, Prichard thought, and fell back without speaking.

That night, at home, he checked the law school directory. Sure enough, Grant and Wilson had the same address, 9 Amelia Street, over in Cabbagetown, same phone number. So much for the immediate and strong reaction.

Four months later—whap, what a *dummy*—Prichard put together the rest of the story. The house at 9 Amelia was a kind of law school boarding house. Wilson and a woman friend from school lived there. So did Grant and a couple of other law students. A law commune. Grant and Wilson were *not* an item.

"A totally missed communication by me," Prichard says.

He put his plans back on track. Still, it wasn't until November of second year, 1973, that Prichard produced enough charm to persuade Wilson into a dinner date. From that night on, it was a fine romance. The following summer, between second and third years, the two moved into a house he bought at 18 Boswell Avenue, a few blocks up Avenue Road north of the law school. Prichard made the house a paying proposition by renting out all the rooms except the two they lived in. The couple was married over the Christmas holidays of 1975, halfway through the year Prichard worked on a master's degree at Yale Law School.

Prichard says the best thing that happened to him at law school was meeting Ann Wilson.

The qualities that law schools demand today in the teachers they hire are the kind that one might expect in, say, the head of a think tank or in an ambassador to the United Nations. They want such qualities as education across many disciplines, depth in writing, distinction in graduate work, perceptive thinking, reflection, the ability to walk on water.

When Rob Prichard was invited to enter law teaching, the schools didn't expect all that fancy stuff. They were interested in marks. Did the person rank first, second, or third in the law class? Yes? Okay, he or she is hired. By that criterion, Prichard was golden. As we know, he stood second to John Zinn in first year and at the top of the class in the other two years. Marty Friedland offered Prichard a job towards the end of the summer between second and third years, to take effect in two years, after Prichard finished law school and put in a year of graduate work.

Was Prichard contemplating a career in teaching?

"If you asked me after first year if I wanted to teach," he says, "I'd have answered, maybe when I'm an established lawyer, I'll come back and teach one course. At the end of second year, I'd have said, gee, teaching wouldn't be so bad. I wasn't driven to teaching. I didn't have a strong career view of teaching. What crystallized things was external. It was when Marty called me in and to my complete astonishment made me an offer. If he hadn't, I would have gone to graduate school, then I would have begun the practice of law quite happily."

But Friedland made his pitch and rewrote Prichard's future. For that matter, he rewrote the University of Toronto's future. In approaching Prichard, in truth Friedland had more than Prichard's glittering marks as motivation. There was a buzz among staff members that Prichard might be someone special. He was working on a research project with the associate dean, Frank Iacobucci, and with a classmate, Marilyn Pilkington, which later appeared as the first book that Prichard's name was attached to, *Canadian Business Corporations*. David Beatty, the labour law and contracts teacher, was developing a mutual admiration society with Prichard. And another professor, the inestimable Michael Trebilcock, was laying plans for a program in law and economics; Prichard, with his economics background at Swarthmore, struck Trebilcock and Friedland as a logical candidate to assist on the project. In many ways, Prichard's name was in the air, a rarefied air at that.

In the late summer of 1975, he headed off for graduate work at the Yale Law School, accompanied by Ann Wilson, who delayed her articles by a year. For the first time, knowing he would be returning to Toronto to teach law, Prichard wrapped his mind around the concept of a career.

"Yale was a transformative year for me," he says. "Without any disrespect for the teachers at Toronto, Yale was when I focused exclusively on what being a law professor would do for me. I was still a student, but I changed my perspective. I began to watch my teachers as role models for myself."

One teacher in particular was Prichard's targeted model, Guido Calabresi, whom he describes as "a dramatically fine teacher." Second in the model category, almost in the Calabresi class, was a prof named Bruce Ackerman. "Those two," Prichard says, "set for me a level of aspiration I've never been able to reach." That last statement may be unnecessary modesty on Prichard's part. In the 1980s, his reputation as a teacher climbed so high and reached so wide that he was recruited to be dean of the Harvard Law School and a full professor at Yale, leading to the dean's job. He turned both down on the grounds that he was committed to Canada. But going back to 1975, when he was fresh at Yale, it was small wonder that the likes of Calabresi and Ackerman opened up splendid new vistas for the kid from Toronto. And it's instructive on many levels to hear Prichard wax on about the almost transcendental experience of studying torts with Calabresi and environmental law with Ackerman. On one level Prichard's description of the classes—his voice pumping up to even greater speed than its normal accelerated flow, his favourite adjective, *fabulous*, getting a thorough work-out—demonstrates his own developing love of legal scholarship and the play of ideas. And on a more general level, it shows just how far the teaching of law had reached from the days when it didn't seem to have as much relevance to the world outside the classroom.

Here's Prichard on Yale: "Both of them, Guido and Bruce, had an incredibly broad view of the law. As law professors, they were principally concerned with the development of wise public policy. In Guido's case, it was on the regulation of accidents, in Bruce's on the regulation of the environment. What was so exhilarating, so *fabulous*, was that they took the best scholarship they were doing, Ackerman having just written his book on environmental law, a case study of the Delaware River basin, and Calabresi in the process of writing a book called *Tragic Choices*, about how we make tough choices in his area of the law and what methods we use, here they were, men of immense scholarship, and they were bringing it right into the classroom. They were *teaching* it. Until then, I didn't have a full appreciation of going above and beyond legal rules and black-letter law and legal doctrine. But at Yale, they showed me that the best scholars could also be the best teachers. They accomplished that by using their scholarship, what they were working on at that very moment, to make their teaching so significant. This was a revelation to me. This was fabulous. And ever since Yale, taking what I saw in Guido and Bruce, I've tried to keep a close link between what I do my research on and what I teach."

Charged up, turned on, the most eager of beavers, Prichard took up teaching at the University of Toronto Law School in the fall of 1976. His subjects were torts, economic analysis of law, and economic regulations. And, oops, calamity struck.

"I knew at the beginning I wasn't a really *good* teacher," Prichard says. "But I was enthusiastic, and if you're honest about being new and enthusiastic, the students will give you the benefit of the doubt."

Well, perhaps, but there seemed to be this problem. Richard Tiberius exposed it. Tiberius was a teaching consultant whom Marty Friedland hired that autumn to help the members of the law faculty brush up on their classroom technique. Tiberius's method was to sit in on a lecturer's classes and afterwards to quiz the students at random on the impressions they were receiving from the lecturer.

"I'd like to paint a picture for you, Rob," Tiberius said to Prichard after he'd questioned a sampling of Prichard's students. "It's the picture the students have passed on to me."

"Paint away," Prichard said, expecting to hear that, for a rookie, he was coming along nicely.

"The picture I'm getting is of a high-volume, high-speed lecturer, a person racing through the material."

Prichard straightened up. "You *are*?"

"People are arriving at your classroom in good shape and leaving with headaches."

"This is terrible!"

"Now, if that's the effect you're trying for, I'll say no more and leave you to it . . . ."

"No, no, that's *not* the effect I want!"

"Well, Rob, why don't we talk about some small changes."

"Oh, *yes.*"

With Tiberius's guidance, Prichard cut back the volume, throttled down the speed, maintained the enthusiasm, injected his own brand of scholarship, and blossomed into one of the magnificent teachers. Not overnight, but in time.

"People think teaching is something you're born to be good at," Prichard says. "I don't believe that for a minute. Teaching is something you work at before you're even remotely close to satisfactory."

That first year, Prichard learned to take pains when he incorporated even the tiniest technique he'd absorbed from his Yale experience. There was, for example, the habit Guido Calabresi had of learning at the first lecture every student's first name, the name he or she liked to be called. Prichard thought he'd give that notion a try in his own classes.

"Tell me how you'd prefer me to address you," he said to the first torts group.

The students smiled, and Prichard ran down the list of names in front of him.

"Ernest Stuart Griffiths," he said, reading a name. "I guess you're Ernie, am I right?"

Prichard didn't hear the student's reply, and for the following weeks, whenever he called on Griffiths, it was as Ernie. Griffiths looked bemused.

"Finally I found out he'd never been an Ernie in his life," Prichard says. "He was a Stuart. To this day, though, whenever I see him, I call him Ernie. He's a good lawyer. A partner at Fasken Campbell."

That's another thing about Prichard as a teacher—he never loses track of anyone he's taught.

"The wonderful thing in being a teacher," Prichard says, "is that, within reason, you can set your own agenda. Compare that with a young lawyer in a big firm—the young lawyer is client-driven. Me, as a starting teacher, I didn't have to respond to the agenda of others. I was free to work on subjects I was interested in, write papers on issues I cared about. Teaching was an unbelievable privilege, especially at a school like ours that's small, incredibly selective, and very diverse. I don't know a better job than teaching at the University of Toronto Law School."

One of the oddities of the class of '75, a nice oddity, is that, just as it produced an inordinately high number of labour lawyers, it turned out more law teachers than any class before it or after it. Some—John Zinn, to cite one—got into teaching early and later switched off to practise law. Others—Dave Murphy—tried practice, found it wanting, and turned to teaching. Most made teaching their immediate and long-term career. David Cohen at UBC is one, Murray Rankin at Victoria, Marilyn Pilkington at Osgoode, Vince Del Buono at McGill. There are others, and the question is, why so many from one class?

David Cohen thinks he has a large part of the answer. "Role models," he says on a day I visit his home in Vancouver. "Some of the teachers at Toronto were spectacular. Michael Trebilcock, Frank Iacobucci, Steve Waddams, Arnie Weinrib. Great teachers like those made teaching seem exciting." Cohen admits he had ambitions to try the academic world before he reached law school. "I was intrigued that you could spend your life asking questions and have other people, the students, try to answer them." But the calibre and attitude of the Toronto profs clinched it for him. "The way our teachers thought about law made it super attractive to be the person leading a class myself."

Cohen is a dark, vibrant man, wears a Tom Selleck moustache, and has a direct way of looking at you that could be unsettling if he didn't happen to be so honest and open. Vitality flies off him in sparks. (Off his wife, too. Gloria—a person of lustrous beauty and, in size, about as big as a minute—is a doctor with a full practice, runs a sports medicine clinic at the Y, and is the official physician to both Canada's national cycling team and Vancouver's triple-A baseball team.) By way of illustrating Cohen's intellectual and physical vigour, it isn't necessary to do more than refer to his early CV: research assistant for British Columbia's Law Reform Commission, law clerk to Mr. Justice Bud Estey of the Supreme Court of Canada, master's degree at Yale, professor at the UBC law school. Arnie Weinrib, a man who hands out praise with care, says of Cohen, "If another school, us for instance, were hiring one teacher away from UBC, it would be, no question, David."

The unavoidable ingredient that Cohen and the other members of the class of '75 who teach have in common is an abundance of energy, the kind I associate with Prichard. Prichardsonian energy. These are people, Prichard, Cohen, the rest, who can't resist a new enterprise, a fresh idea, a galvanizing project. Their brains are in overdrive. They get by on five hours' sleep. They have eight balls in the air at any single moment. They talk fast and often. They seem to be on several cutting edges.

Take Murray Rankin. At law school, he was the guy with the longest hair, the most far-out life style (he lived over a pizza parlour with a modern dancer and he whipped up his own yoghurt, which made his classmates drool for more), and the deepest interest in anarchist theory. In the years since law school, he hasn't lost a step, though the anarchism is directed into straighter channels.

As a teacher at the University of Victoria, beginning in 1977 after a graduate year at Harvard, he was early into environmental law. "It was eight students talking in a little room and afterwards we'd go out for beers," he tells me over lunch in Victoria. "That was how we started. Now, as a subject inside the school and outside, environmental law is mainstream." Rankin is one of the people who have made it mainstream. He's accomplished the job by committee; he functions as one of the more articulate leaders, pamphleteers, and lobbyists for such organizations as Friends of the Earth and the Canadian Environmental Defence Fund. And he's won victories for the environmental cause in the courts; in March 1991, he settled a case in the Cariboo region of British Columbia that ended a savage instance of sewage pollution and set in motion a cleanup. He's indefatigable. He's the chair of the Public Interest Advocacy Centre, a group that does litigation in a wide range of public interest areas. How does Rankin find time to teach? He shrugs. "I love teaching," he says.

Vince Del Buono, another teacher, writer, thinker, doer to come out of the class of '75, has expanded his horizons from Canada to the entire world. Del Buono, a man on whom erudition rests comfortably, taught at McGill Law School, worked for the Canada Law Reform Commission in Ottawa, transferred to the Department of Justice, and taught some more at the University of Ottawa Law School. His specialty all this while was criminal law, particularly its procedural aspects. In July 1987, Del Buono participated in a meeting at the Inns of Court in London, England, with two hundred other experts in criminal law from the Commonwealth countries, Europe, the United States, and Israel. From the meeting, there was born an organization called the Society for the Reform of Criminal Law. What does the society intend to reform? Practically everything that touches on criminal law, from the video-taping of confessions to the role that criminal law can play in promoting human rights. And who is the president of this revolutionary society? Vince Del Buono, operating out of offices in Vancouver.

On the day just before New Year's Day 1992, when I speak with Del Buono and listen at fascinated length to his plans and ambitions, he has just arrived in Toronto from Vancouver. There's been a quick side trip to Ottawa, a meeting planned for the following week in Sweden, all on society business, and he mentions something about the complications of packing the right clothes that'll do for both Sweden and the country he must drop in on first.

"What country?" I ask.

"Saudi Arabia."

That's another thing about these teachers from the class of '75—they're perpetually on the move.

In Rob Prichard's years as a law teacher, 1977 to 1984, his life fell into a rhythm—if your idea of rhythm is a beat that Buddy Rich in his most up-tempo, machine-gun, ra-ta-ta-tat mood would set.

He taught his classes: torts, economic analysis of law, economic regulations, product liability, labour law.

He wrote legal texts and learned articles. Two typical years, 1982 and 1983, show his name as author or co-author of two books and five articles. Not bedside reading, but the kind of deep stuff that fascinates academics with curious minds. *Securing the Canadian Economic Union: Federalism and Internal Barriers to Trade*.

He sat on arbitration panels and served as vice chairman of the Crown Employees Grievance Settlement Board for Ontario from 1977 to 1986.

He found himself in demand at other law schools, hardly backwater schools, either. In 1982–83, he spent a year as Visiting Associate Professor of Law at Yale Law School, and two years later, he did the same thing at Harvard. He made a hit in both places. When he finished delivering his last Harvard lecture, the students rose in tribute and sang *O Canada*. They got the words right, too.

He taught at home, he taught away, he wrote, he arbitrated, he sat on committees by the score, and he signed on for anything else intriguing that happened to pass his way.

The Lysyk Commission in 1977, for instance. Lysyk was Ken Lysyk, a man with credentials (deputy attorney general for Saskatchewan, dean of UBC Law School, currently a justice on the British Columbia Supreme Court), and his commission's assignment was to do for the Yukon what the Berger Commission did earlier for the Northwest Territories—look into the pros and cons of building a natural gas pipeline through the territory. The difference was that, while Tom Berger took a couple of years, Lysyk was allowed a mere three months. Three months of hearings, meetings, brainstorming, and seventeen-hour days in the Yukon. Right up Prichard's alley. He came aboard the commission as one of Lysyk's two principal assistants. The commission worked at such a frenzy that Lysyk, Prichard, and the others wrote the last section of their 171-page report—which concluded that the pipeline could be built through the Yukon on the strict proviso that several conditions were met—while their propeller plane was making the eighthour flight from Whitehorse to the printers who were standing by in Ottawa with the presses set to roll.

*"Exhilarating!"* Prichard says. "That time with Ken in the north was fantastically exhilarating."

On the home front, Rob and Ann bought a house in Toronto in 1979. It's on the same solid, shady street behind Casa Loma where their classmate and the McCarthy Tetrault litigator, Paul Morrison, lives. Ann's legal career picked up after she and Rob returned from his master's year at Yale. She articled at a traditional downtown firm, Tilley Carson, and stayed on with the firm after her articles, first in litigation, then in research. When the first Prichard son arrived in 1980, Ann negotiated a half-time arrangement with Tilley Carson, half the week in the office, half the week at home. Such a deal, virtually unprecedented, made Ann a pioneer of sorts. The year away from Toronto, while Rob taught at Yale, and the birth of another son persuaded Ann to forgo practice—but not the law. She contributed particularly to the Law School Alumni Association and edited its magazine, *Nexus*, for ten years. In 1990, she received the Arbor Award for outstanding volunteer service to the university.

Not everything ran happily for the Prichards through the 1980s. Rob's mother died suddenly of a heart attack, at the age of sixty-nine, in 1983. And when cancer struck Stobo Prichard a couple of years later, Rob and Ann took him into their home and nursed him until he died at seventy-two in 1986. His father's death hit Prichard hard—all those Stobos in the kids' names aren't an empty tribute—and he still grows misty when the subject of Stobo Senior comes up.

A crisis of a different sort bugged Prichard in the early 1980s.

It concerned money. At the beginning of his teaching career, his pay equalled that of his classmates who went into the downtown firms. Five years later, the parity vanished.

"My salary went from sixteen thousand dollars in 1977 to the high twenties in 1982," Prichard says. "That wasn't a lot of money for 1982. It was particularly not a lot of money when I compared it to what Jeannie Fraser and Phil Siller were starting to make. The difference was huge, and I wondered if I could support a young family on what I earned."

Other members of the law faculty had the same doubts, and when complaints surfaced, the university administration moved in a hurry to correct the problem. Salaries went up. Complaints died down.

"It was the only moment of doubt I ever had about teaching," Prichard says.

During his year as visiting professor at Harvard, another emergency that would affect Prichard's future developed back home. Frank Iacobucci had been dean of the law school since 1979. Law school deans usually remain in place for five or six years. But suddenly, in the fall of 1983, Iacobucci was gone, chosen to fly up to the post of university provost. (Iacobucci kept spiralling ever upward until he arrived, in 1990, on the Supreme Court of Canada.)

A search committee was struck to seek out a new dean. Word around the law school was that it would be a short and quick search. Michael Trebilcock was so much the front runner that all other potential contenders were lost in his dust. The rest of the faculty, including Prichard, favoured Trebilcock, and the students whipped up a petition begging for his appointment. There was just one glitch in this apparently effortless process. Michael Trebilcock didn't want to be dean.

"Michael told me one of the reasons he refused the job," Prichard says, "is that he thought I could do it."

In April 1984, the search committee asked Prichard if it could place his name among the contenders. Prichard agreed. "It came at a time when I was struggling with the future," he says. "I wasn't moping around, but I was facing choices and decisions about what to do next." The search committee narrowed its list to four names. Each had approximately the same level of support. But in the end, the committee—which included Michael Trebilcock—chose Prichard.

He was thirty-four years old, and he was dean of the school he had graduated from less than a decade earlier.

I ask Prichard what makes him proudest when he thinks over his six years as the law school's dean, and he says, "The most obvious physical manifestation of the school's moving forward in the time I was there is the Laskin Library, but I actually think the library on its own isn't that significant."

A word about the library: it's elegant. Another word: it's enormous, three floors and tens of thousands of legal volumes. When the law school moved into Flavelle House in 1961, the library was cobbled together from Sir Joseph's sitting room and pantry and other quarters. Frank Iacobucci, during his tenure as dean, started the ball rolling towards a library that offered space and quiet and a measure of comfort (students in the old days, not that long ago, were known to wear gloves against the winter chill and to lose pounds in perspiration in the summer heat). Iacobucci brought in the architects Moffat Kinoshita and performed the rest of the opening legwork. But it fell to Prichard to propel the project to completion. That meant he steered the school through what he calls "three terrible years of construction" and conceived the name and focus of the library. (Putting the name Bora Laskin on it gave the library a nostalgia and sense of historical legitimacy that galvanized everyone associated with the school, past and present.) And it meant he buttonholed everyone—the government, the university, the alumni—for funds to pay the library's costs.

Prichard tells a lovely story about fund raising.

"We wanted to reach law firms for corporate donations. We put a lot of effort into that appeal, and the first firm to come through was Davies, Ward and Beck. They donated one hundred thousand dollars. That set the pace of the other firms who followed. Without the first money from Davies, Ward, we might never have got the library built."

Have you guessed the final line to the story?

"The person at Davies, Ward who talked the firm into the donation wasn't even a senior person in the firm at the time. He was John Zinn."

On March 21, 1991, Pierre Trudeau came to town. The University of Toronto gave him an honorary degree, and Trudeau cut the ribbon that opened the Bora Laskin Law Library. Two thousand people attended the ceremony—an A-list law crowd that included former Chief Justice of Canada Brian Dickson—and it was, in Prichard's description, "a knockout day."

But, as Prichard says, the library was "the physical manifestation" of other, larger things that were going on during his years as dean. Prichard breaks down the rest of the action into three areas. The three are inextricably linked and lead inexorably to something magnificent.

First: reaching out to the legal profession in general and the law school alumni in particular. Why? To get them, and their pocketbooks, on side for the school's heady ambitions. How? By holding annual alumni dinners, circulating an alumni magazine, handing out distinguished-alumni awards.

Second: making the law school an integral part of the university. "You can't build a major law school," Prichard says, "unless you're part of a major university and draw on the university's strength." To that end, the teachers at the law school developed cross-disciplines with other faculties and departments. So Jim Phillips is in law and in history. Jennifer Nedelsky is in law and political science. So is Kathy Swinton. Ernie Weinrib (Arnie's brother) is in law and classics. And so on. "No other law school in North America," Prichard says, "has cross-appointments in the numbers we have. No other law school can offer its students that kind of academic versatility where they're taught to relate law to other subjects and to the world at large."

Which brings us, climactically, to three: making the University of Toronto Law School one of the half dozen finest centres of teaching and legal scholarship in the English-speaking world. "That was our specific goal," Prichard says. "It wasn't just me. It was unanimous in the faculty. We made a commitment together that this was where we were headed."

To get there, two key decisions had to be made.

The faculty must be larger. Not the thirty teachers it had. The minimum number in all the great law schools was forty. Ergo, Toronto would have forty. But not just *any* forty.

"We recruited only people who met international standards," Prichard says. "That meant turning down good people if they weren't good enough. Every year I was dean, we'd have, say, three vacancies, and we'd only fill two of them. The reason was that in each of the years, there were only two out of all the applicants who met the standards, and we'd say, no, sorry, we'll just have to leave the vacancy and hope to recruit better next year. What's happened as a result is that we've got an extraordinary number of young people on the faculty today who are going to be the strongest generation of teachers in the school's history."

Decision number two, in Prichard's words: "We had to focus on our strengths, not try to do everything, not be all things to all people." That entailed jettisoning some of the school's programs. The legal aid clinic—which Prichard was so dedicated to in his own student years—got the axe. Prichard says the decision was personally painful for him, but there had to be a cutoff. What remained, what got the emphasis, was everything that related to theory and policy and doctrine. They became the school's strong suits. They became almost its *only* suit. And with its pre-eminence in those areas, Toronto climbed into the pantheon of law schools, in the exclusive company of Yale and Chicago, Harvard and Stanford.

In the process, Prichard thinks, it became something else that, in the overall scheme of things, may be even more significant.

"The school's an institution that produces leadership," he says. "Not just leaders in law or in business. I mean leaders in all areas. There are very few institutions like that in Canada right now."

It's mid-April 1992. For months, the newspapers have been heavy on stories that moan over the crises that provincial budget cuts have brought down on Ontario's universities, especially the University of Toronto. And Prichard is telling me that the problem over money at the university has to be kept in balance.

We're talking in his university office. It's a glorious room. It's on the second floor of Simcoe Hall, the handsome stone building that looks across the Back Campus towards University College. The room is spacious and bright and casually scattered with pictures—of Prichard's three sons, Wil, Kenny, and Jay, of friends, law school colleagues, a small photo of Bob Rae—that give the surroundings an unexpectedly homey quality. The only formal portrait, and the largest, is a painting of Sir Robert Falconer. When Falconer was named the university's president in 1907, he was forty years old, the only president in this century who was younger at his age of appointment than Prichard. One other way that Falconer has Prichard whipped is in length of service. Sir Robert hung around the office for twenty-five years.

"The focus on money and resources is really a substantial distortion of the role of the president," Prichard begins. "It *is* the case that we have too few resources. It *is* the case we are badly underfunded compared to the other provinces and to the public universities in the United States. And it is *certainly* the case that the president's job is to spend wisely and to assist in attracting more funds."

Prichard sounds just a trifle exasperated, especially for him, and he goes at the money subject from another angle, maybe to make sure I'm getting the point.

"Coming into the job," he says, "I *knew* we were underfunded. I *knew* all that. I knew I had to work every day and every week and every month on money. That was no surprise."

He lets out a whoosh of air, smiles, and I recognize that the Prichard I'm used to, the nonstop optimist, is about to take off on another flight.

"The real thrill, the real surprise to me," he says "is the size of the job. The range of issues that come into the president's office is fantastic. Financial issues, academic issues, resource issues, curriculum issues, issues about people, political issues. There's virtually no issue that doesn't somehow wind up here. Foreign relations, too, they're part of the job, international relations with other universities. No one person can have a background in all of those. Not me, for sure. So I have a need to become familiar with a bunch of new issues, and that's a thrill."

Where, I wonder to myself, is this taking us?

Prichard makes it immediately clear where he's headed. He's on to the subject of leadership.

"With this incredible range of issues," he says, "with the sheer size of the university, the president's job is to try to distill the essence of what the university is all about. It's the same thing I said when I was dean at the law school—we can't be all things to all people. We have to concentrate on what we're good at. On the university level, we can't be a service organization, we can't say yes to every opportunity that comes along, we can't accept every invitation to be a partner in some project, we can't fuzz our focus. What we are is a research-intensive university with outstanding undergraduate, graduate, and professional programs. And the president's job, my job, is to bring shape to that mission, to bring people together, to advance for the long term. Success in this job shouldn't be measured by identifiable achievements of a particularized kind. That's the job of the deans and principals and individual members of the faculties. That's the role of the different people with the imagination and the ideas—to bring their particular parts of the university for-ward. It's the role of the president to create an environment where *those* people can achieve *those* things."

Prichard is soaring now, in his haute cheerleader mode, stim-ulating the troops, even if there's only one trooper, me, in the room.

"I hope at the end of my time in this office," he says, "people will say the university had terrific leadership in the sense that it had hundreds of people leading it in the same direction rather than just one single leader at the head of the institution. My job is to bring a greater sense of community to the university, greater sense of unity, greater commitment to be internationally significant. No matter what happens, I'm going to have a lot of fun because it's such an extraordinarily stimulating job. But if I make the kind of contribution to leadership I want to make, it'll be . . ."

"Fabulous," I say softly, interrupting.

"*Fabulous!*" Prichard repeats.

# EPILOGUE

On May 5, 1992, I spring for fifty-five dollars and go to the annual University of Toronto Law School Alumni Dinner. It's at Hart House, on the university campus. I get a vodka on the rocks from the bar—drinks are included in the fifty-five bucks—and reminisce about the old days with a guy from my class, '57. The guy is Bernie Chernos, a Toronto litigation lawyer who specializes in municipal law.

"You weren't such a terrible student as you thought you were," Bernie tells me.

"I wasn't?" I say. Coming from Bernie, this is high praise. He was our class's gold medalist.

"No," Bernie says, "you just didn't want to be there."

"You got that part right."

"But think about it now," Bernie says. "Aren't you glad you had the experience of going to the place?"

Right again.

A small bubbly woman with a round pretty face approaches me. Her name is Victoria Stuart, and she's from the class of '75, and now practises tax law in Toronto. I didn't interview her for the book, and as she talks, it's clear I should have. She's the only member of the class who came to it from the Maritimes.

"In the summers," she tells me, "I used to go home to Halifax and people would say, 'Why did you go all the way to Toronto for law school? Why didn't you just stay down here and go to Dalhousie law?' And I'd tell them, 'Listen, the people who get

Cs in my class at Toronto are more exciting than the people who get As at Dal.' It was a terribly bright group of people to spend three years with."

We move to Hart House's Great Hall for dinner. The head table files in. I look over its members and feel a sense of *déjà vu*, really recent *déjà vu*. Jim Spence is up there, the treasurer of the law society, and Joan Lax, assistant dean at the law school and the Bencher who brought the motion that ended Bob Topp's pitch to change the law society's discipline procedure. Jim Tory is up there, Brent Belzberg's former boss at the Tory firm. And Frank Iacobucci, dean of the law school immediately before Rob Prichard. And there's Rob himself. Two trumpets blast a fanfare, and the lieutenant-governor of Ontario makes his entrance. Gawd, yes, it's Hal Jackman. Sorry, the Honourable Henry N.R. Jackman. Class of '56.

After dinner, there are speeches. Some are funny. Some are serious. The latter are about raising money for the law school. Prichard talks briefly and says, "From the perspective of Simcoe Hall, the law school is one institution that makes the university great." The remark doesn't come as a surprise, but something Bill Davis says makes me snap to attention. This is William Davis, former premier of Ontario and not a graduate of the University of Toronto Law School. Davis stands at the microphone and takes a slow look along the head table and into the audience of us graduates.

"I'm intimidated," he says.

Well, Bill, I think, you ought to be. I've spent a year and a half hanging out with people from just one of the law school's classes, and *I* feel slightly intimidated. I also feel enlightened and encouraged to have spent time with so many people I've come to admire.

Looking back, I realize that "principled" is a word I found myself writing several times to characterize the men and women from the class of '75. I don't mean by the word that they're a solemn lot, smug about being goody-goody. Not in the least. I did a lot of laughing with these people. Take Brent Belzberg. As you've seen, at the time I called on him, he was in the process of tearing apart the family empire, and he was still laughing. Between the tears, okay, but laughing. I think Brent Belzberg is a guy to be appreciated. So is David Baker, as selfless a man as I've met. And Harriet Lewis, Ellen Murray, and the other women who didn't let the system slow them down for five seconds. And Brent Knazan and Patrick Boyer. Could there exist two such different men? One on the left and the other a Progressive Conservative politician, one guarded in conversation and the other with apparently no secrets. But the same in one way—two men who have a conscience.

If Rob Prichard is right about the law school being one of the few institutions in Canada that is turning out leaders, then the class of '75 is doing more than its share. It's loaded with men and women whom I'd trust with leadership roles in our country. Actually, it's beside the point to say so. Many people from the class have *already* moved into positions of power. It's their turn, and speaking from the vantage point of eighteen months in their company, I feel reassured that some of the people running our courts and businesses and governments and universities are named Prichard and Knazan, Belzberg and Baker, Mike Mitchell and Jim Blacklock, Jean Fraser and Patrick Boyer, David Cohen and Murray Rankin. . . . The class of '75.

# INDEX